AI for Risks

Series Editors

Desheng Wu, School of Economics and Management, University of Chinese Academy of Sciences, Beijing, China

Jim Lambert, University of Virginia, Charlottesville, VA, USA

David L. Olson, Department of Management, University of Nebraska–Lincoln, Lincoln, NE, USA

Risks are widespread in human society, such as in the financial field (various investment risks), in technical fields (risks brought by emerging technologies), in social fields (political risks), and in all aspects of our lives (health risks, natural environment risks, etc.) At the same time, the inherent links between various risks generate systemic risks. The major challenge today is not to deal with new types of risks, but to focus more on those risks that are difficult to distinguish effectively and timely, or risks that have emerged in a different way from the past.

This series of books aims to strengthen discussions on frontier hot topics across disciplines, that is, using AI technologies to solve risks problems that exist in the environment, healthcare, technology, and financial fields. The scope of it focuses on the implementation of artificial intelligence technology in dealing with risks, such as risk prediction, assessment, and mitigation. It includes monographs, edited volumes, textbooks and proceedings etc. on the application of artificial intelligence in risk management in the fields of social media, healthcare, the public sector, financial technology, and regulatory technology.

David L. Olson · Desheng Dash Wu · Cuicui Luo ·
Majid Nabavi

Business Analytics with R and Python

Springer

David L. Olson
Supply Chain Management and Analytics
University of Nebraska-Lincoln
Lincoln, NE, USA

Cuicui Luo
University of Chinese Academy of Science
Beijing, China

Desheng Dash Wu
University of Chinese Academy of Science
Beijing, China

Majid Nabavi
University of Nebraska-Lincoln
Lincoln, NE, USA

ISSN 2731-6327 ISSN 2731-6335 (electronic)
AI for Risks
ISBN 978-981-97-4771-9 ISBN 978-981-97-4772-6 (eBook)
https://doi.org/10.1007/978-981-97-4772-6

© The Editor(s) (if applicable) and The Author(s), under exclusive license to Springer Nature Singapore Pte Ltd. 2024

This work is subject to copyright. All rights are solely and exclusively licensed by the Publisher, whether the whole or part of the material is concerned, specifically the rights of translation, reprinting, reuse of illustrations, recitation, broadcasting, reproduction on microfilms or in any other physical way, and transmission or information storage and retrieval, electronic adaptation, computer software, or by similar or dissimilar methodology now known or hereafter developed.
The use of general descriptive names, registered names, trademarks, service marks, etc. in this publication does not imply, even in the absence of a specific statement, that such names are exempt from the relevant protective laws and regulations and therefore free for general use.
The publisher, the authors and the editors are safe to assume that the advice and information in this book are believed to be true and accurate at the date of publication. Neither the publisher nor the authors or the editors give a warranty, expressed or implied, with respect to the material contained herein or for any errors or omissions that may have been made. The publisher remains neutral with regard to jurisdictional claims in published maps and institutional affiliations.

This Springer imprint is published by the registered company Springer Nature Singapore Pte Ltd.
The registered company address is: 152 Beach Road, #21-01/04 Gateway East, Singapore 189721, Singapore

If disposing of this product, please recycle the paper.

Preface

This book provides an overview of data mining methods in the field of business. Business management faces challenges in serving customers in better ways, in identifying risks, and analyzing the impact of decisions. Of the three types of analytic tools, and descriptive analytics focuses on what has happened, predictive analytics extend statistical and/or artificial intelligence to provide forecasting capability.

Chapter 1 provides and overview of business management problems. Chapter 2 describes how analytics and knowledge management have been used to better cope with these problems. Chapter 3 describes initial data visualization tools. Chapter 4 describes association rules and software support. Chapter 5 describes cluster analysis with software demonstration. Chapter 6 discusses time series analysis with software demonstration. Chapter 7 describes predictive classification data mining tools. Applications of the context of management are presented in Chapter 8. Chapter 9 covers prescriptive modeling in business and applications of artificial intelligence.

Lincoln, NE, USA	David L. Olson
Beijing, China	Desheng Dash Wu
Beijing, China	Cuicui Luo
Lincoln, NE, USA	Majid Nabavi

Contents

1 Data Mining in Business 1
   1.1   Introduction 1
   1.2   Requirements for Data Mining 3
   1.3   Business Data Mining 4
         1.3.1   Frequent Itemset Mining 5
         1.3.2   Customer Relationship Management 5
         1.3.3   Bankruptcy Prediction 5
         1.3.4   Fraud Detection 6
   1.4   Summary 7

2 Data Mining Processes 9
   2.1   KDD 9
   2.2   CRISP-DM 10
         2.2.1   Business Understanding 10
         2.2.2   Data Understanding 11
         2.2.3   Data Preparation 11
         2.2.4   Modeling 12
         2.2.5   Evaluation 13
         2.2.6   Deployment 14
   2.3   SEMMA 14
         2.3.1   Step 1 (Sample) 14
         2.3.2   Step 2 (Explore) 15
         2.3.3   Step 3 (Modify) 15
         2.3.4   Step 4 (Model) 16
         2.3.5   Step 5 (Assess) 16
   2.4   Model Controls 16
   2.5   Evaluation of Model Results 17
         2.5.1   Example Model 18
         2.5.2   Cost Metrics 19

		2.5.3 Other Measures	20
	2.6	Summary	21
	References		21
3	**Data Mining Software**		**23**
	3.1	R	23
	3.2	Rattle	29
	3.3	Python	31
		3.3.1 Installing Python	31
		3.3.2 Running Python	38
	3.4	Summary	40
4	**Association Rules**		**41**
	4.1	Methodology	42
	4.2	Demonstration Dataset	42
		4.2.1 Fit	43
		4.2.2 Lift	45
	4.3	The Apriori Algorithm	48
	4.4	Association Rules from Software	50
		4.4.1 Association Rules in Rattle	52
		4.4.2 R Code	57
		4.4.3 Python Code	61
	4.5	Conclusion	62
	Reference		62
5	**Cluster Analysis**		**63**
	5.1	K-Means Clustering	64
		5.1.1 A Clustering Algorithm	64
		5.1.2 Loan Data	65
	5.2	Clustering Methods Used in Software	67
	5.3	Example Cases	68
		5.3.1 Churn Clustering Model	68
		5.3.2 Credit Risk Assessment Model	69
	5.4	Software	70
		5.4.1 Portuguese Bankruptcy Dataset	70
		5.4.2 Rattle K-Means Clustering	71
		5.4.3 R Clustering	75
		5.4.4 R Code	76
		5.4.5 Python Clustering	80
	5.5	File BostonHousingKaggle.csv	83
		5.5.1 R Code	89
	5.6	Summary	97
	References		97

Contents

6 Regression Algorithms in Data Mining 99
- 6.1 Regression Models 100
- 6.2 Forecasting S&P 500 101
  - 6.2.1 R Code for Simple Regression 102
  - 6.2.2 Python Code for Simple Regression 103
- 6.3 ARIMA Modeling 104
  - 6.3.1 R Code for ARIMA 106
  - 6.3.2 Python Code for ARIMA 108
- 6.4 Multiple Regression 108
  - 6.4.1 R Code for Multiple Regression 110
  - 6.4.2 Python Code for Multiple Regression 112
- 6.5 Stepwise Regression 113
  - 6.5.1 R Code for Stepwise Regression 114
- 6.6 Logistic Regression 117
  - 6.6.1 Tests of the Regression Model 118
  - 6.6.2 Software Demonstrations of Logistic Regression 119
  - 6.6.3 R Code 121
  - 6.6.4 Python Code 123
- 6.7 Summary 124

7 Classification Tools 125
- 7.1 Classification Models 125
  - 7.1.1 Regression 125
  - 7.1.2 Decision Trees 125
  - 7.1.3 Random Forest 126
  - 7.1.4 Extreme Boosting 126
  - 7.1.5 Support Vector Machines 126
  - 7.1.6 Neural Networks 127
- 7.2 Bankruptcy Data Set 128
- 7.3 Logistic Regression 129
  - 7.3.1 R Code Logistic Regression 132
  - 7.3.2 Python Code Logistic Regression 133
- 7.4 Support Vector Machines 135
  - 7.4.1 R Code SVM 137
  - 7.4.2 Python Code SVM 138
- 7.5 Neural Networks 139
  - 7.5.1 R Code Neural Network 140
  - 7.5.2 Python Code Neural Network 142
- 7.6 Decision Trees 143
  - 7.6.1 R Code Decision Tree 145
  - 7.6.2 Python Code Decision Tree 147
- 7.7 Random Forests 148
  - 7.7.1 R Code Random Forest 149
  - 7.7.2 Python Code Random Forest 152
- 7.8 Boosting 154

		7.8.1	R Code XGBoost	155
		7.8.2	Python Code Gradient Boosting	156
	7.9	Comparison		158
	7.10	Loan Default Prediction Model		160
	7.11	Summary		162
	References			163

8 Variable Selection 165
   8.1 Taiwan Bankruptcy Data 166
       8.1.1 Correlation 167
       8.1.2 Logistic Regression Variable Significance 167
       8.1.3 Entropy 171
       8.1.4 Information Content from Random Forest Models 171
       8.1.5 Control Models Using All 94 Variables 172
   8.2 Example Variable Selection Case 173
   8.3 Value of Variable Reduction 174
   References 179

9 Dataset Balancing 181
   9.1 Bankruptcy Datasets 181
   9.2 Balancing 182
   9.3 Process 182
   9.4 Data 183
       9.4.1 Poland Data 183
       9.4.2 Taiwan Data 183
       9.4.3 Slovak Data 184
       9.4.4 U.S. Data 184
   9.5 Results 184
   9.6 Example Credit Card Fraud Detection Case 188
   9.7 Conclusions 191
   References 192

Index 195

Chapter 1
Data Mining in Business

1.1 Introduction

Our life is controlled by computers, which generate data in practically everything we do. Going to the grocery store generates large quantities of data that stores monitor to better control their inventories, as well as increase sales by reminding us of things they think we might want to buy. Going to the doctor (or anywhere in the health system) creates a stream of data that is shared by government, insurers, and health care deliverers. Of course, police systems track violators closely, the efficiency of which has vastly been improved through computer systems.

Data mining refers to the analysis of large quantities of data that are stored in computers. It is a set of processes and algorithms designed to obtain actionable insights, extract patterns, and identify relationships from large datasets. Data mining involves extracting, processing, and modeling data using a variety of methods. The era of big data is here, with many sources pointing out that more data are created over the past year or two than was generated throughout all prior human history. Big data involves datasets so large that traditional data analytic methods no longer work due to data volume. Big data is viewed as:

- Data too big to fit on a single server
- Data too unstructured to fit in a row-and-column database
- Data flowing too continuously to fit into a static data warehouse
- Lack of structure is the most important aspect (even more than the size)
- The point is to *analyze*, converting data into insights, innovation, and business value

Big data has been said to be more about analytics than about the data itself. The era of big data is expected to emphasize focusing on knowing what (based on correlation) rather than the traditional obsession for causality. The emphasis will be on discovering patterns offering novel and useful insights. Data will become a raw material for business, a vital economic input and source of value. Big data has had an impact on statistical analysis in the following ways:

1. There is so much data available that sampling is usually not needed ($n =$ all).
2. Precise accuracy of data is therefore less important as inevitable errors are compensated for by the mass of data (any one observation is flooded by others).
3. Correlation is more important than causality—most data mining applications involving big data are interested in what is going to happen, and you don't need to know why.

The purpose of big data analysis is to identify critical situations, not explain why they occur. Automatic trading programs need to detect trend changes, not figure out that the Greek economy collapsed or whether the Chinese government will devalue their currency. The programs in vehicles need to detect that an axle bearing is overheating, and the vehicle is vibrating and the wheel should be replaced, not whether this is due to a bearing failure or a housing rusting out.

There are many sources of big data. Internal to the corporation, e-mails, blogs, enterprise systems, and automation lead to structured, unstructured, and semi-structured information within the organization. External data is also widely available, much of it free over the Internet, but much also available from commercial vendors. Data can also be obtained from social media.

A knowledge management framework for the product lifecycle, to include classification of knowledge types:

- Customer knowledge—CRM focus in data mining terms;
- Development knowledge—product design involving engineering expertise;
- Production knowledge—knowledge of production processes;
- Delivery & Service knowledge—knowledge of the processes needed to serve customers.

Knowledge of customers is a classical customer profiling matter. The other three bullets are classical business process reengineering matters, often involving tacit knowledge which organizations generate in the form of their employees' expertise. Management of these forms of knowledge require:

- A mechanism to identify and access knowledge;
- A method for collaboration to identify who, how, and where knowledge is;
- A method to integrate knowledge for effectively making specific decisions.

Data can be found in statistics of production measures, which accounting provides and which industrial engineers (and supply chain managers) analyze for decision making. Knowledge also exists in the experience, intuition, and insight found in employees (tacit information). This tacit knowledge includes organizational value systems. Thus, expression of such knowledge is only available through collaboration within organizations. With respect to knowledge management, it means that the factual data found in accounting records needs to be supplemented by expertise, and a knowledge management system is closely tied to the idea of business process mapping. Business process mapping in turn is usually expressed in the form of a flowchart of what decisions need to be made, where knowledge can be found, and the approval authority in the organizations control system.

Data mining is widely used by banking firms in soliciting credit card customers, by insurance and telecommunication companies in detecting fraud, by manufacturing firms in quality control, and many other applications. Data mining is being applied to improve food product safety, criminal detection, and tourism. *Micromarketing* targets small groups of highly responsive customers. Data on consumer and lifestyle data is widely available, enabling customized individual marketing campaigns. This is enabled by *customer profiling*, identifying those subsets of customers most likely to be profitable to the business, as well as *targeting*, determining the characteristics of the most profitable customers.

Data mining involves statistical and artificial intelligence (AI) analysis, usually applied to large-scale datasets. There are two general types of data mining studies. *Hypothesis testing* involves expressing a theory about the relationship between actions and outcomes. This approach is referred to as *supervised*. In a simple form, it can be hypothesized that advertising will yield greater profit. This relationship has long been studied by retailing firms in the context of their specific operations. Data mining is applied to identifying relationships based on large quantities of data, which could include testing the response rates to various types of advertising on the sales and profitability of specific product lines. However, there is more to data mining than the technical tools used. The second form of data min- ing study is *knowledge discovery*. Data mining involves a spirit of knowledge discovery (learning new and useful things). Knowledge discovery is referred to as *unsupervised*. In this form of analysis, a preconceived notion may not be present. Relationships can be identified by looking at the data. This may be supported by visualization tools, which display data, or through fundamental statistical analysis, such as correlation analysis. Much of this can be accomplished through automatic means, as we will see in decision tree analysis, for example. But data mining is not limited to automated analysis. Knowledge discovery by humans can be enhanced by graphical tools and identification of unexpected patterns through a combination of human and computer interaction.

1.2 Requirements for Data Mining

Data mining requires identification of a problem, along with the collection of data that can lead to better understanding, and computer models to provide statistical or other means of analysis. A variety of analytic computer models have been used in data mining. In the later sections we will discuss various types of these models. Also required is access to data. Quite often, systems including data warehouses and data marts are used to manage large quantities of data. Other data mining analyses are done with smaller sets of data, such as can be organized in online analytic processing systems.

Knowledge management consists of the overall field of human knowledge (epistemology) as well as means to record and recall it (computer systems) and quantitative analysis to understand it (in business contexts, business analytics). There are many applications of quantitative analysis, falling within the overall framework of the term business analytics. Analytics has been around since statistics became widespread. With the emergence of computers, we see three types of analytic tools. **Descriptive** analytics focus on reports of what has happened. Statistics are a big part of that. Descriptive models are an example of unsupervised learning, where the algorithm identifies relationships without user direction. They don't predict some target value, but rather try to provide clues to data structure, relationships, and connectedness. **Predictive** analytics extend statistical and/or artificial intelligence to provide forecasting capability. They are directed in the sense that a target is defined. This can be a continuous variable to forecast. It also includes categorical output, especially classification modeling that applies models to suggest better ways of doing things, to include identification of the most likely customer profiles to send marketing materials, or to flag suspicious insurance claims, or many other applications. **Diagnostic** analytics can apply analysis to sensor input to direct control systems automatically. This is especially useful in mechanical or chemical environments where speed and safety considerations make it attractive to replace human monitors with automated systems as much as possible. It can lead to some problems, such as bringing stock markets to their knees for short periods (until humans can regain control). **Prescriptive** analytics applies quantitative models to optimize systems, or at least to identify improved systems. Data mining includes descriptive and predictive modeling. Operations research includes all three. This book focuses on the forecasting component of predictive modeling, with the classification portion of prescriptive analytics demonstrated.

In a more specific sense, knowledge discovery involves finding interesting patterns from data stored in large databases through use of computer analysis. In this context, the term **interesting** implies non-trivial, implicit, previously unknown, easily understood, useful and actionable knowledge. **Information** is defined as the patterns, correlations, rules, or relationships in data providing knowledge useful in decision making.

1.3 Business Data Mining

Data mining has been very effective in many business venues. The key is to find *actionable* information or information that can be utilized in a concrete way to improve profitability. Some of the earliest applications were in retailing, especially in the form of market basket analysis. There are many business data mining applications, four major ones being.

1.3.1 Frequent Itemset Mining

Also known as affinity positioning, or association rule mining, the intent is to identify items that appear together, such as items frequently purchased together in a market basket. The a priori algorithm is the basic computer model, although there have been advances in improving computational efficiency. These methods identify sets of items appearing together more than some level set by the analyst. It can be applied to given datasets as well as to streamed data in real-time. Applications include retail items purchased, analysis of airport traffic flow, analysis of video streaming media content, etc. Web pages, blogs, e-mails and so forth can be mined. There are also interesting medical applications in cancer sample prediction and gene marker identification.

1.3.2 Customer Relationship Management

Customer relationship management (CRM) targets customers for marketing campaigns to maximize profitability (one could also argue that the intent is to serve the customer better if you wish). This requires estimation of the customer lifecycle as well as lifetime customer value based on expected duration of their continued purchasing from the firm, their monthly transactions, and the cost of providing service. Lifetime value of a customer is the net present value of the discounted expected cash flow stream. This concept is very widely used, in credit card operations, banking, catalog marketing, retailing, and insurance. It has been the basis for marketing programs offering favorable pricing, concierge service, and equipment upgrades.

1.3.3 Bankruptcy Prediction

The ability to predict a firm's financial survival is very important to management, stockholders, employees, customers, and other stakeholders. After the 2008 financial crisis, increased emphasis was provided by revised accounting standards from the Financial Accounting Standards Board in the US with increased emphasis on risk management. There is a plethora of financial data available from required accounting reports. Classification models are widely used to predict bankruptcy, which hopefully has highly imbalanced data (far more survival cases than bankruptcies). The ability to focus on important variables is useful when faced with literally hundreds of available explanatory variables.

1.3.4 Fraud Detection

The insurance and credit card businesses face significant risk from fraud. Credit cards are attractive in providing ease of use at any time, place, and amount, in person or over the Internet, but this generates security issues. Data mining has been widely used to detect potential fraud in real-time applications for credit. In evaluating insurance claims, data analysis is needed to detect patterns and hidden trends. It is important to seek understanding of the relationships between cause and effect to aid business decision making. Polity rates are based on actuarial analysis assuming various distributions for claims and claim size.

Table 1.1 shows the general application areas we will be discussing. Note that they are meant to be representative rather than comprehensive.

Assessing credit risk is an important financial decision on the part of lending institutions. Often decision tree models are created to aid this decision. An example decision tree model for a credit risk assessment is demonstrated in Figure 1.1.

Decision trees provide easily followed and implemented sets of rules for loan administrators. They are generated by obtaining a dataset of past loans with measures for all variables used. Then decision tree models are generated, usually using entropy to determine branches and outcomes.

The applications of data mining are unlimited, a matter of analyst ingenuity in identifying key issues and obtaining the best data they can (that includes experimenting to generate new data). The difference between conventional statistical analysis and data mining is the scale of data considered, as well as greater use of machine learning.

Table 1.1 Data mining application areas

Area	Applications	Specifics
Retailing	Affinity position Cross-selling Customer loyalty programs	Position products effectively Generate more purchases Custom-tailor ads
Banking	Customer relationship management (CRM) Credit risk assessment	Identify customer value Tailor advertising Decide to grant loan
Credit card management	Lift Churn	Identify profitable segments Predict customer turnover
Insurance	Fraud detection	Identify cases to investigate
Telecommunications	Churn	Predict customer turnover
Telemarketing	Online recommender systems	Aid telemarketers
Human resource management	Churn (retention)	Identify potential employee turnover

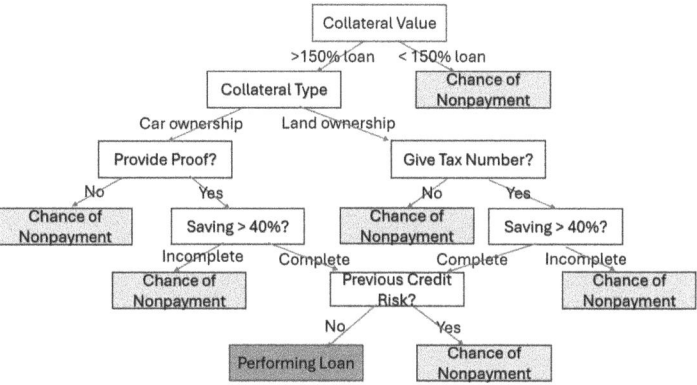

Fig. 1.1 Demonstration credit risk assessment decision tree

1.4 Summary

The presence of big data floods businesses with a variety of data forms, to include numbers, text, and even videos or pictures. Sources of data can be internal from enterprise information systems, but also externally from customers or publicly available data. Data mining provides a tool to turn this data into information leading to improved decision making. Applications can include customer profiling, fraud detection, and churn analysis. The process of data mining relies heavily on data storage support from management information systems as well as data mining software. Chapter 2 will cover the data mining process, and Chapter 3 will discuss some data mining software tools. We will demonstrate various data mining tools with typical data in the remainder of the book. Chapter 4 covers association rule mining, with Rattle, R and Python demonstrations. Chapter 5 does the same with cluster analysis. Chapter 6 covers regression models, including simple time series, multiple regression, and logistic regression. Chapter 7 presents classification models. Variable selection is addressed in Chapter 8 and dataset balancing in Chapter 9.

We provide templates of R and Python code. Note that each system is unique, and variance in coding is possible. We have tested the templates provided but cannot guarantee that they will run as listed on every system. R and Python are computer coding languages. Rattle is an R generalized user interface, with a log that lists R code. Like all machine generated code it tends to be generic and long. But these provide some templates for R coding.

Chapter 2
Data Mining Processes

Data mining projects usually follow a structured process. In order to conduct data mining analysis, a general methodology specifying tasks, inputs, outputs, and ways to execute tasks is useful. This chapter describes an industry standard process, which is often used, and a shorter vendor process. While each step is not needed in every analysis, this process provides a good coverage of the steps needed, starting with data exploration, data collection, data processing, analysis, inferences drawn, and implementation.

Plotnikova et al. (2020) discussed three standard processes for data mining. KDD (Knowledge Discovery in Databases) was the original conceptual process model of computational theories and tools to support information extraction leading to knowledge. CRISP-DM (cross-industry standard process for data mining) is an industry standard, and SEMMA (sample, explore, modify, model, and assess) was developed by the SAS Institute Inc., a leading vendor of data mining software (and a premier statistical software vendor). Industry surveys indicate that CRISP-DM is used by over 70% of the industry professionals, while about half of these professionals use their own methodologies. SEMMA has a lower reported usage, as per the KDNuggets.com survey.

2.1 KDD

KDD consists of nine steps leading to knowledge discovery. KDD distinguishes between data analytics (the entire KDD process) and data mining, which is aimed at finding hidden information in the data. The nine steps are:

1. Learning the application domain and prior knowledge followed by identification of the customer's goal;
2. Dataset creation: select a dataset and identify the variables involved;

3. Data cleaning and processing: remove noise or outliers, decide on strategy to handle missing data, account for data types;
4. Data reduction and projection: apply transformation as needed to find the optimal features for the data;
5. Choose the data mining function: summarization, classification, regression, clustering, etc.;
6. Choose data mining algorithm: select models and parameters (often multiple models);
7. Data mining: search for interesting patterns, obtaining classification rules or trees, regression models, or clustering;
8. Interpretation: filter out redundant or irrelevant patterns interpret and visualize relevant patterns to make results understandable to users;
9. Use discovered knowledge: incorporate results into the performance system, document, report to stakeholders, use results as the basis for decisions.

This KDD process led to evolution to extend the framework. CRISP-DM appeared in 2000, while SAS introduced SEMMA in 2015.

2.2 CRISP-DM

CRISP-DM is widely used by the industry members. This model consists of six phases intended as a cyclical process: This six-phase process is not a rigid, by-the-numbers procedure. There is usually a great deal of backtracking. Additionally, experienced analysts may not need to apply each phase for every study. But, CRISP-DM provides a useful framework for data mining.

2.2.1 Business Understanding

The key element of a data mining study is understanding the purpose of the study. This begins with the managerial need for new knowledge and the expression of the business objective of the study to be undertaken. Goals in terms of things, such as which types of customers are interested in each of our products or what are the typical profiles of our customers, and how much value do each of them provide to us, are needed. Then, a plan for finding such knowledge needs to be developed, in terms of those responsible for collecting data, analyzing data, and reporting. At this stage, a budget to support the study should be established, at least in preliminary terms.

2.2 CRISP-DM

2.2.2 Data Understanding

Once the business objectives and the project plan are established, data understanding considers data requirements. This step can include initial data collection, data description, data exploration, and verification of data quality. Data exploration, such as viewing summary statistics (which includes visual display of the categorical variables), can occur at the end of this phase. Models such as cluster analysis can also be applied during this phase, with the intent of identifying patterns in the data.

Data sources for data selection can vary. Normally, the types of data sources for business applications include *demographic data* (such as income, education, number of households, and age), *sociographic data* (such as hobby, club membership, and entertainment), *transactional data* (sales record, credit card spending, and issued checks), and so on. The data type can be categorized as quantitative and qualitative data. *Quantitative data* is measurable by numerical values. It can be either discrete (such as integers) or continuous (such as real numbers). *Qualitative data*, also known as categorical data, contains both nominal and ordinal data.

Nominal data has finite nonordered values, such as gender data having two values: male and female. Ordinal data has finite ordered values. For example, customer credit ratings are ordinal data since ratings can be excellent, fair, or bad.

2.2.3 Data Preparation

The purpose of data preprocessing is to clean the selected data for better quality. Some selected data may have different formats because they are chosen from different data sources. If selected data are from flat files, voice messages, and web texts, they should be converted to a consistent electronic format. In general, data cleaning means to filter, aggregate, and fill the missing values (*imputation*). By filtering data, the selected data are examined for outliers and redundancies. Outliers have huge differences from the majority of data or data that are clearly out of range of the selected data groups. For example, if the income of a customer included in the middle class is $250,000, it is an error and should be taken out from the data mining project examining aspects of the middle class. Outliers may be caused by many reasons, such as human errors or technical errors, or may naturally occur in a dataset due to extreme events. Suppose the age of a credit card holder is recorded as 12. This is likely a human error. However, there may be such an independently wealthy preteenager with important purchasing habits. Arbitrarily deleting this outlier could lose valuable information.

Redundant data are the same information recorded in several different ways. The daily sales of a particular product are redundant to seasonal sales of the same product, because we can derive the sales from either daily data or seasonal data. By aggregating data, the data dimensions are reduced to obtain aggregated information. Note that although an aggregated dataset has a small volume, the information will remain. If a marketing promotion for furniture sales is considered in the next three or four years, then the available daily sales data can be aggregated as annual sales data. The size of the sales data is dramatically reduced. By smoothing data, the missing values of the selected data are found and new or reasonable values will be added. These added values could be the average number of the variable (mean) or the mode. A missing value often causes no solution when a data mining algorithm is applied to discover the knowledge patterns.

Usually, we think of data as real numbers, such as age in years or annual income in dollars (we would use RANGE in those cases). Sometimes, variables occur as either and or types, such as having a driving license or not, an insurance claim being fraudulent or not. This case could be dealt with by real numeric values (such as 0 or 1). But, it is more efficient to treat them as FLAG variables. Often it is more appropriate to deal with categorical data, such as age in terms of the set {young, middle-aged, elderly} or income in the set {low, middle, high}. In that case, we could group the data and assign the appropriate category in terms of a string, using a set. The most complete form is RANGE, but sometimes data does not come in that form, and analysts are forced to use SET or FLAG types.

Sometimes, it may actually be more accurate to deal with SET data types than RANGE data types.

Each software tool will have a different data scheme, but the primary types of data dealt with are represented in these two lists.

There are many statistical methods and visualization tools that can be used to preprocess the selected data. Common statistics, such as max, min, mean, and mode, can be readily used to aggregate or smooth the data, while scatter plots and box plots are usually used to filter outliers. More advanced techniques, including regression analysis, cluster analysis, decision tree, or hierarchical analysis, may be applied in data preprocessing depending on the requirements for the quality of the selected data. Because data preprocessing is detailed and tedious, it demands a great deal of time. In some cases, data preprocessing could take over 50% of the time of the entire data mining process. Shortening data processing time can reduce much of the total computation time in data mining. The simple and standard data format resulting from data preprocessing can provide an environment of information sharing across different computer systems, which creates the flexibility to implement various data mining algorithms or tools.

2.2.4 Modeling

Data modeling is where the data mining software is used to generate results for various situations. Cluster analysis and or visual exploration of the data is usually applied first. Depending on the type of data, various models might then be applied. If the task is to group data and the groups are given, discriminant analysis might be appropriate. If the purpose is estimation, regression is appropriate if the data is continuous (and logistic regression, if not). Neural networks could be applied for both tasks. Decision trees are yet another tool to classify data. Other modeling tools are available as well. The point of data mining software is to allow the user to work with the data to gain understanding. This is often fostered by the iterative use of multiple models.

Data treatment: Data mining is essentially analysis of the statistical data, usually using very large datasets. The standard process of data mining is to take this large set of data and divide it using a portion of the data (the *training set*) for the development of the model (no matter which modeling technique is used) and reserving a portion of the data (the *test set*) for testing the model that is built. The principle is that if you build a model on a particular set of data, it will of course test quite well. By dividing the data and using part of it for model development, and testing it on a separate set of data, a more convincing test of model accuracy is obtained.

This idea of splitting the data into components is often carried to the additional levels in the practice of data mining. Further portions of the data can be used for refinement of the model.

2.2.5 Evaluation

In this phase data mining models can be applied. Data mining can lead to understanding through association rules, classification, clustering, predictions, sequential patterns, and similar time sequences. In *association rule mining*, the relationship of some item in a data transaction with other items in the same transaction is used to predict patterns. For example, if a customer purchases a laptop PC (X), then he or she also buys a mouse (Y) in 60% of the cases. This pattern occurs in 5.6% of laptop PC purchases. An association rule in this situation can be "X implies Y, where 60 percent is the confidence factor and 5.6 percent is the support factor." When the confidence factor and support factor are represented by linguistic variables "high" and "low," respectively, the association rule can be written in the fuzzy logic form, such as "when the support factor is low, X implies Y is high." In the case of many qualitative variables, fuzzy association is a necessary and promising technique in data mining.

Sequential pattern analysis seeks to find similar patterns in data transaction over a business period. These patterns can be used by the business analysts to identify relationships among data. The mathematical models behind sequential patterns are logic rules, fuzzy logic, and so on. As an extension of sequential patterns, *similar time sequences* are applied to discover sequences similar to a known sequence over the past and current business periods. In the data mining stage, several similar sequences can be studied to identify the future trends in transaction development. This approach is useful in dealing with databases that have time-series characteristics.

Important data mining functions include clustering, prediction, and classification.

2.2.6 Deployment

Deployment is to put data mining analysis to use. The data interpretation stage is very critical. It assimilates knowledge from mined data. There are two essential issues. One is how to recognize the business value from knowledge patterns discovered in the data mining stage. Another issue is which visualization tool should be used to show the data mining results. Determining the business value from discovered knowledge patterns is similar to playing "puzzles." The mined data is a puzzle that needs to be put together for a business purpose. This operation depends on the interaction between data analysts, business analysts, and decision makers (such as managers or CEOs). Because data analysts may not be fully aware of the purpose of the data mining goal or objective, while business analysts may not understand the results of sophisticated mathematical solutions, interaction between them is necessary. In order to properly interpret knowledge patterns, it is necessary to choose an appropriate visualization tool. There are many visualization packages or tools available, including pie charts, histograms, box plots, scatter plots, and distributions. A good interpretation will lead to productive business decisions, while a poor interpretation analysis may miss useful information. Normally, the simpler the graphical interpretation, the easier it is for the end users to understand.

2.3 SEMMA

In order to be applied successfully, the data mining solution must be viewed as a process, rather than a set of tools or techniques. In addition to the CRISP-DM, there is yet another well-known methodology developed by the SAS Institute Inc., called SEMMA. The acronym SEMMA stands for sample, explore, modify, model, and assess. Beginning with a statistically representative sample of your data, SEMMA intends to make it easy to apply the exploratory statistical and visualization techniques, select and transform the most significant predictive variables, model the variables to predict outcomes, and finally, confirm a model's accuracy.

By assessing the outcome of each stage in the SEMMA process, one can determine how to model new questions raised by the previous results, and thus, proceed back to the exploration phase for additional refinement of the data. That is, as is the case with CRISP-DM, SEMMA is also driven by a highly iterative experimentation cycle.

2.3.1 Step 1 (Sample)

This is where a portion of a large dataset (big enough to contain the significant information, yet small enough to manipulate quickly) is extracted. For optimal cost and computational performance, some (including the SAS Institute Inc.) advocate a sampling strategy, which applies a reliable, statistically representative sample of the full-detailed data. In the case of very large datasets, mining a representative sample instead of the whole volume may drastically reduce the processing time required to get crucial business information. If general patterns appear in the data as a whole, these will be traceable in a representative sample. If a niche (a rare pattern) is so tiny that it is not represented in a sample and yet so important that it influences the big picture, then it should be discovered using the exploratory data description methods. It is also advised to create partitioned datasets for better accuracy assessment.

Datasets are sometimes divided into three (or may be more) groups if a lot of model development is conducted. The basic idea is to develop models on the training set and then test the resulting models on the test set. When developing models with the data, a validation set is also often used. It is typical to try to develop multiple models (such as various decision trees, logistic regression, and neural network models) for the same training set and to evaluate errors on the test set.

- Training—used for model fitting.
- Validation—used for assessment and for preventing over fitting.
- Test—used to obtain an honest assessment of how well a model generalizes.

2.3.2 Step 2 (Explore)

This is where the user searches for unanticipated trends and anomalies in order to gain a better understanding of the dataset. After sampling your data, the next step is to explore them visually or numerically for inherent trends or groupings. Exploration helps refine and redirect the discovery process. If visual exploration does not reveal clear trends, one can explore the data through statistical techniques, including factor analysis, correspondence analysis, and clustering. For example, in data mining for a direct mail campaign, clustering might reveal the groups of customers with distinct ordering patterns. Limiting the discovery process to each of these distinct groups individually may increase the likelihood of exploring richer patterns that may not be strong enough to be detected if the whole dataset is to be processed together.

2.3.3 Step 3 (Modify)

This is where the user creates, selects, and transforms the variables upon which to focus the model-construction process. Based on the discoveries in the exploration phase, one may need to manipulate data to include information, such as the grouping of customers and significant subgroups, or to introduce new variables. It may also be necessary to look for outliers and reduce the number of variables, to narrow them down to the most significant ones. One may also need to modify data when the "mined" data change. Because data mining is a dynamic, iterative process, you can update the data mining methods or models when new information is available.

2.3.4 Step 4 (Model)

This is where the user searches for a variable combination that reliably predicts a desired outcome. Once you prepare your data, you are ready to construct models that explain patterns in the data. Modeling techniques in data mining include artificial neural networks, decision trees, rough set analysis, support vector machines, logistic models, and other statistical models, such as time-series analysis, memory-based reasoning, and principal component analysis. Each type of model has particular strengths and is appropriate within the specific data mining situations, depending on the data. For example, artificial neural networks are very good at fitting highly complex nonlinear relationships, while rough sets analysis is known to produce reliable results with uncertain and imprecise problem situations.

2.3.5 Step 5 (Assess)

This is where the user evaluates the usefulness and reliability of the findings from the data mining process. In this final step of the data mining process, the user assesses the models to estimate how well it performs. A common means of assessing a model is to apply it to a portion of dataset put aside (and not used during the model building) during the sampling stage. If the model is valid, it should work for this reserved sample as well as for the sample used to construct the model. Similarly, you can test the model against known data. For example, if you know which customers in a file had high retention rates and your model predicts retention, you can check to see whether the model selects these customers accurately. In addition, practical applications of the model, such as partial mailings in a direct mail campaign, help prove its validity.

The SEMMA approach is completely compatible with the CRISP-DM approach. Both aid the knowledge discovery process. Once the models are obtained and tested, they can then be deployed to gain value with respect to a business or research application.

2.4 Model Controls

A key part of modeling is to obtain models that provide useful information to aid decision making. There are a variety of purposes. Table 2.1 displays models, common uses, and controls available to users: occurrence.

Analytics is the process of applying tools to data to improve understanding in specific problem contexts. Table 2.1 lists the most commonly used tools (there are others, such as naïve Bayes models that have special purposes). The important part of modeling is to apply appropriate models, know which controls to use to gain understanding, and improve performance of whatever system is being analyzed.

Table 2.1 Data mining models

Model	Uses	Purposes	Controls
Association rules	Identify co-occurrence	Cross-selling Symptom relationships	Support Confidence
Cluster analysis	Group data	Similarity identification	K (number of clusters)
Regression	Simple regression ARIMA Multiple regression	Predict Forecast Relationships	Data P D Q Select variables
Classification	Decision trees Logistic regression Support vector machines Neural networks Ensembles	Classify " " " Random forest, boosting	Complexity Select variables Hidden layers

2.5 Evaluation of Model Results

Models with involving continuous variables such as regression are measured in various ways. Regressions have r-squared measures, reflecting the proportion of variance in the dependent variable that has been explained by the model. Time series accuracy can also be measured by sum of squared errors or other related metrics. Classification errors are commonly displayed in *coincidence matrixes* (called confusion matrixes by some). A coincidence matrix shows the count of cases correctly classified as well as the count of cases classified in each incorrect category. But, in many data mining studies, the model may be very good at classifying one category, while very poor at classifying another category. The primary value of the coincidence matrix is that it identifies what kinds of errors are made. It may be much more important to avoid one kind of error than another. Assume a loan vice president suffers a great deal more from giving a loan to someone who's expected to repay and does not, than making the mistake of not giving a loan to an applicant who actually would have paid. Both instances would be classification errors, but in data mining, often one category of error is much more important than another. Coincidence matrixes provide a means of focusing on what kinds of errors particular models tend to make.

Deployment is the act of using data mining analyses. New knowledge generated by the study needs to be related to the original project goal. Once developed, models need to be monitored for performance. The patterns and relationships developed based on the training set need to be changed if the underlying conditions generating the data change. For instance, if the customer profile performance changes due to the changes in the economic conditions, the predicted rates of response cannot be expected to remain the same. Thus, it is important to check the relative accuracy of data mining models and adjust them to new conditions, if necessary.

2.5.1 Example Model

Westerski et al. (2021) reported the modeling of a procurement fraud detection system developed for government procurement in Singapore. Four years of procurement activity involved 216,000 transactions. Procurement savings are generated through purchase consolidation obtaining price reductions because of volume. Savings also are obtained by close collaboration with long-term vendor relationships. Almost always, government procurement relies upon competitive bidding. However, these sources of savings also have been taken advantage of to fraudulently take money from procuring agencies. Procurement agency employees have been exploited to cheat governments. Collusion among bidders is another major source of procurement fraud.

The procuring agency under study had a procurement portal intended to manage all purchase orders. Procurement activity was systematically audited. The first step was to generate a risk score for each procurement transaction in order to detect potential fraudulent activity. Unsupervised computer analysis was implemented to investigate procurer-vendor relationships, activity to reduce order values in order avoid approval procedures, and identification of price variances for the same products ordered across purchase orders. Initial experience identified a need for the system to not only identify risky cases, but to be able to explain why they were risky to procurement officers. Further, models that were understandable by users and capable of expansion were needed, and that would execute in reasonable time. The second stage of the analysis (a matter of years) refined the framework and algorithms.

Transaction stages included invitations for vendor quotations, bid placement and approval, and issuance of a purchase order. Over the period 2010 through 2013 the 216,771 purchase orders were identified involving over 607,000 items. The four key aspects were found to be who (requester), what (item), from whom (vendor), and when (creation and approval dates). Of the 607,369 purchase order items, information was missing in 291,333 records due to data input issues. Analysis of the overall system led to identification of an ensemble of risk indicators. The risk indicators, all of which generated tools for auditors to identify risk and trace logic.

As an example, the unusual vendor indicator looked as relationships between requesting officers, approving officers, vendors, approval date, and total value of the purchase. If the requesting officer bought common goods from a vendor that nobody else dealt with, that was considered an indicator of potential collusion. The focus was on seeking pattern abnormalities. The item spending indicator employed natural language processing followed by cluster analysis to enable detection of outlier cases. The focus in this indicator was numeric values deviating from reference levels. The third indicator was to analyze order splitting.

This case gives an example of the process of a data mining study. The system needed to be defined, data gathered and cleaned, followed by modeling. Once initial results were obtained, users were involved to critique the output of the system, which was refined over a period of years.

2.5 Evaluation of Model Results

When classifying data, in the simplest binary case, there are two opportunities for the model to be wrong. If the model is seeking to predict true or false, correctly classifying true is *true positive* (TP), and correctly classifying false is *true negative* (TN). One type of error is to incorrectly classify an actual false as true (*false positive* (FP), *type I error*).

A second type of error is to incorrectly classify an actual true case as false (*false negative* (FN), *type II error*).

2.5.2 Cost Metrics

A way to reflect the relative error importance is through cost. This is a relatively simple idea, allowing the user to assign relative costs by the type of error. For instance, if our model predicted that an account was insolvent, that might involve an average write-off of $1000. On the other hand, waiting for an account that ultimately was repaid might involve a cost of $50. Thus, there would be a major difference in the cost of errors in this case. Treating a case that turned out to be repaid as a dead account would risk the net loss of $950 in addition to alienating the customer (which may or may not have future profitability implications). Conversely, treating an account that was never going to be repaid may involve carrying the account on the books longer than needed, at an additional cost of $50. Here, a cost function for the coincidence matrix could be:

$$\$950 \times (\text{closing good account}) + \$50 \times (\text{keeping bad account open})$$

(Note that we used our own dollar costs for purposes of demonstration and were not based on the real case.) This measure (like the correct classification rate) can be used to compare alternative models. We assume a model is built on a training set of 1,000,000 cases which is then applied to a test set of 100,000 cases predicting 10,000 defaults. Of the test set of 100,000 cases, 500 defaulted and 99,500 paid back (or were OK). The coincidence matrix for this model is displayed in Table 2.2.

The overall classification accuracy is obtained by dividing the correct number of classifications (400 + 89,900 = 90,300) by the total number of cases (100,000). Thus, the test data was correctly classified in 0.903 of the cases. The cost function value here was:

Table 2.2 Demonstration coincidence matrix

	Model default	Model OK	
Actual default	400	100	500
Actual OK	9600	89,900	99,500
	10,000	90,000	100,000

$$\$1000 \times 100 + \$50 \times 9600 = \$580,000$$

This can be compared with the results of other models (typically a variety of classification models are run, such as random forests, extreme boosting, support vector machines, neural networks, etc., and confusion matrices and cost functions can be used to select which model to use).

2.5.3 Other Measures

There are a number of other measures obtainable from the confusion matrix. Most are self-defining, such as:

True positive rate (TPR), which is equal to TP/(TP + FN) (also called *sensitivity*)

$$\text{Example}: 89900/(89900 + 9600) = 0.9035$$

True negative rate (TNR) equal to TN/(FP + TN) (also called *specificity*)

$$\text{Example}: 400/(9600 + 400) = 0.04$$

Positive predictive value (PPV) equal to TP/(TP + FP) (also called *precision*)

$$\text{Example}: 89900/(89900 + 100) = 0.9989$$

Negative predictive value (NPV) equal to TN/(TN + FN)

$$\text{Example}: 400/(400 + 100) = 0.80$$

False positive rate (FPR) equal to FP/(FP + TN) (also called *fall-out*) *False discovery rate* (FDR) equal to FP/(FP + TP)

$$\text{Example}: 100/(100 + 400) = 0.20$$

False negative rate (FNR) equal to FN/FN + TP) (also called *miss rate*).

$$\text{Example}: 9000/(9000 + 89900) = 0.091$$

Accuracy is equal to (TP + TN)/(TP + TN + FP + FN)

$$\text{Example}: (89900 + 400)/(89900 + 400 + 100 + 9600) = 0.903$$

A *receiver operating characteristic* (ROC) curve is obtained by plotting TPR versus FPR for various threshold settings. This is equivalent to plotting the cumulative distribution function of the detection probability on the *y* axis versus the cumulative distribution of the false-alarm probability on the *x* axis.

2.6 Summary

KDD was the first data mining process framework. The industry standard CRISP-DM process has six stages: (1) business understanding, (2) data understanding, (3) data preparation, (4) modeling, (5) evaluation, and (6) deployment. SEMMA is another process outline with a very similar structure. Using the CRISP-DM framework, data selection and understanding, preparation, and model interpretation require teamwork between data mining analysts and business analysts, while data transformation and data mining are conducted by data mining analysts. Each stage is a preparation for the next stage. In the remainder chapters of this book, we will discuss the details of this process from a different perspective, such as data mining tools and applications. This will provide the reader with a better understanding of why the correct process, sometimes, is even more important than correct performance of the methodology.

Deployment is the act of using data mining analyses. New knowledge generated by the study needs to be related to the original project goal. Once developed, models need to be monitored for performance. The patterns and relationships developed based on the training set need to be changed if the underlying conditions generating the data change. For instance, if the customer profile performance changes due to the changes in the economic conditions, the predicted rates of response cannot be expected to remain the same. Thus, it is important to check the relative accuracy of data mining models and adjust them to new conditions, if necessary.

References

Plotnikova V, Dumas M, Milani F (2020) Adaptations of data mining methodologies: a systematic literature review. Peer J Comput Sci 6:e267. https://doi.org/10.7717/peerj-cs.267

Westerski A, Kanagasabai R, Shaham E, Narayanan A, Wong J, Singh M (2021) Explainable anomaly detection for procurement fraud identification—lessons from practical deployments. Int Trans Oper Res 28:3276–3302

Chapter 3
Data Mining Software

There are many excellent commercial data mining software products, although these tend to be expensive. These include SAS Enterprise Miner and IBM's Intelligent Miner, as well as many more recent variants and new products appearing regularly. Datamation ranks data mining software, shown in Table 3.1.

Note that some products such as KNIME and RapidMiner have basic versions available as open-source, with commercial variants. R and Python are open-source programming languages that are highly popular. Rattle is a graphical user interface (GUI) system for R (also open-source) and is also highly recommended.

3.1 R

To install R, visit https://cran.rstudio.com/ Open a folder for R.

Select Download R for Windows.

R is a command line software. R Studio, a Graphical User Interface (GUI) and integrated programming environment developed for R, provides a user-friendly programming environment by making screen menus for packages, functions, and files, surfing and saving utilities, and concurrent access to multiple scripts, files, and directories. You can download both R and RStudio (Fig. 3.1) from the following URL: https://posit.co/download/rstudio-desktop/.

Install R first, by clicking on "Download and Install r". This will redirect you to https://cran.rstudio.com where you can download R compatible to your operations system. Follow the instructions in next step and install R (Fig. 3.2).

After completing R installation, go back to https://posit.co/download/rstudio-desktop/ and download the executable file that will install RStudio on your computer. There is a button available for RStudio desktop for Windows. If you have a different operating system, scroll down the page and find the proper release.

Table 3.1 Data mining software by popularity (Datamation.com)

Rank	Commercial	Open-source
1	SAS Enterprise Miner	WEKA
2	Oracle Data Miner	KNIME
3	IBM SPSS Modeler	Orange
4	TIBCO Data Science	RapidMiner
5	MonkeyLearn	Apache Mahout

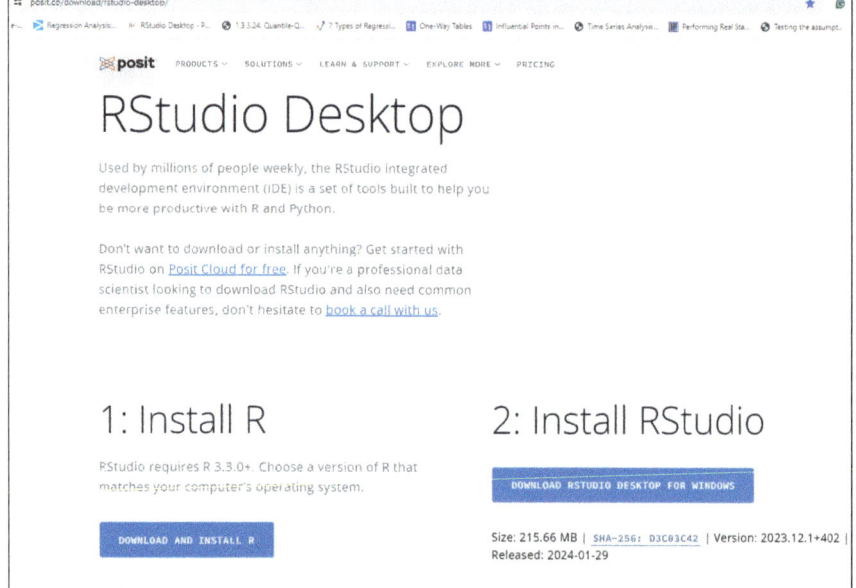

Fig. 3.1 R and RStudio download page

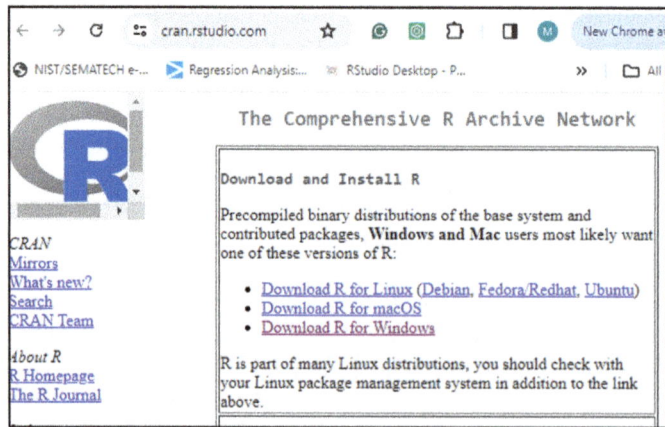

Fig. 3.2 R download page

3.1 R

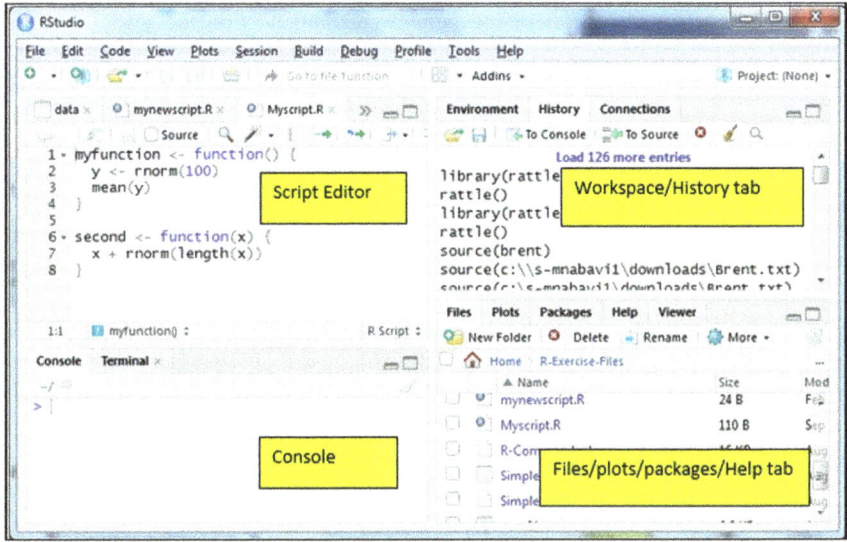

Fig. 3.3 RStudio programming environment

RStudio will be the default interface of R. There are four major areas in RStudio interface (see Fig. 3.3).

- **Workspace/History/Connections**: This area on the upper-right of the interface window is the current working environment and includes all objects defined by user, including functions, variables, and all data structure elements such as vectors, data frames, and lists. These elements and all scripts are saved in your working directory, the default location of storing R files. You may use two commands in the console to find out where your working directory is, or change it. '#' is the comment character and R will ignore anything typed in a line after this character.
- **Files/Plots/Packages/Help**: At the lower-right section of the window you can explore the working directory, demonstrate plots, and help content. You may open any file from the Files tab in this area and display or import data from compatible formats into R environment.
- **Script editor**: on the upper-left of the window, a script writing environment and data file demonstration. Can save the script as a.R file. To start a new file use the menu: File > New File > R Script, or use the key combination Ctrl + Shift + N. For opening an existing file use menu File > Open or key combination Ctrl + O. A good introduction to RStudio script editor can be found here: https://support.posit.co/hc/en-us/articles/200484448-Editing-and-Executing-Code. To run script command(s) put the cursor on the line you are going to execute, then click the run button (green arrow) from the menu or use key combination Ctrl + Enter. For running multiple lines, highlight them, then use one of these options.

- **Console**: on the lower-left of the window. Command-line execution area that does not save the script. You may directly type and run commands here. This area demonstrates the output as well.

Since R is an open-source developing environment and evolving frequently, by the time you use this material there might be a few changes in control and performance of the language, but they are mostly in the form of additions to packages and libraries, unlikely to change the basic syntax and performance of the tools we use here. Before starting with the R command line instructions please note that R is a case sensitive language.

To create a new script file use File/New File/R Script (Fig. 3.4). Save your script using File/Save As menu. For opening existing files use File/Open File… from menu. When opening or creating several files, they are all available under their own tabs.

Code completion is another feature of RStudio. When typing commands in script editor or console, screen menu makes variables, functions, or libraries available in your workspace and potentially match the partial string you are typing. You may select options using down arrow and tab to select and complete the string (Fig. 3.5).

Find and edit/replace is invoked by pressing Ctrl + F, or Edit/Find menu. You can search and find variable, function, or arguments in script using this feature.

Comment lines start with # and automatically color coded (Fig. 3.6). You can comment anywhere in your script starting the line with #. If you have a long comment that needs multiple lines, select all lines and use Ctrl + Shift + C to convert them to comment lines altogether.

To execute each line of code in script editor, put the cursor on the line and click on Run button on top of the editor, or use Ctrl + Enter key combination. You may

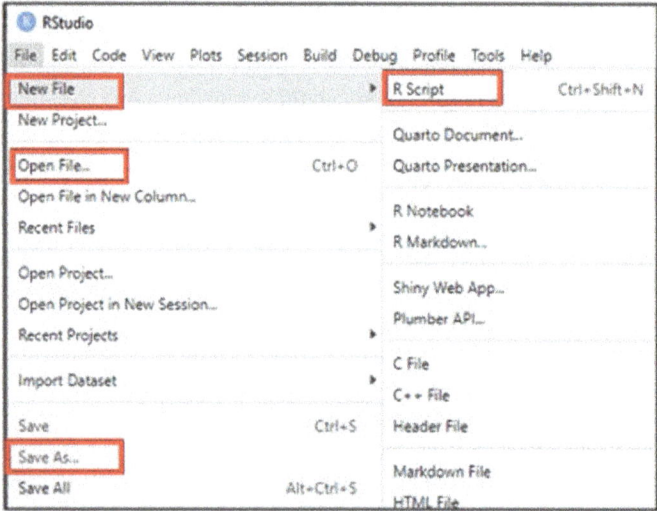

Fig. 3.4 RStudio file creation, saving, and opening

3.1 R

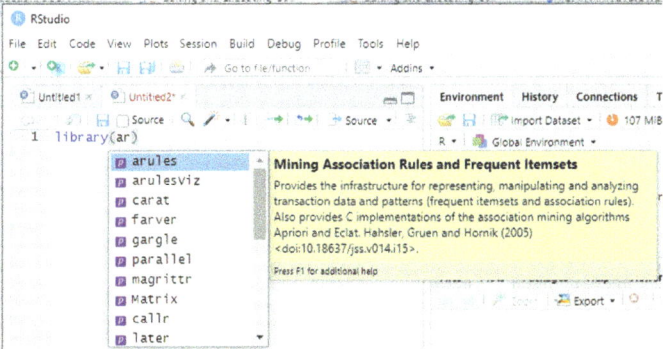

Fig. 3.5 RStudio auto-complete feature

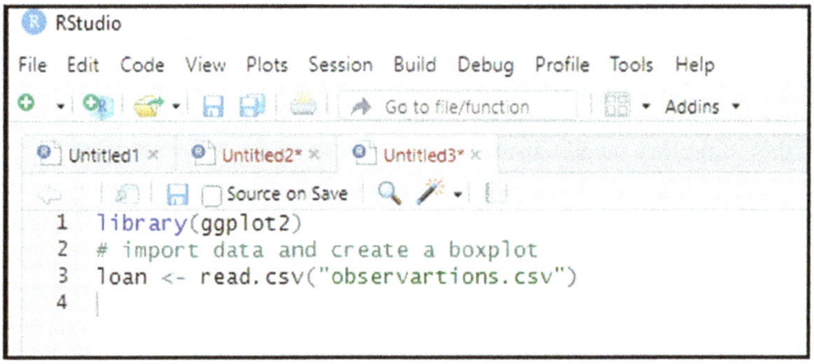

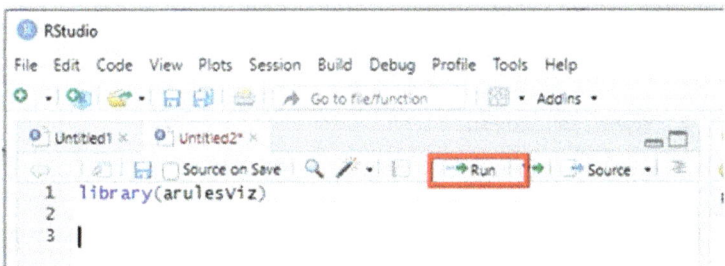

Fig. 3.6 Commenting R code

select multiple lines of code and use Ctrl + Enter. To run the entire script, use Ctrl + Shift + Enter (Fig. 3.7).

When using the console, using Enter key will execute each line of code.

Fig. 3.7 Code execution in RStudio

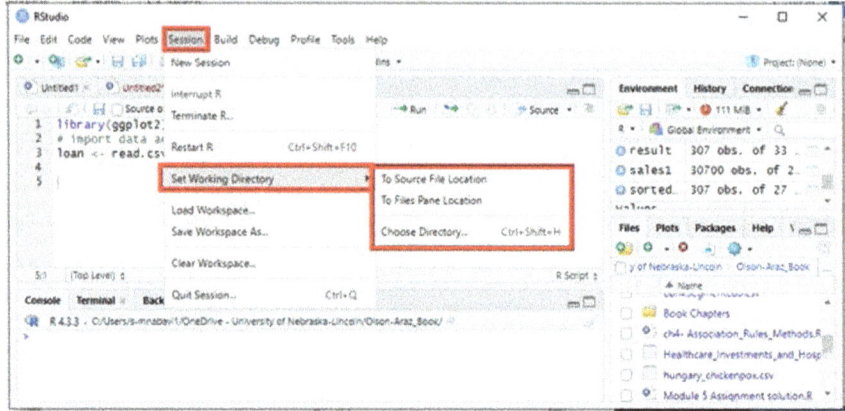

Fig. 3.8 Change working directory in RStudio

Working directory: Every R script is created in the current working directory. This script has direct access to all files in that directory. Access to files out of this directory needs using the complete path. You can find this directory by typing the following command in script editor or console and return the full path of the directory: getwd( ).

Set the working directory using setwd( ) command, or use the convenient options available under "Session/Set Working Directory" menu (Fig. 3.8). "To Source File Location" will set the working directory to the current file location, saved previously and open at that time. The last option, "Choose Directory" is more flexible in choosing or creating the working directory of choice.

R packages provide pre-programmed functions for a variety of analytical processes. These functions are only available to programmers if their library is already loaded into the working space. For example, ggplot() function will not work unless the library ggplot2 is loaded prior to call for this function:

```
library(ggplot2)
```

Loading all libraries required for a script first, is a good practice. These libraries need to be installed prior to loading too. R will download on computers with basic functionality. Thousands of additional libraries however, are available for download. We can download them using either the command line or RStudio menu (Fig. 3.9). Command line syntax for ggplot2 library is:

```
Install.packages("ggplot2")
```

Menu "Tools/Install Packages…" will open a dialog box for typing the package name. Enter the package you need and make sure the "Install dependencies" checkbox is checked. R packages are often developed relying on existing packages, so when they are called for operation, those packages should be available as well.

3.2 Rattle

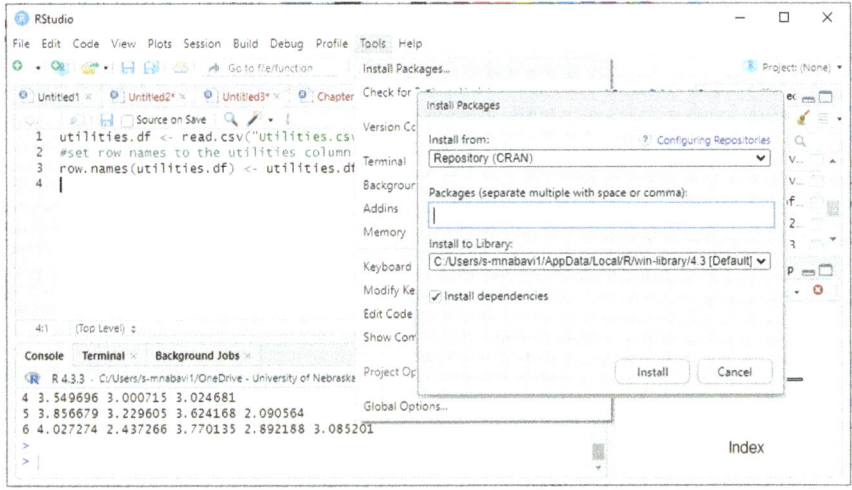

Fig. 3.9 Install R packages in RStudio

3.2 Rattle

To install Rattle:

Open the R Desktop icon (32-bit or 64-bit) and enter the following com- mand at the R prompt. R will ask for a CRAN mirror. Choose a nearby location.

> install.packages("rattle")

Enter the following two commands at the R prompt. This loads the Rattle package into the library and then starts up Rattle.

> library(rattle)

> rattle()

If the RGtk2 package is yet to be installed, there will be an error popup indicating that libatk-1.0–0.dll is missing from your computer. Click on the OK button and then, you will be asked if you would like to install GTK+. Click on OK to do so. This then downloads and installs the appropriate GTK+ libraries for your computer. After this has finished, do exit from R and restart it so that it can find the newly installed libraries.

When running Rattle, a number of other packages will be downloaded and installed as needed, with Rattle asking for the user's permission before doing so. They only need to be downloaded once.

The installation has been tested to work on Microsoft Windows, 32-bit and 64-bit, XP, Vista, and 7 with R 3.1.1, Rattle 3.1.0, and RGtk2. If you are missing something, you will get a message from R asking you to install a package. I read nominal data (string), and was prompted that I needed "stringr." On the R console (see Fig. 3.1), click on the "Packages" tab on the top line.

Give the command "Install packages," which will direct you to HTTPS CRAN mirror. Select one of the sites (like "USA(TX) [https]") and find "stringr" and click on it. Then, upload that package. You may have to restart R.

We will demonstrate on a small file of appliance loan applicants. Data was divided into a training set of 400 cases (LoanTrainPredictive.csv) and a test set of 250 (Loan-TestPredictive.csv). Variables are age, income, assets, debts, loan amount requested, a risk measure based on the relationship of debts, a categorical credit rating, FICO score and a categorical risk rating. The risk rating was generated by formula using assets, debts, and amount requested. The outcome variable was on-time payment or not (late or default).

To run a model, on the *Filename* line, click on the icon and browse for the file "LoanTrainPredictive.csv." Click on the *Execute* icon on the upper left of the Rattle window. This yields Fig. 3.10.

Here variable "Risk" is a function "Assets," "Debt," and "Want." Rattle treated "Debt" as an identifier variable and deleted it from the analysis. This can be adjusted by the user so desires.

Select the *Model* tab, yielding Fig. 3.11.

This yields options to set parameters for a decision tree, which we will examine later in the book. For now, we can use the default settings shown, *Execute*, and obtain Fig. 3.12.

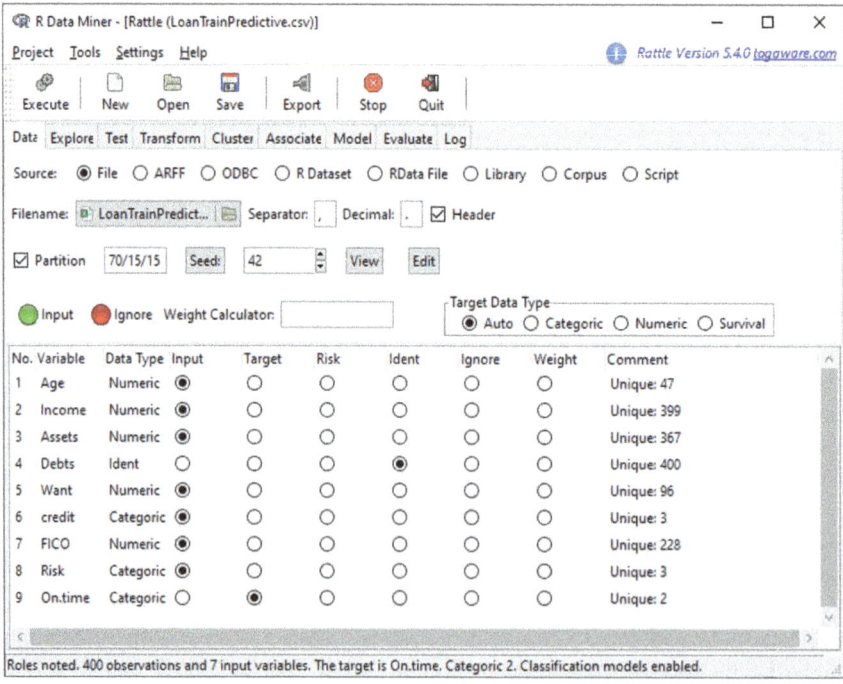

Fig. 3.10 LoanTrainPredictive.csv data read

3.3 Python

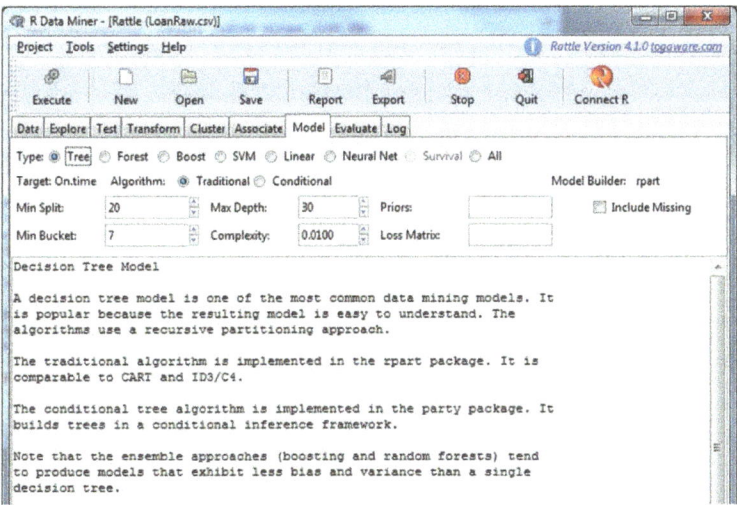

Fig. 3.11 Model tab with Tree selected

Rattle can also provide a descriptive decision tree by selecting the *Rules* button, yielding Fig. 3.13.

Selecting the *Draw* button yields Fig. 3.14, a graphic decision tree.

3.3 Python

Python is also a command line programming language. Python base is a limited library, available to download with a standard command line editor.

3.3.1 Installing Python

Installing Python is a straightforward process. Here are the step-by-step instructions:

1. Download Python Installer:

   Go to the official Python website at https://www.python.org/. On the homepage, you'll see a prominent download button (Fig. 3.15).

2. Select Operating System:

   Python is available for various operating systems like Windows, macOS, and Linux. Choose the installer that corresponds to your operating system. For

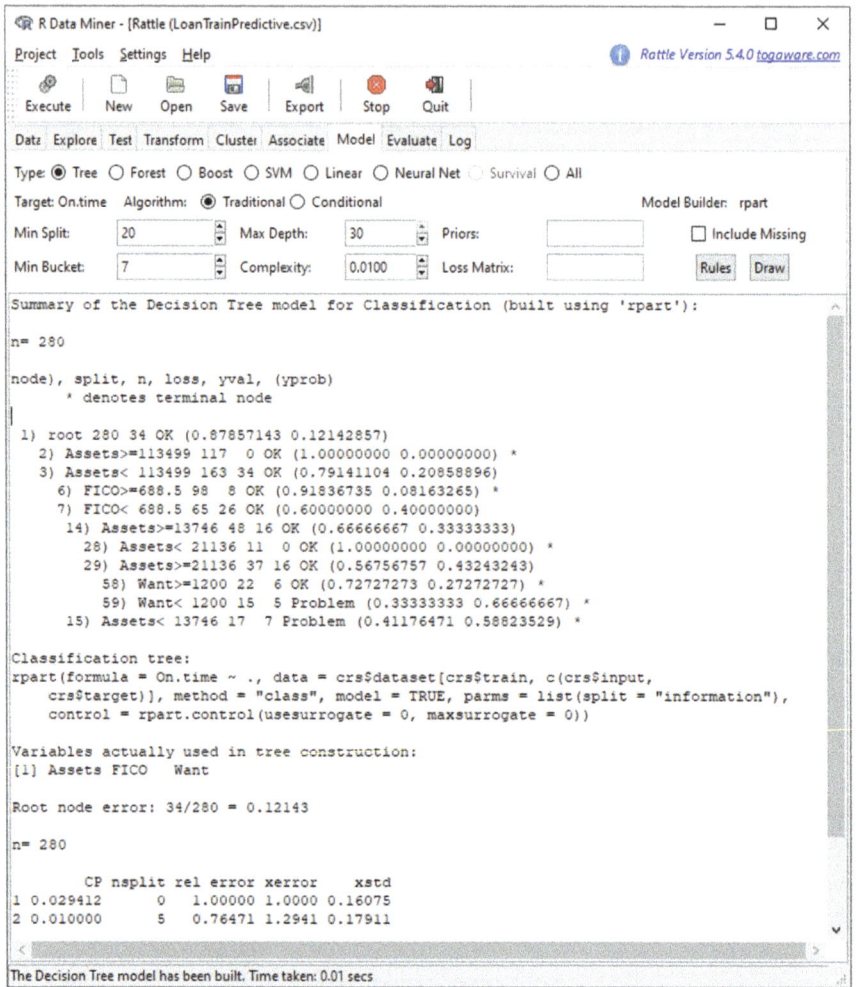

Fig. 3.12 Decision tree model for LoanTrainPredictive.csv data

example, if you're using Windows, download the Windows installer. If you're using macOS, download the macOS installer.

3. Choose Python Version:

   Click on "Downloads" to expand and then click on "Windows" to jump to the download Python version page. Choose the latest stable version available, which should be displayed on the downloads page (Fig. 3.16).

4. Download Installer:

   Click on the download button for the installer corresponding to your operating system. The installer file will start downloading. Wait for the download to complete (Fig. 3.17).

3.3 Python

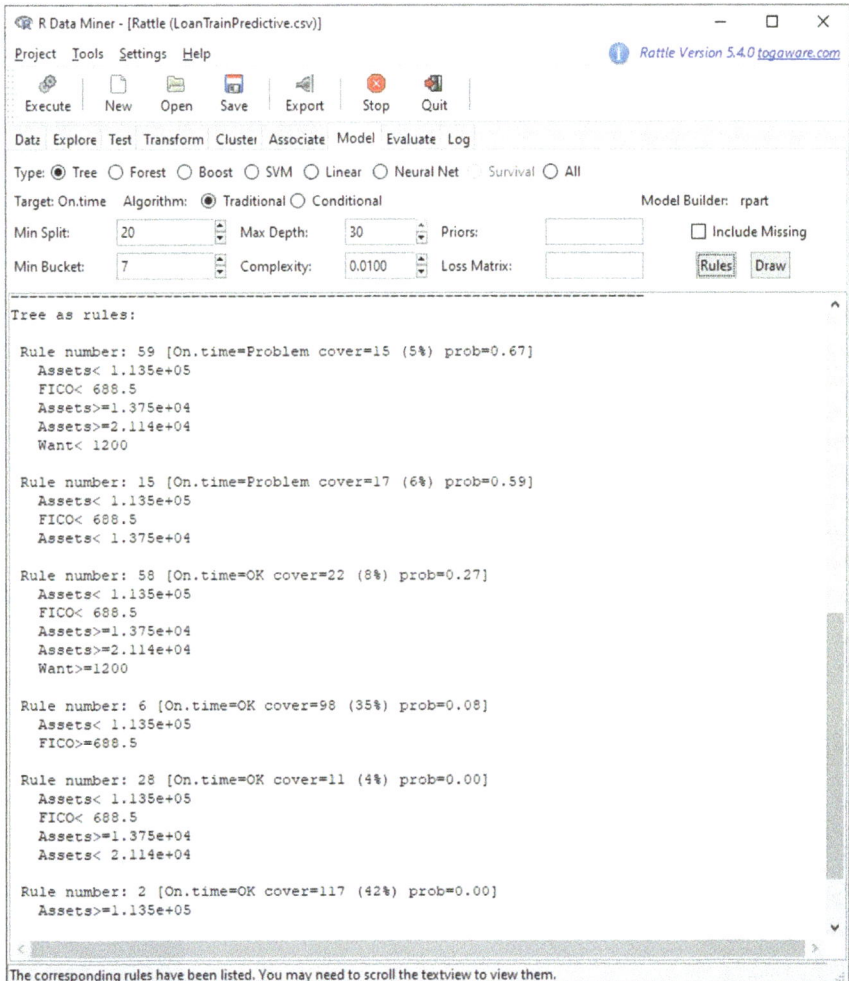

Fig. 3.13 Rules from the decision tree model

5. Run Installer:

   Once the installer is downloaded, locate the installer file in your downloads folder or wherever your browser saves downloads. Double-click on the installer to run it. This will start the Python installation process (Fig. 3.18).

6. Customize Installation (Optional):

   During the installation process, you may be given the option to customize the installation. You can choose the installation location, add Python to your system PATH (recommended), and select additional features. For most users, the default options are fine, but feel free to customize according to your preferences (Fig. 3.19).

Fig. 3.14 Draw results for decision tree

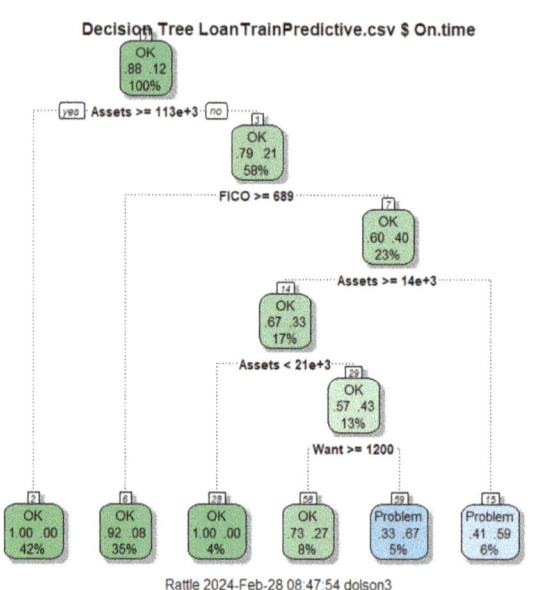

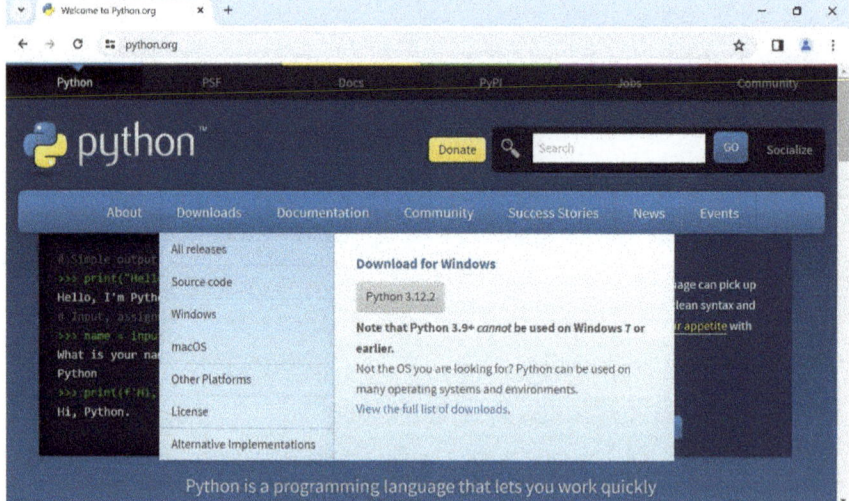

Fig. 3.15 Python introductory screen

7. Install Python:

   Proceed with the installation by clicking on the "Install" or "Next" buttons. The installer will copy Python files to your system and set everything up automatically (Fig. 3.20).

3.3 Python

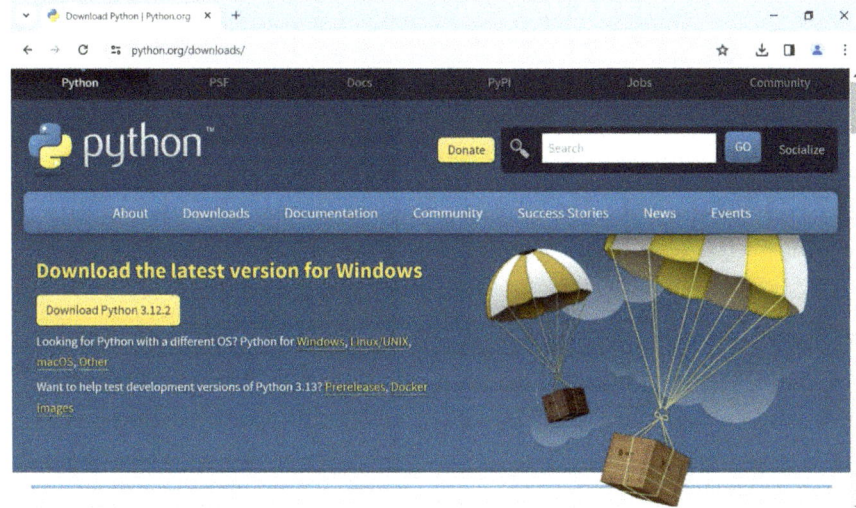

Fig. 3.16 Python version page

Fig. 3.17 Completion message

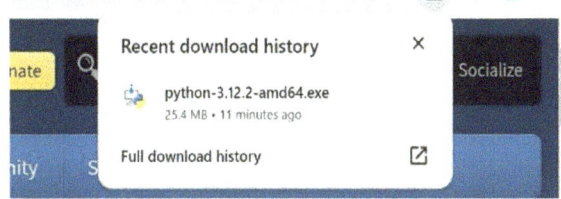

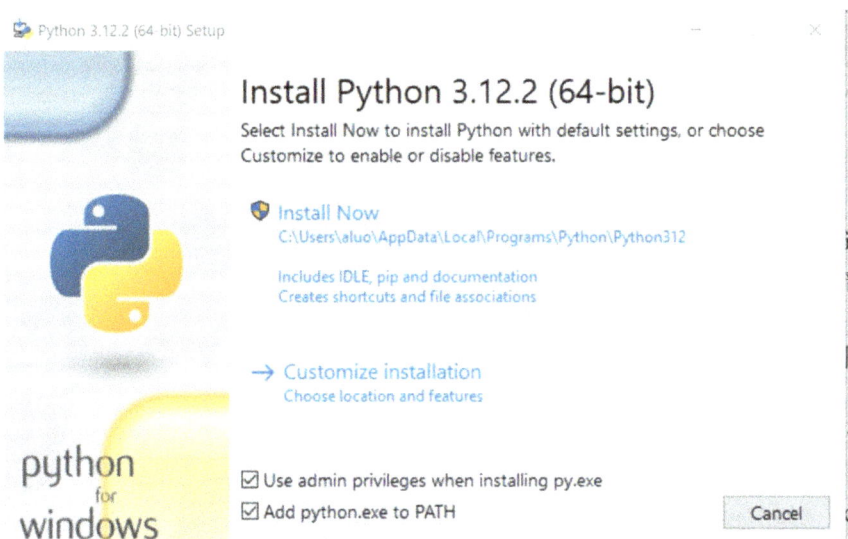

Fig. 3.18 Python installation start

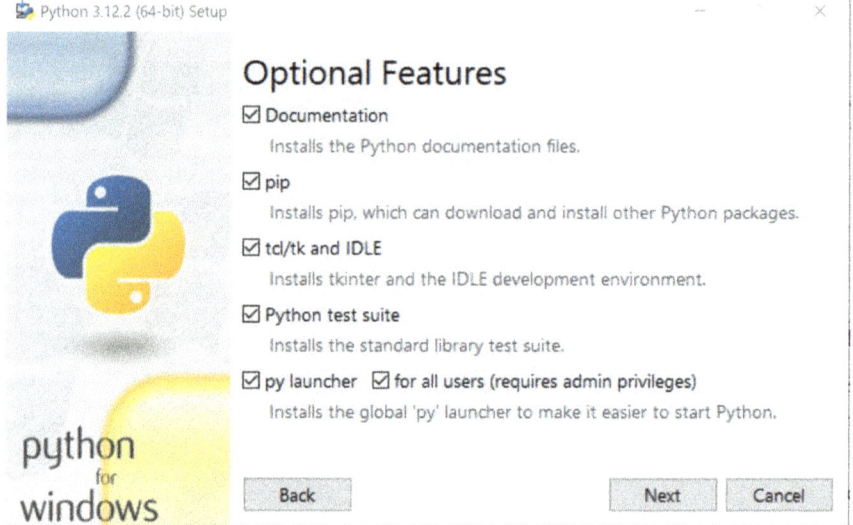

Fig. 3.19 Optional features selection

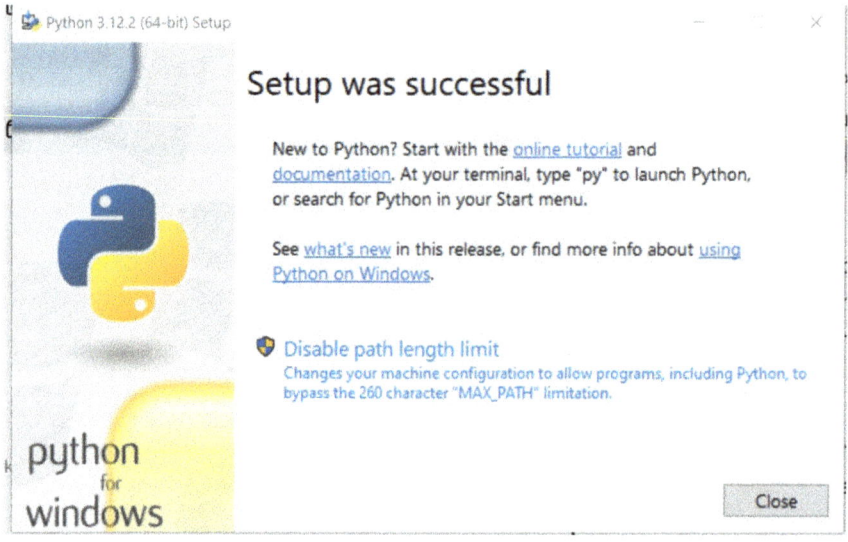

Fig. 3.20 Success message

8. Verify Installation:

   After installation is completed, open the command line (cmd can be used by Windows users, and terminal can be used by Mac and Linux users), and enter the 'Python - V' command to view Python version information. If the correct version

3.3 Python

number is displayed, it indicates that Python has been successfully installed. Enter Python to enter the Python environment. When you see the command prompt ">>>", it means you have entered the Python environment. When you have successfully installed Python on your system. You can now start writing and running Python programs.

A number of other editors have been developed for Python programming, among them Jupyter notebook is a popular tool. Jupyter and a number of other programming tools are packaged in Anaconda suite. An advantage of Anaconda suite is providing a Python distribution that includes many additional libraries, eliminating the need for finding, downloading, and install them as required in basic editors. This suite is available for download the executable file at https://www.anaconda.com/download.

Run this executable file to install the suite. During the installation, choose personal option once asked (Just Me) if this tool is intended for personal/individual use. After installation, you will have a number of Anaconda products on your machine's start menu. Start "Anaconda Navigator" (Fig. 3.21).

The navigator homepage offers a number of popular tools including Jupyter lab. Click on the "Launch" button of Jupyter lab menu to open the Python programming environment which is the Jupyter notebook (Fig. 3.22). This notebook opens on the default Web browser. The left-side pane of this window is a file explorer. Decide about the folder you will save your work.

Use the file browser to change the path to your desired folder, or use the New Folder icon to create one. After selecting or creating the folder, click on the "Python 3" icon on the left pane to create your Python script file. This file is saved and highlighted in your current folder. You may right-click on the untitled and highlighted file in the left-side file explorer, select "Rename" from the pop-up menu, and change the filename (Fig. 3.23). Storing the data files you are going to use in this script is recommended.

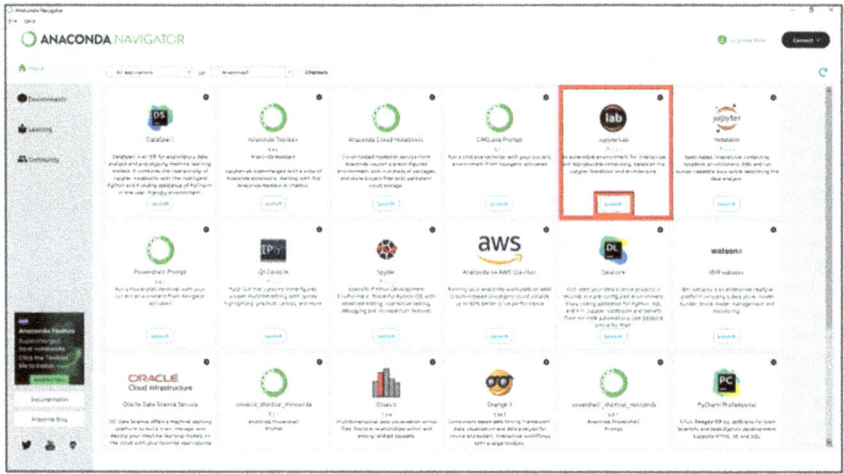

Fig. 3.21 Anaconda Navigator tools

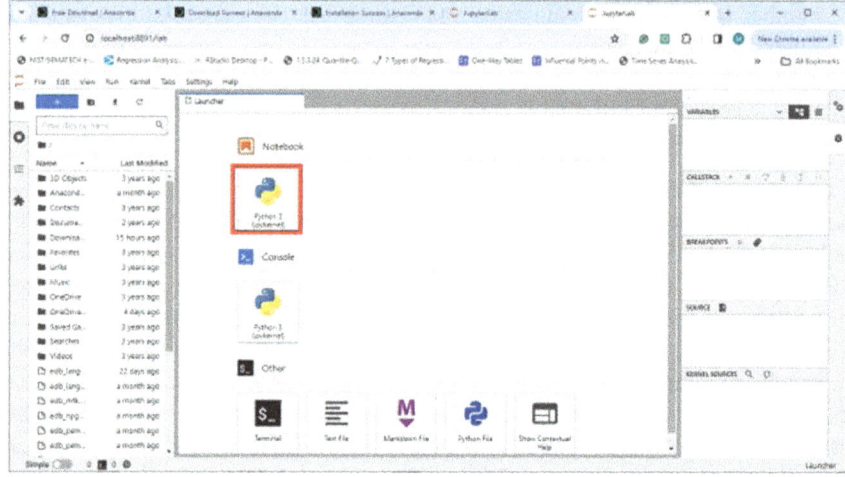

Fig. 3.22 Jupyter lab and notebook creation

When importing data files within this folder only calling the file name is needed, while working with files from other folders requires referencing their path.

Anaconda distribution includes popular Python libraries used in data analysis. In case of need for packages not available, you can install them using Anaconda Powershell Prompt. This is a command line utility. The standard code you need to type (Fig. 3.24) after the prompt is:

```
conda install -c conda-forge module_name
```

The powershell will install the package and its dependencies, if needed. For example, if you want numpy package installed, the following code is required:

```
conda install -c conda-forge numpy
```

3.3.2 Running Python

Before running any part of the code, make sure you've completed two essential steps:

1. Install Python correctly.
2. Install the required dependencies.

Please note that this code should be executed in the console terminal, not within a Python Integrated Development Environment (IDE) like PyCharm. For commonly used dependencies in data mining, within the Python console type:

3.3 Python

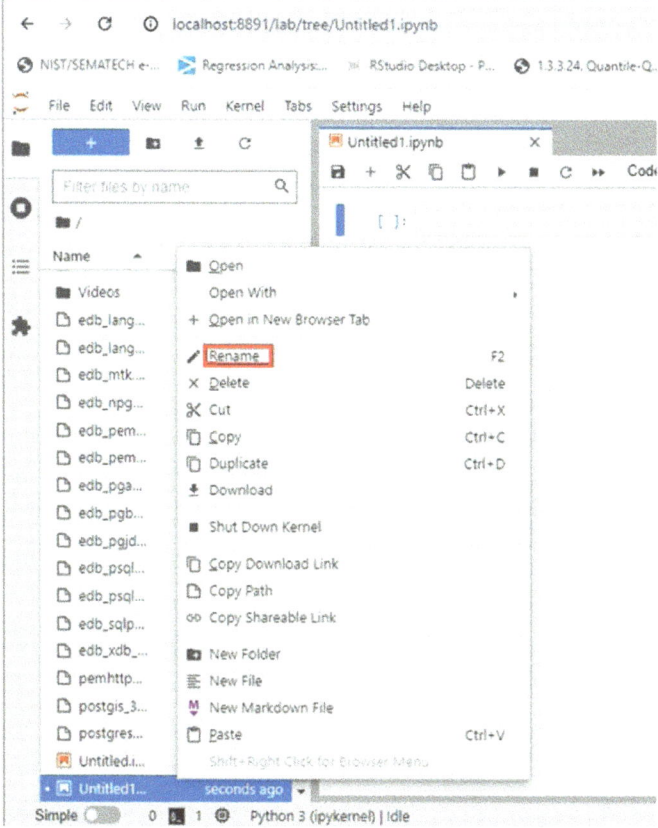

Fig. 3.23 Rename notebooks

Fig. 3.24 Install packages in Anaconda Powershell Prompt

```
pip install numpy
pip install pandas
pip install matplotlib
pip install -U scikit-learn
pip install statsmodels
pip install mlxtend
```

These provide access to Python dependencies.

3.4 Summary

There are many excellent data mining software products, commercial (which are often expensive, but quite easy to use) as well as open-source. R has grown to be viable for major data mining, and the Rattle GUI makes it easy to implement. Python has joined it as a standard open-source product.

Chapter 4
Association Rules

Association rules seek to identify patterns in the form of combinations of things that frequently occur together (**affinity analysis**). This is also the basis of market basket analysis. Association rules take things a step further by applying a form of machine learning, the most common of which is the Apriori algorithm.

Association rules can provide information can be useful to retailers in a number of ways:

- Identify products that could be placed together when customers interested in one are likely to be interested in the other;
- Targeting customers through campaigns (coupons, mailings, e-mailings, etc.) seeking to get them to expand the products they purchase;
- In on-line marketing, drive recommendation engines.

Outside of retailing, there are many other uses for association rules, to include the relationship of symptoms to diseases. Classically, they were applied to retail transaction analysis, akin to market basket analysis. With the emergence of big data, the ability to apply association rules to streams of real-time data is highly useful, enabling a great deal of Web mining for many applications, including e-business retail sales. Association rule mining is one of the most widely used data mining techniques. This can be applied to target marketing, by customer profile, space allocation strategy within stores, but can also be extended to business applications such as international trade and stock market prediction. In the sciences, remotely sensed imagery data has been analyzed to aid precision agriculture and resource discovery (to include oil). It has been used in manufacturing to analyze yield in semiconductor manufacturing.

Key libraries for R association rule and frequent itemsets mining are:

- **arules**: functions for reading and manipulating transactional data and for generating association rules and evaluating their quality.
- **arulesViz**: package for visualizationfunctions for creating plots and charts to aid understanding and interpretation of association rule mining.

- **arulesSequences**: functions for reading and manipulating sequential data, generating association rules and evaluating their quality.

Key libraries for Python association rule mining:

- **apyori**: library to implement the Apriori algorithm with functions for reading and manipulating transactional data, generating association rules and evaluating their quality.
- **mlxtend**: library to implement machine learning algorithms and tools to include association rule mining—functions for reading and manipulating transactional data, generating association rules and evaluating their quality.
- **PyCaret**: open-source low-code machine learning library to automate machine learning workflows providing a wrapper on top of mlxtend for easy implementation of the Apriori algorithm.

4.1 Methodology

Association rules deal with **items**, with are the objects of interest. In the case of the pseudo-Amazon data generated to demonstrate association rule modeling, these would be the products marketed. Association rules group items into sets representing groups of items tending to occur together (an example being a transaction). Rules have the form of an item set on the left (antecedent) with a consequence on the right. For instance, if a customer bought an ebook, correlation indicated a strong likelihood of buying a paperback book.

4.2 Demonstration Dataset

We generated a set of pseudo-Amazon data selecting twelve of these categories, while expanding books into e-books, hard back books, and paperback books. The next step is to determine what percentage of each of these categories was in each market basket. Here we make up numbers to demonstrate. Market baskets are assigned to each profile based on greatest dollar value. These profiles were viewed as capturing the reason the shopper was at the site. Market-basket analysis reveals that customers do not shop based on product groupings, but rather on personal needs. The consumer orientation allows understanding combinations of product purchases. For instance, hardback books, paperbacks, and e-books are different products, but all are part of the books purchase profile. Particular customers could buy a market basket in one profile (say books) during one visit, and another profile (say Movies & TV) later. The focus is on the market basket, not customers as individuals.

4.2 Demonstration Dataset

Table 4.1 Pseudo-Amazon data for correlation

Auto	Baby	EBooks	Hard	Paper	Music	Elect	Health	GiftC	Luggage	Mag	Movies
0	0	1	0	0	0	0	0	0	0	0	0
0	0	1	1	0	0	0	0	0	0	0	0
0	1	0	0	0	0	0	0	0	0	0	0
0	0	1	0	1	0	0	0	0	0	0	0
0	0	1	0	0	1	0	0	0	0	0	0

4.2.1 Fit

Correlation works best for this type of data (due to the large number of combinations). Data has to be numerical for correlation, but we can obtain Table 4.1 from Excel showing an extract of this data:

This data then is used to generate the correlations in Table 4.2:

The combinations with correlations over 0.3 in absolute value are:

Hard cover and Paperback books	+0.724
Ebooks and Paperback books	+0.705
Ebooks and Hard cover books	+0.683
Baby and Toys	+0.617
Ebooks and Movies	−0.447
Paperback books and Movies	−0.358
Ebooks and Software	−0.348
Hard cover books and Movies	−0.320

One might question the data with respect to movies and books, but maybe people that go to movies don't have time to read books. Otherwise these numbers seem plausible.

A limitation of association rule analysis is the enormous number of combinations. Furthermore, the data includes many null entries. Software deals with this quite well, but it leads to burying interesting rules within many meaningless negative relationships. Our correlation finds that the pseudo-Amazon dataset is dominated by ebooks, hardbacks, and paperbacks. Table 4.3 provides the counts of the transactions for eight combinations of these three book products:

Totals are 619 ebook sales 493 hardbacks, and 497 paperbacks. There are 12 pairs of these three variables plus 8 triplets, There are 48 rules from only one antecedent, plus another 24 with two antecedents, yielding 72 possible rules. An example rule might be:

IF{ebook} THEN {paperback}

Table 4.2 Pseudo-Amazon correlations

	Auto	Baby	EBooks	Hard	Paper	Music	Elect	Health	GiftC	Luggage	Mag	Movies	Software	Toys
Auto	1													
Baby	−0.029	1												
EBooks	−0.161	−0.212	1											
Hard	−0.105	−0.204	0.683	1										
Paper	−0.123	−0.170	0.705	0.724	1									
Music	−0.045	−0.072	−0.194	−0.243	−0.295	1								
Elect	−0.025	−0.002	−0.234	−0.099	−0.152	0.226	1							
Health	0.134	−0.007	−0.058	−0.057	−0.067	0.042	0.029	1						
GiftC	−0.030	−0.058	−0.061	−0.113	−0.124	0.057	0.016	−0.030	1					
Luggage	−0.008	−0.015	−0.050	−0.031	−0.031	−0.023	−0.013	−0.017	−0.016	1				
Mag	−0.021	0.017	−0.076	−0.090	−0.079	0.016	−0.003	0.031	0.065	−0.011	1			
Movies	−0.048	−0.078	−0.447	−0.320	−0.358	0.041	0.131	0.077	0.172	0.116	0.117	1		
Software	−0.044	−0.040	−0.348	−0.227	−0.243	−0.011	0.237	−0.042	−0.059	−0.022	−0.020	−0.034	1	
Toys	−0.044	0.617	−0.285	−0.249	−0.220	−0.022	−0.024	0.009	−0.033	−0.023	0.000	−0.073	−0.075	1
Wine	−0.030	0.020	−0.249	−0.173	−0.184	−0.023	−0.028	−0.065	0.033	−0.016	0.012	0.044	0.050	−0.019

4.2 Demonstration Dataset

Table 4.3 Pseudo-Amazon cases

Ebooks	Hardbacks	Paperbacks	Count
Yes	Yes	Yes	419
Yes	Yes	No	56
Yes	No	Yes	64
Yes	No	No	80
No	Yes	Yes	7
No	Yes	No	11
No	No	Yes	7
No	No	No	356

This can be extended to multiple conditions:

IF{ebook & hardback} THEN {paperback}

There are measures of interest for rules. The **support** of an item or item set is the proportion of transactions containing that item set. In the pseudo-Amazon dataset, there are 619 cases out of 1000 where an ebook was purchased. Its support is 0.619. Rules have **confidence** measures, defined as the consequent occurs if the antecedent is present. Confidence gives the probability of paperbacks being bought should ebooks have been bought in the example above. Of the 619 customers who purchased on or more ebooks, 483 also purchased one or more paperbacks. Confidence in this case is 483/619 = 0.780. The conventional **lift** formula is support{antecedent & consequent} divided by the support of the antecedent times the support of the consequent. This is equivalent to the confidence of the rule divided by (support of the consequent). For the ebook and paperback rule above, this would be 0.780 divided by the average propensity for customers who purchased paperbacks (497/1000), yielding lift of 1.57. Most sources give lift as support for the rule divided by (the independent support of the antecedent times the independent support of the consequent), or in this case (483/1000) / [(619/1000 × 497/1000] also equal to 1.57. Cursory inspection of course explains this as the support for the rule is 483/619 = 0.780. Algorithm users are allowed to set minimum support and confidence levels. **Frequent sets** are those for which support for the antecedent is at least as great as the minimum support level. **Strong sets** are frequent and have confidence at least as great as the minimum confidence level.

4.2.2 Lift

This section demonstrates the concept of lift used in customer segmenta- tion models. We can divide the data into groups as fine as we want (here, we divide them into 10 equal portions of the population, or groups of 10% each). These groups have some identifiable features, such as zip code, income level, and so on (a profile). We can then sample and identify the portion of sales for each group. The idea behind lift is to send promotional material (which has a unit cost) to those groups that have the greatest probability of positive response first. We can visualize lift by plotting the responses against the proportion of the total population of potential customers, as shown in Table 4.4. Note that the segments are sorted by expected customer response.

The purpose of lift analysis is to identify the most responsive segments. Here, the greatest lift is obtained from the first five segments. We are probably more interested in profit, however. We can identify the most profitable policy. What needs to be done is to identify the portion of the population to send promotional materials to. For instance, if an average profit of $100 is expected for each positive response and a cost of $8 is expected for each set of promotional material sent out, it obviously would be more profitable to send to the first segment containing an expected 0.17 positive responses ($100 times 0.17 equals an expected revenue of $17, covering the cost of $8 leaving $9 profit). It still might be possible to improve the overall profit by sending to other segments as well (always selecting the segment with the larger response rates in order). The plot of cumulative profit is shown in Fig. 4.1 for this set of data. The second most responsive segment would also be profitable, collecting $100 times 0.15 or $15 per $8 mailing for a net profit of $7. The sixth most responsive segment collects 0.09 times $100 ($18) for a net profit of $1, while the seventh most responsive segment collects $100 times 0.06 ($6) for a net loss of $2.

Both the cumulative responses and cumulative proportion of the population are graphed to identify the lift. Lift is the difference between the two lines in Fig. 4.1. Profit calculation is not the same, as shown in Table 4.5:

Table 4.4 Lift calculation

Ordered segment	Expected Customer Response	Proportion {expected responses}	Cumulative response proportion	Cumulative random	LIFT
0	0	0	0	0	0
1	0.17	0.1828	0.1828	0.1	0.0828
2	0.15	0.1613	0.3441	0.2	0.1441
3	0.13	0.1398	0.4839	0.3	0.1839
4	0.12	0.1290	0.6129	0.4	0.2129
5	0.10	0.1075	0.7204	0.5	0.2204
6	0.09	0.0968	0.8172	0.6	0.2172
7	0.06	0.0645	0.8817	0.7	0.1817
8	0.05	0.0538	0.9355	0.8	0.1355
9	0.04	0.0430	0.9785	0.9	0.0785
10	0.02	0.0215	1.0000	1	0.0000
Sum	0.93				

4.2 Demonstration Dataset

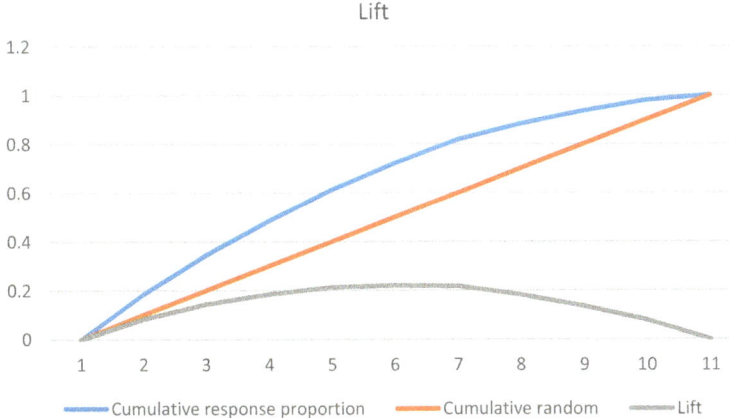

Fig. 4.1 Lift for scenario

Table 4.5 Profit calculation

Segment	Revenue	Cost	Profit
0	0	0	0
1	17	8	9
2	32	16	16
3	45	24	21
4	57	32	25
5	67	40	27
6	76	48	28
7	82	56	26
8	87	64	23
9	91	72	19
10	93	80	13

The profit function in Fig. 4.2 reaches its maximum with the sixth segment.

It is clear that the maximum profit is found by sending to the six most responsive segments of the ten in the population. The implication is that in this case, the promotional materials should be sent to the six segments expected to have the largest response rates. If there was a promotional budget, it would be applied to as many segments as the budget would support, in order of the expected response rate, up to the sixth segment.

It is possible to focus on the wrong measure. The basic objective of lift analysis in marketing is to identify those customers whose decisions will be influenced by marketing in a positive way. In short, the methodology described earlier identifies those segments of the customer base that would be expected to purchase. This may or may not have been due to the marketing campaign effort. The same methodology

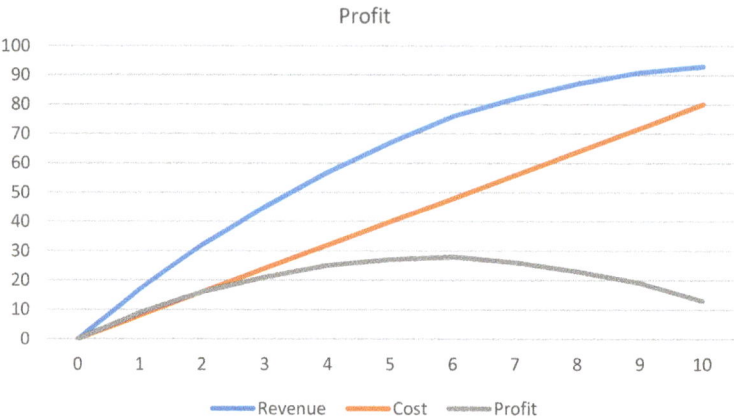

Fig. 4.2 Profit impact of lift

can be applied, but more detailed data is needed to identify those whose decisions would have been changed by the marketing campaign, rather than simply those who would purchase.

Understanding lift enables understanding the value of specific types of customers. This enables more intelligent customer management.

4.3 The Apriori Algorithm

The most common association rule mining algorithms are the Apriori algorithm, the frequent pattern growth (FP.Growth) algorithm, and the equivalence class clustering and bottom-up lattice traversal (ECLAT) algorithm. The Apriori algorithm operates by systematically considering combinations of variables, and ranking them on either support, confidence, or lift at the user's discretion. It uses a bottom-up approach, beginning with individual items and building up to more complex itemsets. However, it is inefficient in that at each step it needs to build candidate sets through repeated scanning of the database. The FP-Growth algorithm constructs a tree-like structure encoding frequent itemsets, which is used to generate rules similarly to the Apriori algorithm, but it is generally faster, especially for large datasets. The ECLAT algorithm is another variation of the Apriori algorithm, using a top-down approach. It divides items into equivalence classes based on their support, then generates rules by combining equivalence classes into a lattice-like structure. It is more efficient and scalable than the basic Apriori algorithm. The FP.Growth algorithm is considered more efficient for large datasets, and has been reported widely used in market basket analysis, bioinformatics, and on-line usage.

The Apriori algorithm is credited to Agrawal et al. (1993) who applied it to market basket data to generate association rules. Association rules are widely used, usually

4.3 The Apriori Algorithm

applied to binary data where customers either purchase or don't purchase particular products.

The Apriori algorithm operates by finding all rules satisfying minimum confidence and support specifications. First, the set of frequent 1-itemsets is identified by scanning the database to count each item. Next, 2-itemsets are identified, gaining some efficiency by using the fact that if a 1-itemset is not frequent, it can't be part of a frequent itemset of larger dimension. This continues to larger-dimensioned itemsets until they become null. The magnitude of effort required is indicated by the fact that each dimension of itemsets requires a full scan of the database. The algorithm is:

To identify the candidate itemset C_k of size k

1. Identify frequent items L_1
    For $k = 1$ generate all itemsets with support $\geq$ Support$_{min}$
    If itemsets null, STOP
        Increment k by 1
        For itemsets of size k identify all with support $\geq$ Support$_{min}$
    END
2. Return list of frequent itemsets
3. Identify rules in the form of antecedents and consequents from the frequent items
4. Check confidence of these rules
    If confidence of a rule meets Confidence$_{min}$ mark this rule as strong

The output of the Apriori algorithm can be used as the basis for recommending rules, considering factors such as correlation, or analysis from other techniques, from a training set of data. This information may be used in many ways, including in retail where if a rule is identified indicating that purchase of the antecedent occurred without that customer purchasing the consequent, then it might be attractive to suggest purchase of the consequent.

The Apriori algorithm can generate many frequent itemsets. Association rules can be generated by only looking at frequent itemsets that are strong, in the sense that they meet or exceed both minimum support and minimum confidence levels. It must be noted that this does not necessarily mean such a rule is useful, that it means high correlation, nor that it has any proof of causality. However, a good feature is that you can let computers loose to identify them (an example of machine learning).

To demonstrate using data from Table 4.1, establish Support$_{min}$ = 0.4 and Confidence$_{min}$ = 0.5:

1. L_1 = Ebooks (support 0.619), Paperbacks (support 0.497), and Hardbacks (support 0.493); noHardbacks (support 0.507), no Paperbacks (support 0.503)
    The item noEbooks fails because it's support of 0.381 is below Support$_{min}$.
2. L_2 = Ebooks & Hardbacks (support 0.475), Ebooks & Paperbacks (support 0.483), Hardbacks & Paperbacks (support 0.426), and noHardbacks & noPaperbacks (support 0.436)
    Itemsets Ebooks & noHardbacks fail with support of 0.144, Ebooks & noPaperbacks with support of 0.136, Hardbacks & noPaperbacks with support of

0.067, Paperbacks & noEbooks with support of 0.014, Paperbacks & noHardbacks with support of 0.071, noEbooks & noPaperbacks with support of 0.367,
3. L_3 = Ebooks & Hardbacks & Paperbacks (support 0.419)
    Itemsets Ebooks & Hardbacks & noPaperbacks fail with support of 0.056, Ebooks & Paperbacks & noHardbacks with support of 0.064, and Hardbacks & Paperbacks & Ebooks with support of 0.007.
4. There aren't four items, so L_4 is null.
5. Identify rules from frequent items:

Ebooks → Hardbacks	Confidence 0.767
Ebooks → Paperbacks	Confidence 0.780
Hardbacks → Ebooks	Confidence 0.963
Hardbacks → Paperbacks	Confidence 0.850
Paperbacks → Ebooks	Confidence 0.972
Paperbacks → Hardbacks	Confidence 0.843
noHardbacks → noPaperbacks	Confidence 0.860
noPaperbacks → noHardbacks	Confidence 0.867
Ebooks & Hardbacks → Paperbacks	Confidence 0.882
Ebooks & Paperbacks → Hardbacks	Confidence 0.886
Hardbacks & Paperbacks → Ebooks	Confidence 0.984

All other combinations of frequent itemsets in L_3 failed the minimum support test.

These rules now would need to be evaluated, possibly subjectively by the users, for interestingness. Here the focus is on cases where a customer who buys one type of book might be likely according to this data to buy the other type of books. Another indication is that if a customer never bought a paperback, they are not likely to buy a hardback, and vice versa.

4.4 Association Rules from Software

There are two basic controls in association rule mining: support and confidence levels. R also call for minimum rule length. It has other options as well. We will set support and confidence (as well as lift, which is an option for sorting output) below. Our pseudo-Amazon database has 1000 customer entries (which we treat as transactions).

The data needs to be put into a form the software will read. In R and Python, you either need categorical data, or else you need to transform it to that form. Rattle requires data be categorical rather than numerical. The rules generated will be positive cases (IF you buy diapers THEN you are likely to buy baby powder) and negative

4.4 Association Rules from Software

cases are ignored (IF you **didn't** buy diapers THEN you are likely to do whatever). If you wish to study the negative cases, you would need to convert the blank cases to No. Here we will demonstrate the positive case.

Rattle's Association Rule screen is shown in Fig. 4.3:

Selecting the options given in Fig. 4.3 yields nine rules after Execute (see Fig. 4.4).

This shows that nine rules are generated. Minimum support and confidence control the number of rules. Since the minimum support in the dataset is 0.419 and minimum confidence 0.7552, one should obtain nine rules up to those levels, which is the case (see Fig. 4.5):

The nine rules generated are displayed in Fig. 4.6:

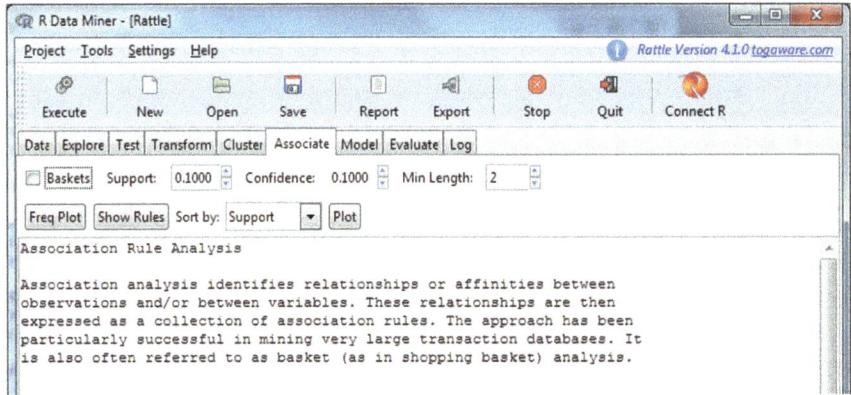

Fig. 4.3 Screen of Rattle's Association Rule Tab

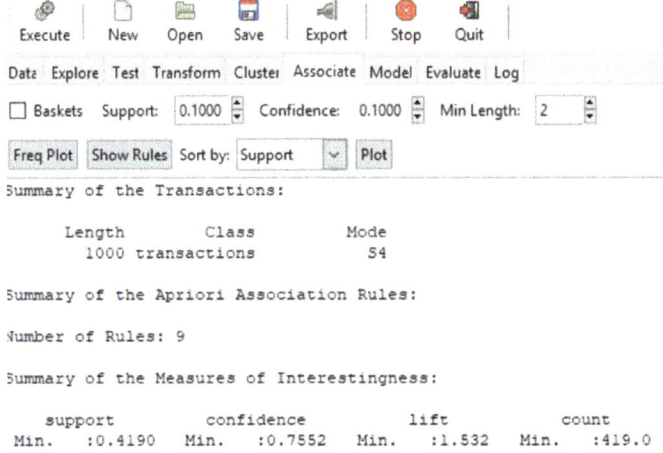

Fig. 4.4 Rattle Association Screen

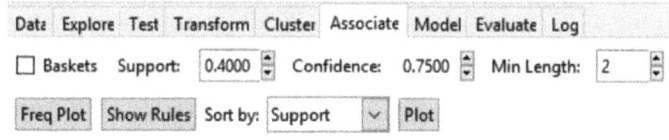

Fig. 4.5 Setting support and confidence

```
All Rules

        lhs                         rhs              support confidence lift     count
[1]  {Paper=Yes}              => {EBooks=Yes}    0.483   0.9718310  1.545041  483
[2]  {EBooks=Yes}             => {Paper=Yes}     0.483   0.7678855  1.545041  483
[3]  {Hard=Yes}               => {EBooks=Yes}    0.475   0.9634888  1.531779  475
[4]  {EBooks=Yes}             => {Hard=Yes}      0.475   0.7551669  1.531779  475
[5]  {Paper=Yes}              => {Hard=Yes}      0.426   0.8571429  1.738626  426
[6]  {Hard=Yes}               => {Paper=Yes}     0.426   0.8640974  1.738626  426
[7]  {Hard=Yes,Paper=Yes}     => {EBooks=Yes}    0.419   0.9835681  1.563701  419
[8]  {EBooks=Yes,Paper=Yes}   => {Hard=Yes}      0.419   0.8674948  1.759624  419
[9]  {EBooks=Yes,Hard=Yes}    => {Paper=Yes}     0.419   0.8821053  1.774860  419
```

Fig. 4.6 Rattle Association Rules

4.4.1 Association Rules in Rattle

Baskets is used for market basket data. An Ident variable is required if this option is used. Our data is not of that type. Support, confidence, and Min length are controls for rule display. Using 0.5 for support as well as confidence, and a minimum rule length of 2, Freq Plot gives a frequency plot (Fig. 4.7):

Figure 4.8 demonstrates a common feature of market basket data—a heavy preponderance of negatives. **Show Rules** gives the output satisfying the support and confidence set.

While clustering requires all data be numeric, association rules require data to be categorical. Setting different levels for support and confidence resulted in rule counts given in Table 4.6:

It can be seen the lower support and confidence yield more rules. Running support and confidence of 0.5 yielded the output shown in Fig. 4.8. The list of rules with support, confidence and lift can be obtained by clicking the Show Rules button:

Figure 4.9 shows the Plot output for the smaller set of six variables, support and confidence set to 0.5:

Table 4.7 gives the rules obtained with the six variable set using support of 0.6 and confidence of 0.6 (Min length 2). Note that only four give positive conclusions (indicated in bold), and that none of the 16 rules involves a positive antecedent. Executing with support of 0.6 and confidence of 0.6 resulted in 16 rules, the only positive outcomes being the three combinations of movies, wine and ebooks.

Here the three positive outcomes are displayed in bold, indicating EBook readers don't drink wine nor attend movies much (the dataset was generated by the author, so this relationship may not be true). Running association rules involves having the computer do enormous numbers of combinatorial calculations. They are quite good at

4.4 Association Rules from Software

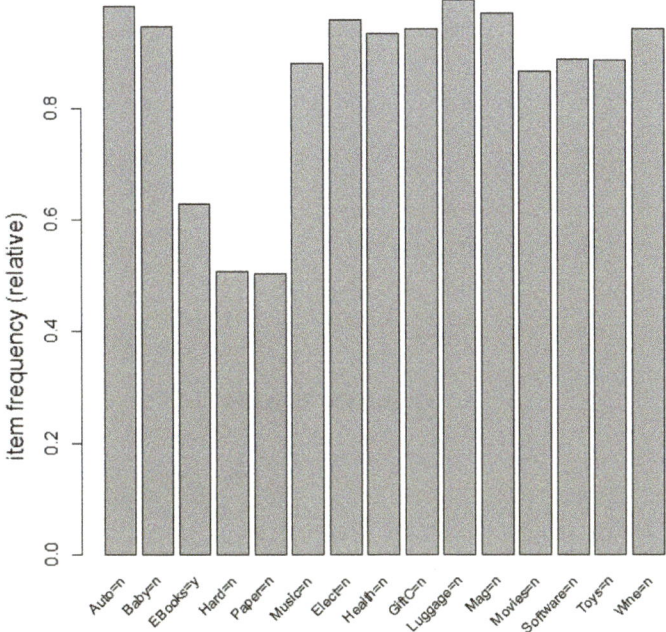

Fig. 4.7 Frequency plot for data

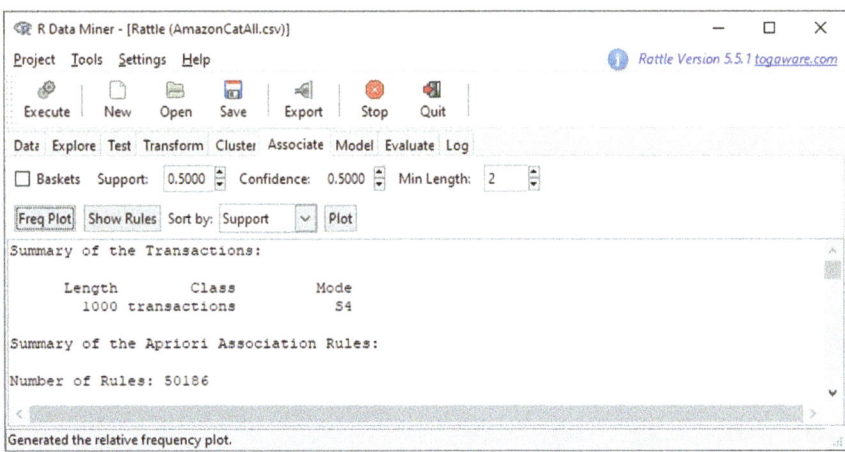

Fig. 4.8 Rattle Association Rule executed

that. Software allows users to specify minimum support and confidence. The impact of different support levels is indicated in Table 4.8, where mean values for support, confidence, and lift are given, along with the number of rules obtained.

Table 4.6 Rules at different support and confidence levels

Support	Confidence	All twelve variables	Six variables
0.2	0.2	285,020	309
0.3	0.3	234,896	239
0.4	0.4	178,633	194
0.5	0.5	50,186	28
0.6	0.6	18,909	16
0.7	0.7	7593	9
0.8	0.8	1483	4
0.9	0.9	111	0

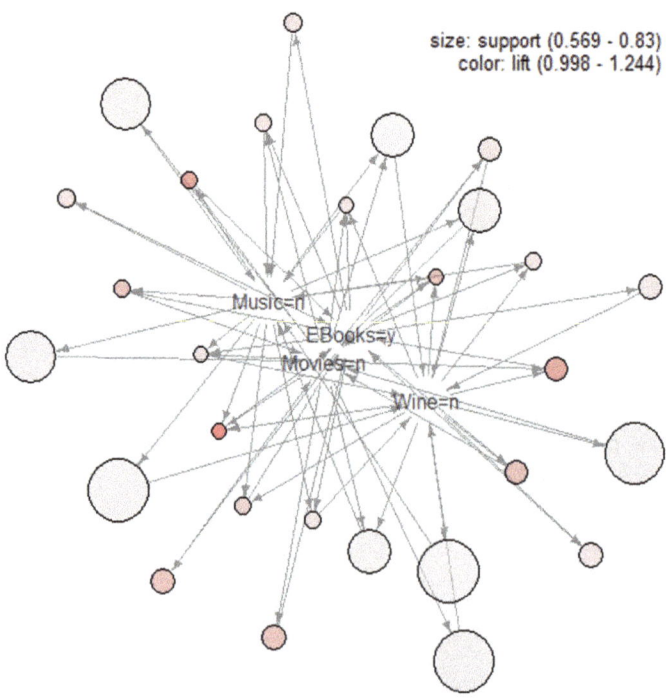

Fig. 4.9 Plot output—support and confidence 0.5, six variables

Table 4.8 focuses on support. Confidence and lift go up and down, although lift tends to drop with tighter controls. The number of rules is what is controlled, declining with tighter controls as expected.

To demonstrate what is going on, we focus on only three of these variables: Ebooks, Hardbacks, and Paperbacks. Table 4.9 shows the association rules generated by R sorted by lift:

4.4 Association Rules from Software

Table 4.7 Rules for support and confidence set to 0.6, set of 6 variables

	Lhs		rhs	support	confidence	coverage	lift	count
[1]	{Music = n}	=>	{Wine = n}	0.830	0.941	0.882	0.998	830
[2]	{Wine = n}	=>	{Music = n}	0.830	0.880	0.943	0.998	830
[3]	{Movies = n}	=>	{Wine = n}	0.822	0.947	0.868	1.004	822
[4]	{Wine = n}	=>	{Movies = n}	0.822	0.872	0.943	1.004	822
[5]	{Movies = n}	=>	{Music = n}	0.770	0.887	0.868	1.006	770
[6]	{Music = n}	=>	{Movies = n}	0.770	0.873	0.882	1.006	770
[7]	{Music = m, Movies = n}	=>	{Wine = n}	0.727	0.944	0.770	1.001	727
[8]	{Movies = n, Wine = n}	=>	{Music = n}	0.727	0.884	0.822	1.003	727
[9]	{Music = n, Wine = n}	=>	{Movies = n}	0.727	0.876	0.830	1.009	727
[10]	{EBooks = y}	=>	{Wine = n}	0.621	0.987	0.629	1.005	621
[11]	**{Wine = n}**	=>	**{EBooks = y}**	**0.621**	**0.659**	**0.943**	**1.047**	**621**
[12]	{EBooks = y}	=>	{Movies = n}	0.619	0.984	0.629	1.134	619
[13]	**{Movies = n}**	=>	**{EBooks = y}**	**0.619**	**0.713**	**0.868**	**1.134**	**619**
[14]	{EBooks = y, Movies = n}	=>	{Wine = n}	0.612	0.989	0.619	1.048	612
[15]	{EBooks = y, Wine = n}	=>	{Movies = n}	0.612	0.986	0.621	1.135	612
[16]	{Movies = n, Wine = n}	=>	{EBooks = y}	0.612	0.744	0.822	1.183	612

Table 4.8 Rules obtained by support level specified

Specified Support	Specified Confidence	Min Length	Support Obtained	Confidence Obtained	Lift	Rules
0.1	0.1	2	0.3029	0.7838	1.3246	503
0.2	0.2	2	0.4094	0.8451	1.2945	309
0.3	0.3	2	0.4529	0.8676	1.2962	239
0.4	0.4	2	0.4781	0.8959	1.3095	194
0.5	0.5	2	0.6516	0.8829	1.0690	28
0.6	0.6	2	0.7088	0.8854	1.0474	16
0.7	0.7	2	0.7806	0.9005	1.0032	9

Table 4.9 Rattle Association Rules

ID	Antecedent	Consequent	Support	Confidence	Lift	Count
1	EBooks, Hard	Paper	0.42	0.88	1.77	419
2	EBooks, Paper	Hard	0.42	0.87	1.76	419
3	Hard	Paper	0.43	0.86	1.74	426
4	Paper	Hard	0.43	0.86	1.74	426
5	Hard, Paper	EBooks	0.42	0.98	1.56	419
6	Paper	EBooks	0.48	0.97	1.55	483
7	EBooks	Paper	0.48	0.77	1.55	483
8	EBooks	Hard	0.48	0.76	1.53	475
9	Hard	EBooks	0.48	0.96	1.53	475

What are the implications? For this data, grouping EBooks, Hard Cover Books, and Paperback Books together yields the greatest lift. Confidence is the proportion of the examples covered by the premise that are also covered by the consequence (Class association rules can only be mined using confidence). Lift is confidence divided by the proportion of all examples that are covered by the consequence. This is a measure of the importance of the association that is independent of support. Leverage is the proportion of additional examples covered by both the premise and consequence above those expected if the premise and consequence were independent of each other. The total number of examples that this represents is presented in brackets following the leverage. Conviction is another measure of departure from independence. Conviction is given by:

[1 − Support(consequent)]/[1 − confidence(IF antecedent THEN consequent)]

This is the ratio of the probability of the antecedent occurring without the consequent divided by the observed frequency of incorrect cases.

Correlation found the strongest relationship between purchase of hard cover books and paperbacks. Rattle ranked the rules combining these two options number 11, 12,

4.4 Association Rules from Software

13 & 14 based on lift. The point is that there are lots of options in measuring what things go together, and different metrics will yield different results.

4.4.2 R Code

This script uses the **arules** package to load and preprocess transaction data from a CSV file of binary (0–1) data. We demonstrate using the Apriori algorithm to find frequent itemsets and generate association rules based on specified support (**supp = 0.419**) and confidence (**conf = 0.7552**) thresholds. Note that this input file only has three columns of products. A major problem with association rules is the scale of results. Using all columns yields too many rules for R Studio to run.

```
# Call the data loading and preprocessing function
trans <- load_data_set("./AmazonEHP.csv")

# Use the Apriori algorithm to find frequent itemsets
frequent_itemsets <- apriori(trans, parameter = list(supp =
0.419, target = "frequent itemsets"))

# Generate association rules
rules <- apriori(trans, parameter = list(supp = 0.419, conf =
0.7552, target = "rules"))

# Print frequent itemsets
inspect(frequent_itemsets)

# Print association rules
inspect(rules)
```

This code yielded 8 rules displayed in Fig. 4.10:

Faster alternatives to the apriori algorithm include the FP Growth and ECLAT algorithms. R also has the ECLAT (equivalence class clustering and bottom-up lattice traversal) algorithm, demonstrated in the following code:

```
library(arules)

# Data loading and preprocessing function
load_data_set <- function(path) {
    # Assume each row in the file corresponds to a transaction
    # and each item is represented as 1 (purchased) or 0 (not
purchased).
        df <- read.csv(path, header = FALSE)
        transactions <- list()
        labels <- c('Auto', 'Baby', 'EBooks', 'Hard', 'Paper',
'Music', 'Elect',
```

```
> # Print frequent itemsets
> inspect(frequent_itemsets)
    items                support            count
[1] {Hard}                0.7538226         493
[2] {Paper}               0.7599388         497
[3] {EBooks}              0.9617737         629
[4] {Hard, Paper}         0.6513761         426
[5] {EBooks, Hard}        0.7262997         475
[6] {EBooks, Paper}       0.7385321         483
[7] {EBooks, Hard, Paper} 0.6406728         419
>
> # Print association rules
> inspect(rules)
     lhs                rhs        support    confidence coverage
[1]  {}              => {Paper}    0.7599388  0.7599388  1.0000000
[2]  {}              => {EBooks}   0.9617737  0.9617737  1.0000000
[3]  {Hard}          => {Paper}    0.6513761  0.8640974  0.7538226
[4]  {Paper}         => {Hard}     0.6513761  0.8571429  0.7599388
[5]  {Hard}          => {EBooks}   0.7262997  0.9634888  0.7538226
[6]  {Paper}         => {EBooks}   0.7385321  0.9718310  0.7599388
[7]  {EBooks}        => {Paper}    0.7385321  0.7678855  0.9617737
[8]  {Hard, Paper}   => {EBooks}   0.6406728  0.9835681  0.6513761
[9]  {EBooks, Hard}  => {Paper}    0.6406728  0.8821053  0.7262997
[10] {EBooks, Paper} => {Hard}     0.6406728  0.8674948  0.7385321
     lift      count
[1]  1.000000  497
[2]  1.000000  629
[3]  1.137062  426
[4]  1.137062  426
[5]  1.001783  475
[6]  1.010457  483
[7]  1.010457  483
[8]  1.022661  419
[9]  1.160758  419
[10] 1.150794  419
>
```

Fig. 4.10 R output for support of 0.419, confidence of 0.7552

```
              'Health', 'GiftC', 'Luggage', 'Mag', 'Movies',
    'Software',
              'Toys', 'Wine')
    for (i in 1:nrow(df)) {
        items <- labels[df[i,] == 1]
                    if (length(items) > 0) transac-
tions[[length(transactions) + 1]] <- items
    }
    return(as(transactions, "transactions"))
    }

# Convert the dataset to transaction format
trans <- load_data_set("./AmazonBinaryAll.csv")

# Mining for frequent itemsets with min_support = 0.419
# Note: This support level is unusually high and may not return
many itemsets,
# you might need to adjust this value based on your actual data.
```

4.4 Association Rules from Software

```
frequent_itemsets <- eclat(trans, parameter = list(supp =
0.419, maxlen = 15))

# Mining for association rules with min_support = 0.419 and
min_conf = 0.7552
rules <- apriori(trans, parameter = list(supp = 0.419, conf =
0.7552, minlen = 2))

# Print out the association rules
inspect(rules)

# Since direct support data extraction for 1-itemsets, 2-
itemsets, and 3-itemsets
# was requested, and related rules' confidences:
# This part can be achieved by filtering the 'rules' or
'frequent_itemsets' object.
```

The resulting output is shown in Fig. 4.11:

The following code is for a dataset of 15 products. It uses a binary (0–1) input file which is converted to categorical data needed for the apriori algorithm.

```
library(arules)
library(arulesViz)
# Load and preprocess data
load_data_set <- function(path) {
  # Read the CSV file
  df <- read.csv(path, header = FALSE, colClasses = "char-
acter")
  # Initialize the list of transactions
  transactions <- list()
  # Iterate through each row of data
```

```
        lhs                  rhs       support confidence coverage lift
[1] {Paper}           => {Hard}     0.426   0.8571429  0.497    1.738626
[2] {Hard}            => {Paper}    0.426   0.8640974  0.493    1.738626
[3] {Paper}           => {EBooks}   0.483   0.9718310  0.497    1.545041
[4] {EBooks}          => {Paper}    0.483   0.7678855  0.629    1.545041
[5] {Hard}            => {EBooks}   0.475   0.9634888  0.493    1.531779
[6] {Hard, Paper}     => {EBooks}   0.419   0.9835681  0.426    1.563701
[7] {EBooks, Paper}   => {Hard}     0.419   0.8674948  0.483    1.759624
[8] {EBooks, Hard}    => {Paper}    0.419   0.8821053  0.475    1.774860
    count
[1] 426
[2] 426
[3] 483
[4] 483
[5] 475
[6] 419
[7] 419
[8] 419
```

Fig. 4.11 ECLAT rule output

```
    for (i in 1:nrow(df)) {
    # Initialize the list of items for the current transaction
    items <- c()
    # Convert binary to categorical
    if (df[i, 1] == "1") items <- c(items, 'EBooks')
    if (df[i, 2] == "1") items <- c(items, 'Hard')
    if (df[i, 3] == "1") items <- c(items, 'Paper')
    if (df[i, 3] == "1") items <- c(items, 'Music')
    if (df[i, 3] == "1") items <- c(items, 'Elect')
    if (df[i, 3] == "1") items <- c(items, 'Health')
    if (df[i, 3] == "1") items <- c(items, 'Giftc')
    if (df[i, 3] == "1") items <- c(items, 'Luggage')
    if (df[i, 3] == "1") items <- c(items, 'Mag')
    if (df[i, 3] == "1") items <- c(items, 'Movies')
    if (df[i, 3] == "1") items <- c(items, 'Software')
    if (df[i, 3] == "1") items <- c(items, 'Toys')
    if (df[i, 3] == "1") items <- c(items, 'Wine')
    if (df[i, 1] == "1") items <- c(items, 'Auto')
    if (df[i, 2] == "1") items <- c(items, 'Baby')

  # If the current transaction contains at least one item, add
it to the transactions list
    if (length(items) > 0) transactions[[length(transactions)
+ 1]] <- items
  }
  # Convert the list of transactions into a transactions object
  return(as(transactions, "transactions"))
}

# Call the data loading and preprocessing function
trans <- load_data_set("./AmazonBinaryAll.csv")

# Use the Apriori algorithm to find frequent itemsets
frequent_itemsets <- apriori(trans, parameter = list(supp =
0.6, target = "frequent itemsets"))

# Generate association rules
rules <- apriori(trans, parameter = list(supp = 0.6, conf =
0.6, target = "rules", minlen=2, maxlen = 3))

# Print frequent itemsets
inspect(frequent_itemsets)

# Print association rules
inspect(rules)

#View and save rules in a csv file
write.csv(DATAFRAME(rules), "rules.csv")

plot(rules, method = "scatterplot", measure=c("support",
"lift"), shading = "confidence")

plot(rules, method = "graph", shading = "confidence")
```

4.4.3 Python Code

The following code reads a file with 0 s for no purchase and 1 for one or more purchases for each item. Association rule algorithms work with character data. The first line accesses a needed Python function. Then the file is linked in the second line. The data frame df is defines, and the data converted from 0/1 to character data (using the short form of product names).

```
pip install mlxtend
import pandas as pd
from mlxtend.frequent_patterns import apriori
from mlxtend.frequent_patterns import association_rules

df = pd.read_csv("AmazonBinaryAll.csv")

itemsets = apriori(df, min_support = 0.4, use_colnames = True)

rules = association_rules(itemsets, metric = 'confidence',
min_threshold = 0.7)
rules.sort_values(by = ['lift'], ascending = False).head(6)
print(rules.sort_values(by  =  ['lift'],  ascending  =
False).drop(columns = ['antecedent support',
'consequent support', 'conviction']))
```

Results are given in Table 4.10, sorted by Lift:

Table 4.10 Python rule output

ID	Antecedent	Consequent	Support	Confidence	Lift	Leverage	Zhang's
1	EBooks, Hard	Paper	0.419	0.882	1.775	0.183	0.832
2	Paper	EBooks, Hard	0.419	0.843	1.775	0.183	0.868
3	EBooks, Paper	Hard	0.419	0.867	1.760	0.181	0.835
4	Hard	EBooks, Paper	0.419	0.850	1.760	0.181	0.851
5	Hard	Paper	0.426	0.864	1.739	0.181	0.838
6	Paper	Hard	0.426	0.857	1.739	0.181	0.845
7	Hard, Paper	EBooks	0.419	0.984	1.564	0.151	0.628
8	Paper	EBooks	0.483	0.972	1.545	0.170	0.701
9	EBooks	Paper	0.483	0.768	1.545	0.170	0.951
10	Ebooks	Hard	0.475	0.755	1.532	0.165	0.936
11	Hard	EBooks	0.475	0.963	1.532	0.165	0.685

These results match the Rattle results given in Table 4.9, with the exception of adding two rules having two consequents. Rattle generated a rule for IF EBooks THEN Hardback, which had a confidence at the limit used with Python.

Leverage measures the correlation between item sets by comparing the support of item set5s. Leverage of item{x} and item{y} would be support for the union of item{x} and item{y} − (support(item{x} x support(item{y})). While lift uses a ratio, leverage uses a difference. Zhang's metric measures the strength of association between two items considering both co-occurrence and non-co-occurrence. It's numerator is the support(item{x} & item{y}) minus the product of (support(item{x} x item{y}). The denominator is the maximum[support(item{x} & item{y}) x (1 − support(item{x})) and support(item{x} x item{y} − support(item{x} & item{y})).

4.5 Conclusion

Association rules are very useful in that they provide a machine-learning mechanism to deal with the explosion of big data. This can be for good or bad, as in any data mining application. Real-time automatic trading algorithms have caused damage in stock markets, for instance. However, they provide great value not only to retail analysis (to serve customers better), but also in the medical field to aid in diagnosis, in agriculture and manufacturing to suggest greater efficient operations, and in science to establish expected relationships in complex environments.

Implementing association rules is usually done through the Apriori algorithm, although refinements have been produced. This requires software for implementation, although that is available in most data mining tools, commercial or open source. The biggest problem with association rules seems to be sorting through the output to find interesting results.

Reference

Agrawal R, Imieliński T, Swami A (1993) Mining association rules between sets of items in large databases. In: Buneman P, Jajodia S (eds.) Proceedings of the 1993 ACM SIGMOD international conference on management of data, 201–216. Association for Computer Machinery, New York.

Chapter 5
Cluster Analysis

This chapter covers several aspects of cluster analysis. Initially, it presents clustering manually, using standardized data. This is to show how basic algorithms work. The second section shows how software works.

Cluster analysis is usually used as an initial analytic tool, enabling data mining analysts the ability to identify general groupings in the data. It often follows initial graphical display of data, and provides a numeric means to describe underlying patterns. This can include pattern identification. Cluster analysis is thus a type of model, but one that is usually applied in the process of data understanding.

Clustering has been applied in many areas. In finance, it has been used to support credit appr4oval decisions in credit scoring, as well as in portfolio selection of investments and selection of trading strategies. In healthcare, cost change patterns in claims data have been identified through clustering. Clustering has also supported prediction based on groups, hypothesis generation, and analysis of genes to identify those with similar biological functions. Clustering has also aided in identification of patient groups most in need of targeted intervention. There also have be4en applications in customer service, dividing customers into groups based on shared characteristics. Textual clustering has been widely applied in social media analysis.

Clustering involves identification of groups of observations measured over variables. Here we distinguish between discriminant analysis (where the groups are given as part of the data, and the point is to predict group membership) and cluster analysis (where the clusters are based on the data, and thus not pre-determined, and the point is to find items that belong together rather than to predict group membership). Cluster analysis is an unsupervised technique, where data is examined without reference to a response variable. (You can include outcome variables in cluster analysis, but they are treated just as any other variable, and if included will yield different clusters than if they weren't included.) Cluster analysis is an example of machine learning, where their value is their ability to capture interesting data groupings. The technique requires a large enough dataset to establish statistical significance, but conversely suffers from the curse of dimensionality in that the more variables and values these variables can take on, the more difficult the computational task. A typical use is to initially apply clustering models to identify segments of the data that are used in subsequent predictive analyses. There are a number of techniques used for cluster analysis, the basic method being K-means clustering.

5.1 K-Means Clustering

The most general form of clustering analysis allows the algorithm to determine the number of clusters. At the other extreme, the number of clusters may be pre-specified. Partitioning is used to define new categorical variables that divide the data into a fixed number of regions (k-means clustering, for example). A common practice is to apply factor analysis as a pre-processing technique to get a reasonable idea of the number of clusters, as well as to give managers a view of which types of items go together. Given a number (k) of centers, data observations are assigned to that center with the minimum distance to the observation. A variety of distance measures are available, although conventionally the centroid (a centroid has the average value—mean, median, etc.—for each variable) of each cluster is used as the center, and squared distance (or other metric) is minimized. This is the most widely used form of cluster analysis in data mining.

Cluster analysis has been used by data miners to segment customers, allowing customer service representatives to apply unique treatment to each segment. Data needs to be numerical for clustering algorithms to work. We will demonstrate methods with standardized data (ranging from 0 to 1) because metrics will be warped by different measurement scales. This isn't necessary with software, as most datamining software does this for you in the algorithm.

5.1.1 A Clustering Algorithm

The following is a simple k-means algorithm:

1. Select the desired number of clusters k (or iterate from 2 to the maximum number of clusters desired).
2. Select k initial observations as seeds (could be arbitrary, but the algorithm would work better if these seed values were as far apart as possible).
3. Calculate average cluster values over each variable (for the initial iteration, this will simply be the initial seed observations).
4. Assign each of the other training observations to the closest cluster, as measured by squared distance (other metrics could be used, but squared distance is conventional).
5. Recalculate cluster averages based on the assignments from Step 4.

5.1 K-Means Clustering

6. Iterate between steps 4 and 5 until the same set of assignments are obtained twice in a row.

Note that this algorithm does not guarantee the same result no matter what the initial seeds are. However, it is a relatively straightforward procedure. The problem of how to determine k can be dealt with by applying the procedure for 2 clusters, then for 3, and so forth until the maximum desired number of clusters is reached. Selecting from among these alternatives may be relatively obvious in some cases, but can be a source of uncertainty in others.

There are some drawbacks to k-means clustering. The data needs to be put in standardized form to get rid of the differences in scale. However, even this approach assumes that all variables are equally important. If there are some variables more important than others, weights can be used in the distance calculation, but determining these weights is another source of uncertainty.

5.1.2 Loan Data

This data set consists of information on applicants for appliance loans, and was used in Chapter 2 to demonstrate visualization. We will use the loan application dataset to demonstrate clustering software. The business purpose here is to identify the type of loan applicants least likely to have repayment problems. In the dataset, an outcome of On-Time is good, and Late is bad. Distance metrics are an important aspect of cluster analysis, as they drive algorithms, and different scales for variable values will lead to different results. Thus we will transform data for demonstration of how clustering works. We will use 400 of the observations for cluster analysis. Transformation of data to standardized form (between 0 and 1) is accomplished as follows:

Age	< 20	0
	20 to 50	(age-20)/30
	50 to 80	1−(age-50)/30
	> 80	0
Income	< 0	0
	0 to $100,000	income/100000
	> $100,000	1
Risk	Max 1, min 0	assets/(debts + want) (higher is better)
Credit	Green	1
	Amber	0.3
	Red	0

Standardized values for the data are given in Table 5.1.

Dividing the data into 400 for a training set and retaining 250 for testing, simply identifying average attribute values for each given cluster, we begin with sorting

Table 5.1 Standardized loan data

Age	Income	Risk	Credit	OnTime
0	0.17152	0.531767	1	1
0.1	0.25862	0.764475	1	1
0.266667	0.26169	0.903015	0.3	0
0.1	0.21117	0.694682	0	0
0.066667	0.07127	1	0.3	1
0.2	0.42083	0.856307	0	0
0.133333	0.55557	0.544163	1	1
0.233333	0.34843	0	0	1
0.3	0.74295	0.882104	0.3	1
0.1	0.38887	0.145463	1	1
0.266667	0.31758	1	1	1
0.166667	0.8018	0.449404	1	0
0.433333	0.40921	0.979941	0.3	0
0.533333	0.63124	1	1	1
0.633333	0.59006	1	1	1
0.633333	1	1	0.3	1
0.833333	0.80149	1	1	1
0.6	1	1	1	1
0.3	0.81723	1	1	1
0.566667	0.99522	1	1	1

Table 5.2 Group standard score averages for loan application data

Cluster	On-time	Age	Income	Risk	Credit
C1 (355 cases)	1	0.223	0.512	0.834	0.690
C2 (45 cases)	0	0.403	0.599	0.602	0.333

the 400 training cases into on-time and late categories, and identifying the average performance by variable for each group.

These averages are shown in Table 5.2

Cluster 1 included members that tended to be younger with better risk measures and credit ratings. Income tended to be the same for both, although Cluster 1 members had slightly lower incomes.

Step 3 of the k-means algorithm calculates the ordinary least squares distance to these cluster averages. This calculation for test case 1 to Cluster 1, using Age, Income, Risk and Credit standardized scores, would be:

$$(0.223 - 0.967)^2 + (0.512 - 0.753)^2 + (0.834 - 1)^2 + (0.690 - 0)^2 = 1.115.$$

The distance to Cluster 2 is:

$$(0.403 - 0.967)^2 + (0.599 - 0.753)^2 + (0.602 - 1)^2 + (0.333 - 0)^2 = 0.611.$$

Because the distance to Cluster 2 (0.611) is closer than to Cluster 1 (1.115), the algorithm would assign Case 1 to Cluster 2.

If there were a reason to think that some variables were more important than others, you could apply weights to each variable in the distance calculations. In this case, there clearly are two interesting classes, so we might stop at two clusters. However, in principle, you can have as many clusters as you want. The basic distance calculation is the same. Analyzing the differences in clusters accurately depends upon knowledge of the underlying data.

5.2 Clustering Methods Used in Software

The most widely used clustering methods are hierarchical clustering, Bayesian clustering, K-means clustering, and self-organizing maps. Hierarchical clustering algorithms do not require specification of the number of clusters prior to analysis. However, they only consider local neighbors at each stage, and cannot always separate overlapping clusters. The two-step method is a form of hierarchical clustering. Two-step clustering first compresses data into subclusters, and then applying a statistical clustering method to merge subclusters into larger clusters until the desire number of clusters is reached. Thus the optimal number of clusters for the training set will be obtained. Bayesian clustering also is statistically based. Bayesian clustering is based on probabilities. Bayesian networks are constructed with nodes representing outcomes, and decision trees constructed at each node. K-means clustering involves increasing the number of clusters as demonstrated earlier. Software allows you to specify the number of clusters in K-means. Self-organizing maps use neural networks to convert many dimensions into a small number (like two), which has the benefit of eliminating possible data flaws such as noise (spurious relationships), outliers, or missing values. K-means methods have been combined with self-organizing maps as well as with genetic algorithms to improve clustering performance.

K-means algorithms work by defining a fixed number of clusters, and iteratively assigning records to clusters. In each iteration, the cluster centers are redefined. The reassignment and recalculation of cluster centers continues until any changes are below a specified threshold.

Kohonen self-organizing maps (SOM, or Kohonen networks) are neural network applications to clustering. Input observations are connected to a set of output layers, with each connection having a strength (weight). A general four-step process is applied (Kohonen 1997):

1. **Initialize map:** A map with initialized reference vectors is created, and algorithm parameters such as neighborhood size and learning rate are set.
2. **Determine winning node:** For each input observation, select the best matching node by minimizing distance to an input vector. The Euclidean norm is usually used.
3. **Update reference vectors:** Reference vectors and its neighborhood nodes are updated based upon the learning rule.
4. **Iterate:** Return to step 2 until the selected number of epochs is reached, adjusting neighborhood size.

Small maps are recommended. Large neighborhood sizes and learning rates are recommended initially, but can be decreased. With small maps, these parameters have not been found to be that important. There are a number of variants, to include self-organizing tree maps and self-organizing time maps (Sarlin 2013). Self-organizing maps are a useful tool for machine learning as applied to cluster analysis.

5.3 Example Cases

The next section will present two cases applying cluster analysis. The first deals with churn analysis. The second applies credit risk assessment.

5.3.1 Churn Clustering Model

Telecom companies participate in a highly competitive environment. New customers are attracted through incentive programs, which cost the telecom firm money. This money is wasted if a customer takes advantage of the incentive program and then leaves for a competitor (churn). Therefore, the ability to predict churn is critical to telecom success.

Jafari-Marandi et al. (2020) developed a method to systematically leverage information obtained from machine learning to estimate the value of each type of customer profile. This model was then employed in supervised churn classification. The system included calculation of customer value for each profile. This was followed by a self-organizing map (SOM) neural network clustering model involving fine-tuning of parameters, which was adjusted with experience. The SOM provided targets for a neural network classification model.

A key evaluation metric was identification of misclassification cost. Customer lifetime value for each profile was replaced with lifetime revenue as data was unavailable for costs. The time horizon used was cluster average age until age 65. Average monthly revenue for a cluster was estimated using average number of text messages and average seconds of call usage along with their respective prices.

The self-organizing map generated clusters divided into churn and non-churn categories. This categorization was refined in the later step optimizing cluster assignments, using calculated misclassification costs. The system was compared with other algorithms, to oinclude decision trees. The churn clustering model developed was found to save an average $43,000 compared to the best cost-sensitive approaches reported in the literature.

5.3.2 Credit Risk Assessment Model

Granting loans and issuing credit cards are the primary concern of banks. A major risk is non-payment. In Europe, Basel II guidelines require banks to develop their own credit risk assessment systems. This environment is challenging due to changing economic and political conditions. This is especially true in Iran, under US sanctions over the period 2008–2016,

Moradi and Mokhatab Rafiei (2019) developed a model intended to be flexible in considering 35 loan applicant factors. The model was dynamic in that it was updated monthly. Each month a list of customers who had not paid their debt for the last 2 months or so was identified. Then fuzzy clustering was applied to identify customer clusters (low risk, medium risk, high risk). High risk customers were rejected, low risk customers accepted. Then an adaptive-network fuzzy inference system was applied to those applicants in the medium risk category, applying the new credit risk factors to assign customers to higher risk (applications rejected) and medium risk (loan granted under special conditions).

Banks prefer to build static models once, and use them for years. But Iran faced conditions with severe change in political and economic conditions. After applying the dynamic modeling system, Moradi and Mokhatab Rafiei (2019) found the most important variables (based on correlation) to be age, monthly income, number of dependents, marital status, occupation code, type of home, and bill payment experience. Clustering methods considered were k-means, fuzzy clustering, and subtractive approaches. Fuzzy clustering worked best in this study. It had the advantage of not having crisp borders between clusters, as was the case with K-means models.

The bank customer database consisted of 9000 profiles, divided into 7920 records (6668 2 to 6 months late falling into the medium-risk category and 1262 high-risk with no payment for over 6 months) to design and train the adaptive-network fuzzy inference system, and 1080 held out for testing. The model proved to fit the real data much better than the old static model.

5.4 Software

Chapter 3 introduced Rattle, a GUI interface for the open software R and Python. We will demonstrate clustering with a publicly available dataset involving a Portuguese bank's telemarketing application. Rattle has four algorithms—Kmeans, Ewkm (entropy weighted k-means), Hierarchical, and BiCluster. K-means clustering assigns records to a specified number of clusters through iteratively adjusting the cluster centers (much as described earlier in this chapter).

5.4.1 Portuguese Bankruptcy Dataset

This data comes from the UCI Machine Learning Repository at archive.ics.uci.edu/dataset/222/bank+marketing hosted by the University of California-Irvine. The study was reported by Moro et al. (2012) and Moro et al. (2014). Data is shown in Table 5.3.

Table 5.3 Bank marketing variables

Variable name	Type	Description	End type	Result
Age	Integer		Numeric	
Job	Categoric	Type of Job		Excluded
Marital	Categoric	Marital Status		Binary
Education	Categoric	Education level	Numeric	
Default	Categoric	Does the client have credit in default?		Binary
Balance	Integer	Average yearly balance	Numeric	
Housing	Categoric	Does the client have a housing loan?		Binary
Loan	Categoric	Does the client have a personal loan?		Binary
Contact	Categoric	Contact communication type		Excluded
Day_of_week	Categoric	Last contact day of the week		Excluded
Month	Categoric	Last contact month of the year		Excluded
Duration	Numeric	Last contact duration	Numeric	
Campaign	Numeric	Number of contacts performed during this campaign	Numeric	
Pdays	Numeric	Number of days passed since the client was last contacted	Numeric	
Previous	Numeric	Number of contacts performed before the start of the campaign	Numeric	
Poutcome	Categoric	Outcome of the previous marketing campaign		Binary
Y	Categoric	Has the client subscribed to a term deposit?		Binary

5.4 Software

5.4.2 Rattle K-Means Clustering

Clustering is adversely affected by binary variables—K-means clustering algorithm is based on assuming normality, and binary variables aren't distributed at all normally. They are in effect all outliers. Therefore, we delete binary variables from the Portuguese Bankruptcy dataset to demonstrate clustering.

In Rattle's Explore page, asking for Distributions and selecting Box Plots for each variable yields Fig. 5.1

These are box-and-whisker plots displaying the means (asterisks), quartiles (box ends) and outliers (outlying dots). The last plot in Fig. 5.1 shows that Subscribe is a binary variable, which is not best for the normality assumption of the K-Means algorithm. However, there is a tradeoff in many cases if that variable is the focus of analysis. Here we leave the binary variable in the data analyzed.

Another useful tool is correlation, which can be obtained by selecting the **Correlation** radio button, yielding Fig. 5.2.

The graphic shows Previous and Pdays as well as Duration and Subscribe have strong positive relationships. There are negative relationships, but not very strong.

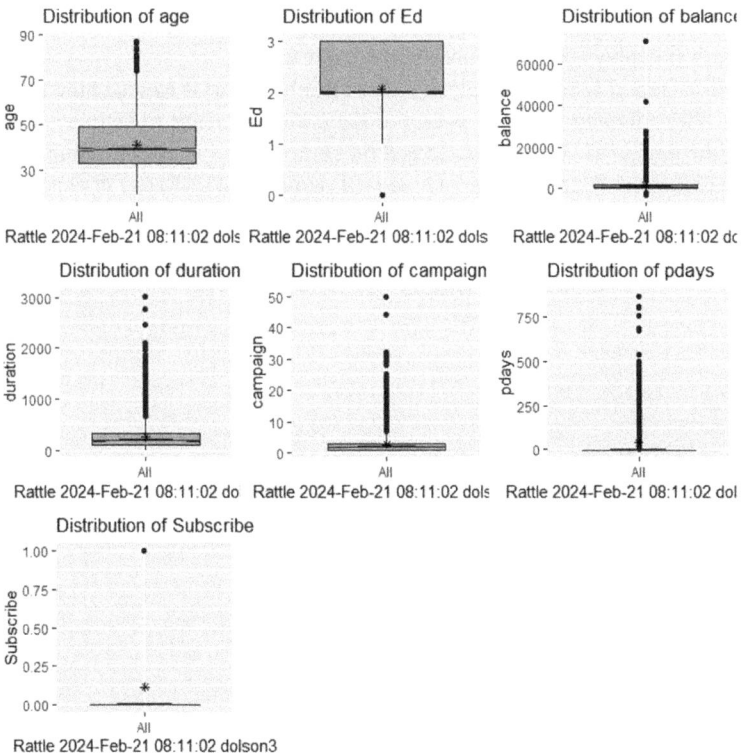

Fig. 5.1 Box plot distributions output from Rattle

Fig. 5.2 Rattle correlation graphic

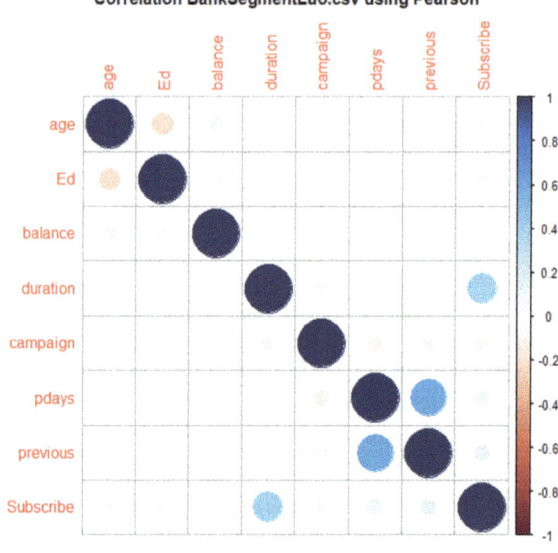

Table 5.4 displays this information in tabular form.

The first step in K-means analysis (after cleaning data) is to select the number of clusters. The silhouette method is one of the stronger means to estimate a K value that fits the data well. This approach is a bit complex and is not available on Rattle. (It is available on R and Python, as we will demonstrate.) Rattle does have a tool obtained by clicking on the iterate clusters box (see Fig. 5.3).

This yields Fig. 5.4, plotting sum of squared errors versus K.

5.4 Software

Table 5.4 Correlation—Bank marketing data

	Age	Ed	Balance	Duration	Campaign	Pdays	Previous	Subscribe
Age	1.000							
Ed	−0.199	1.000						
Balance	0.084	0.036	1.000					
Duration	−0.002	−0.003	−0.016	1.000				
Campaign	−0.005	0.019	−0.010	−0.068	1.000			
Pdays	−0.009	0.007	0.009	0.010	−0.093	1.000		
Previous	−0.004	0.027	0.026	0.018	−0.068	0.578	1.000	
Subscribe	0.045	0.050	0.018	0.401	−0.061	0.104	0.117	1.000

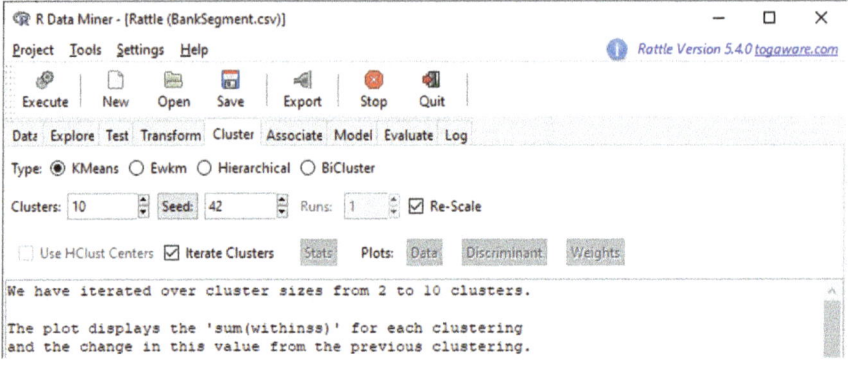

Fig. 5.3 Rattle iterate clusters screen

Fig. 5.4 Rattle's iterate clusters output

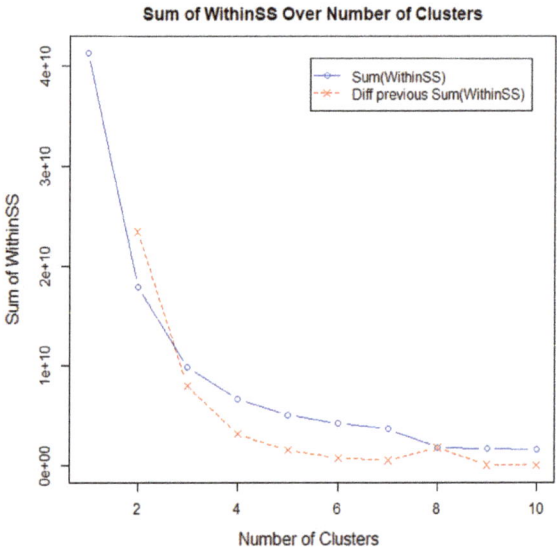

This plots the sum of within sum of squared errors by K from 1 to 10. It (the line with the o icons) has to decline as K increases. Rattle also plots the derivative, change in sum of within sum of squares (the line with the x icon). The idea of the "elbow" method is to pick the K that is obtained when the sum of within sum of squares flattens out. Here you could argue for 4, or 8.

5.4 Software

5.4.3 R Clustering

The silhouette method to determine K is more complete than the visual elbow method. The silhouette score is a measure of how similar a data point is within-cluster (cohesion) compared to other clusters (separation). The R code for three plots to aid in selecting K is in the code above.

```
# Elbow method
fviz_nbclust(dt, kmeans, method = "wss") +
  geom_vline(xintercept = 4, linetype = 2)+
  labs(subtitle = "Elbow method")
# Silhouette method
fviz_nbclust(dt, kmeans, method = "silhouette")+
  labs(subtitle = "Silhouette method")
# Gap statistic
set.seed(1)
fviz_nbclust(dt, kmeans, nstart = 25, method = "gap_stat",
nboot = 50)+
  labs(subtitle = "Gap statistic method")
```

The output from R Studio is given in Fig. 5.5, with a recommendation for $K = 4$.

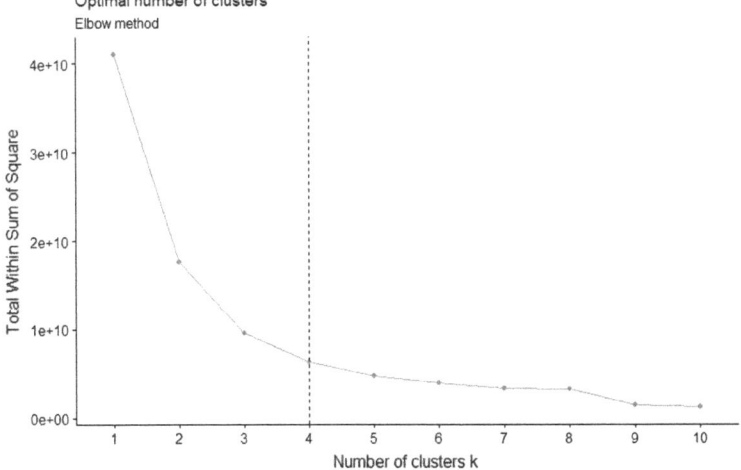

Fig. 5.5 R Studio elbow output for BankSegmentLuo.csv

5.4.4 R Code

```
library(scales)
library(arules)
library(factoextra)
library(NbClust)
BankSegmentLuo=read.csv("BankSegmentLuo.csv")
str(BankSegmentLuo)
dt=BankSegmentLuo[,-c(4)]
str(dt)
# Elbow method
fviz_nbclust(dt, kmeans, method = "wss") +
  geom_vline(xintercept = 4, linetype = 2)+
  labs(subtitle = "Elbow method")
# Silhouette method
fviz_nbclust(dt, kmeans, method = "silhouette")+
  labs(subtitle = "Silhouette method")
# Gap statistic
set.seed(1)
fviz_nbclust(dt, kmeans, nstart = 25, method = "gap_stat",
nboot = 50)+
  labs(subtitle = "Gap statistic method")
#K-means
set.seed(42)
k2=kmeans(dt,2,nstart = 25)
k3=kmeans(dt,3,nstart = 25)
k4=kmeans(dt,4,nstart = 25)
k5=kmeans(dt,5,nstart = 25)
k6=kmeans(dt,6,nstart = 25)
par(mfrow=c(1,3))
fviz_cluster(k2, dt,
    palette = c("#2E9FDF", "#00AFBB"),
    geom = "point",
    ellipse.type = "convex",
    ggtheme = theme_bw()
)
fviz_cluster(k3, dt,
    palette = c("#2E9FDF", "#00AFBB", "#E7B800"),
    geom = "point",
    ellipse.type = "convex",
    ggtheme = theme_bw()
)
fviz_cluster(k4, dt,
    palette = c("#2E9FDF", "#00AFBB", "#E7B800","#FF9999"),
    geom = "point",
    ellipse.type = "convex",
    ggtheme = theme_bw()
)
fviz_cluster(k5, dt,
                    palette =   c("#2E9FDF",   "#00AFBB",
"#E7B800","#FF9999","#33FFFF"),
```

5.4 Software

```
        geom = "point",
        ellipse.type = "convex",
        ggtheme = theme_bw()
)
fviz_cluster(k6, dt,
                    palette  =  c("#2E9FDF",  "#00AFBB",
"#E7B800","#FF9999","#33FFFF","#CC99FF"),
        geom = "point",
        ellipse.type = "convex",
        ggtheme = theme_bw()
)
k2
k3
k4
k5
k6
```

The silhouette output from RStudio is shown in Fig. 5.6.
Python has functionality to identify the silhouette score.

```
Sklearn.metrics.silhouette_score(,         labels,           *,
metric='Euclidean',   sample_size=None,  random_state=None,
**kwds)
```

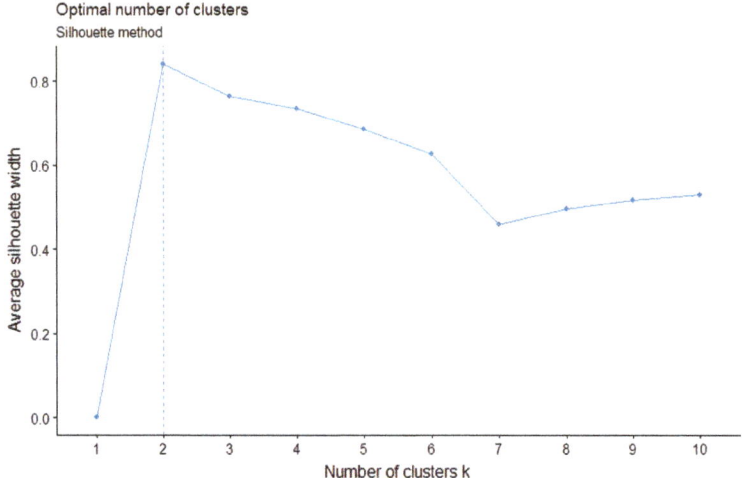

Fig. 5.6 Silhouette output from R Studio

From R Studio we obtain the following cluster centers for K = 1 to 6 using data that is not re-scaled, sorting on Age and identifying the extreme values (larger in bold; smaller in italic) (Table 5.5).

Note that the oldest group tends to be the smallest, have the largest balance, as well as the largest days in promotion (pdays). They also have lower subscription rates. This indicates that older wealthier buyers are less interested in term deposits. As K is increased, the oldest group gets smaller (more focus)

We demonstrate with K of 6. The K-means clustering output using re-scaling (giving output on the same 0–1 scale for all variables) is given in Table 5.6.

Here cluster 1 has 1280 younger borrowers. This cluster had low values for balance, and no subscribers. Cluster 2 was the next youngest cluster (1151 members) with high education level and high number of contacts during this marketing

Table 5.5 R Clusters for bank segment data

Cluster	Count	Age	Ed	Balance	Duration	Campaign	Pdays	Previous	Subscribe
K = 2									
1	229	41	2.1	*901*	265	2.8	39	0.53	0.12
2	4292	44	2.2	**11,339**	236	2.8	45	0.74	0.09
K = 3									
1	3875	41	2.1	*549*	264	2.8	40	0.53	0.11
2	577	43	2.1	5250	**273**	2.7	36	0.59	**0.16**
3	69	45	2.3	**18,457**	*202*	**3.0**	49	0.77	*0.06*
K = 4									
1	3676	41	2.1	*444*	264	2.8	40	0.53	0.11
2	672	43	2.1	3860	**275**	2.8	36	0.57	0.17
3	150	43	2.2	10,670	236	2.9	41	**0.72**	0.08
4	23	46	2.2	**26,354**	*173*	*2.3*	53	0.57	0.09
K = 5									
1	3402	41	2.1	*336*	263	2.8	39	0.51	0.10
2	761	43	2.1	2673	**278**	2.6	41	0.61	0.17
3	73	43	2.3	13,674	215	2.8	*33*	0.59	0.05
4	266	43	2.1	6502	256	2.9	46	**0.77**	0.14
5	19	47	2.2	**27,766**	*168*	2.5	65	0.68	*0.05*
K = 6									
1	2959	41	2.0	*209*	259	2.9	39	0.50	0.10
2	896	42	2.1	1619	**278**	2.5	44	0.62	0.15
3	415	43	2.1	3973	**283**	2.8	*33*	0.59	0.18
4	68	43	2.3	13,919	215	2.8	35	0.63	0.06
5	164	44	2.1	7542	260	2.8	44	**0.75**	0.11
6	19	47	2.2	**27,766**	*168*	2.5	65	0.68	*0.05*

5.4 Software

Table 5.6 Cluster output with K = 6 with re-scale

Cluster	Count	Age	Ed	Balance	Duration	Campaign	Pdays	Previous	Subscribe
1	1280	0.211	0.667	*0.058*	0.078	0.036	0.051	0.020	0.000
2	1151	0.301	**1.000**	0.068	*0.069*	**0.041**	0.041	0.022	0.000
3	430	0.310	0.816	0.063	**0.181**	*0.026*	**0.082**	**0.047**	1.000
4	782	0.396	*0.262*	0.063	0.073	0.037	0.040	*0.018*	0.000
5	787	0.467	0.669	0.064	0.072	0.038	*0.033*	*0.014*	0.000
6	91	0.512	*0.293*	**0.076**	**0.186**	*0.026*	**0.071**	0.029	1.000

campaign. The last contact duration was low (recent). The cluster had no subscriptions. Cluster 3 had high values for last contact (duration) and days past since last contact (Pdays), but a high number of contacts prior to this marketing campaign. This cluster's 430 members all subscribed. Cluster 4 had lower education and a low number of contacts prior to this marketing campaign, and none of the 782 members subscribed. Cluster 5 had low values for number of days since last contact and low value for number of contacts prior to this campaign. None of the 787 members subscribed. The last cluster's 91 members all subscribed. The major differences with Cluster 3 were that Cluster 6 had high average yearly balance, and lower number of contacts prior to this campaign. Note that here each of the six clusters were uniform with respect to subscription. That's beyond analyst control (a matter of luck).

It often is easier to see what the variables say if you don't re-scale, which reports clusters in nominal variable terms. However, this results in an entirely different set of clusters.

Re-scaling should provide greater balance, and here it also provided more differential information.

There are other tools provided by Rattle clustering. The Stats button gives detailed statistics which don't usually have much interest. The Data button, however, provides a view of how each variable is grouped by cluster, as shown in Fig. 5.7

Rattle warns us that over five variables are cluttered, and only displays the first five. But we can see from FICO that the higher values are displayed in red, indicating that red must be cluster 2. Then we can see that Age, income, and safety are spread out a lot. Credit had three ratings—0 for poor, 0.3 for not that good, and 1.0 for OK. The OK rated observations are all red (cluster 2), the others black (cluster 1).

The Discriminant button provides a plot of the first two eigen vectors (see Fig. 5.8).

The Components here are assigned by Rattle based on discriminant analysis, essentially compressing the six variables into two. Circles are for cluster 1 and triangles for cluster 2, and here there is clear difference, indicated by the ovals.

Radar charts provide useful visuals to differentiate among clusters. Figure 5.9 displays the radar chart for the data in Table 5.6 (re-scaled data, where all variables were on a 0–1 range). Radar charts were obtained through Excel by importing the cluster centers and using Excel plots.

This enables us to see the relationships how the features of the clusters change.

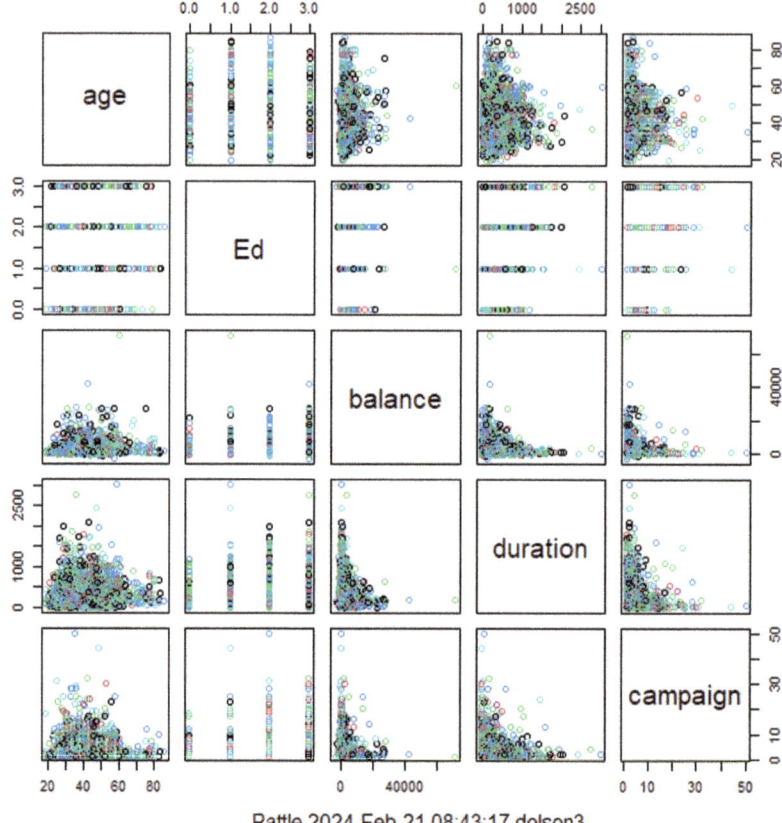

Fig. 5.7 Data output from Rattle for re-scaled Clusters

5.4.5 Python Clustering

The Python Code for this data file:

```
from sklearn.cluster import KMeans
from sklearn.manifold import TSNE

import pandas as pd
import numpy as np

# First step: read the data (original data need to put into a file
named "data")
df = pd.read_csv('./data/BankSegmentLuo.csv')
datalist = []
target_label = []
```

5.4 Software

Fig. 5.8 Discriminant plot for re-scaled Clusters

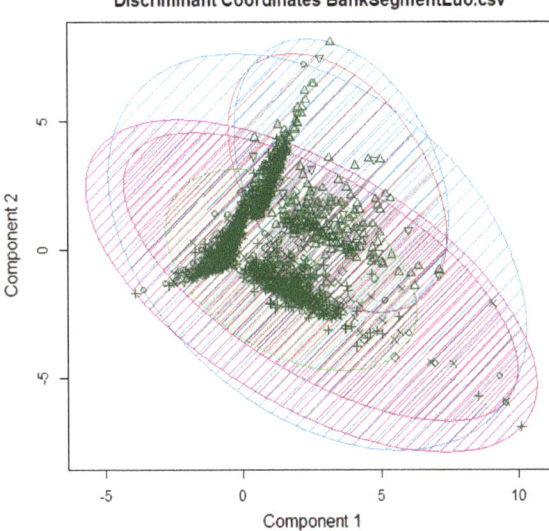

Fig. 5.9 Hierarchical Cluster radar plot for the clusters as shown in Table 5.6

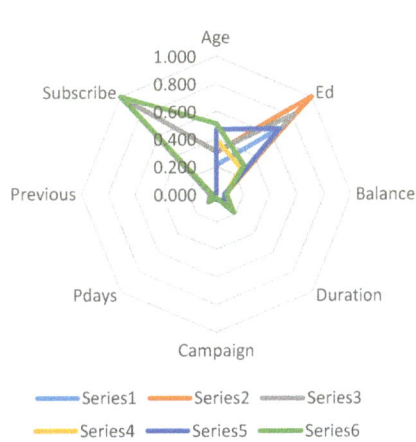

```
# Second step: data preprocessing
for index, row in df.iterrows():
    temp = list(row)
    datalist.append(temp)
datalist = np.array(datalist)

# Third step: set parameter K for K-Means Algorithm
K = [6, 10]
```

```python
tsne = TSNE(n_components=2, init='pca', random_state=0)
embed = tsne.fit_transform(datalist)
result = {} # Initialize an empty dictionary
for k in K:
    print(f"When k is: {k}")
    # K-Means Algorithm
    kmeans    =    KMeans(n_clusters=k,    random_
state=0).fit(datalist)
    # print the center of parameter K
    print("cluster_centers")
    print(kmeans.cluster_centers_)
    # sample counts for each cluster
    print("sample counts of each cluster:")
    print(np.bincount(kmeans.labels_))
        # record the result of parameter K which indicates the
category of each sample
        result.update({f'k={k}_cluster_label': kmeans.labels_})

# Fourth step: output the result of different parameter K to a
csv file
result = pd.DataFrame(result)
result.to_csv('./data/BankSegmentLuoResult.csv',
index=False, header=True)
```

Table 5.7 gives results from Python using K of 6. This data is not re-scaled, so can be compared to Rattle output in Table 5.5. Both are sorted by age.

There is some similarity between Table 5.6 and Table 5.7, but they are different. A feature of cluster analysis is that there is very little control over the output obtained. An interesting feature of Cluster 6 in Table 5.7 is that it consists of 1 member, with a high average yearly balance. That makes it an outlier.

Table 5.8 gives the ten cluster centers obtained from Python, sorted by age (in Excel).

Table 5.9 gives cluster centers from Rattle (not re-scaled) for K of 10.

In both cases clusters were sorted by subscription rate. Both had the single individual with the high balance in the last cluster. Otherwise little pattern is observed.

Table 5.7 K = 6 Python

Cluster	Count	Age	Ed	balance	duration	campaign	pdays	previous	Subscribe
1	3393	40.6	2.05	*333*	263	2.82	39	0.51	0.10
2	762	42.6	2.09	2639	**277**	2.65	42	0.61	**0.17**
3	71	43.0	2.25	13,232	212	2.92	34	0.61	*0.04*
4	272	43.2	2.09	6419	257	2.88	44	**0.75**	0.14
5	22	45.9	2.27	24,316	*171*	2.36	**56**	0.59	0.09
6	1	60.0	*1*	71,188	205	*1*	−1	0	0

Table 5.8 K = 10 Python

Cluster	Count	Age	Education	Balance	Duration	Campaign	P Days	Previous	Subscribe
1	427	42.7	2.08	2823	**285**	2.74	38	0.54	**0.19**
2	245	43.2	2.03	4836	270	2.76	39	0.70	0.16
3	1021	41.4	2.10	1169	**288**	2.54	47	0.68	0.13
4	124	43.7	2.16	7859	254	2.84	49	**0.76**	0.12
5	2612	40.4	2.04	*135*	253	**2.91**	37	0.46	0.09
6	17	46.0	2.18	24,372	*163*	2.65	**72**	**0.76**	0.06
7	51	41.9	2.18	12,264	212	**2.96**	34	0.51	0.06
8	22	45.9	2.45	16,942	221	2.45	32	**0.77**	0.05
9	1	42.0	**3.00**	**42,045**	205	2.00	−1	0	0
10	1	**60.0**	*1.00*	**71,188**	205	*1.00*	−1	0	0

Table 5.9 K = 10 Rattle

Cluster	Count	Age	Education	Balance	Duration	Campaign	P Days	Previous	Subscribe
1	365	40.7	2.03	398	**825**	2.67	45	0.58	**0.39**
2	417	42.6	2.08	2849	283	2.77	35	0.53	**0.19**
3	249	43.2	2.04	4883	269	2.73	40	0.70	0.16
4	864	41.5	2.11	1256	235	2.55	47	0.65	0.11
5	132	43.5	2.12	8223	248	2.81	45	0.70	0.11
6	228	39.5	2.02	−487	276	2.54	27	0.36	0.09
7	22	45.9	2.27	24,315	*171*	2.36	**56**	0.59	0.09
8	2188	40.6	2.05	*204*	*179*	2.95	38	0.48	0.06
9	55	43.1	2.35	14,001	230	**3.09**	40	**0.75**	0.05
10	1	**60.0**	*1.00*	**71,188**	205	*1.00*	−1	0	0

5.5 File BostonHousingKaggle.csv

The dataset is from government sources. It has 506 observations over 14 variables:

- CRIM—per capita crime rate by town
- ZN—proportion of residential land zoned for lots over 25,000 sq.ft.
- INDUS—proportion of non-retail business acres per town.
- CHAS—Charles River dummy variable (1 if tract bounds river; 0 otherwise)
- NOX—nitric oxides concentration (parts per 10 million)
- RM—average number of rooms per dwelling
- AGE—proportion of owner-occupied units built prior to 1940
- DIS—weighted distances to five Boston employment centres
- RAD—index of accessibility to radial highways

Fig. 5.10 Elbow output for BostonHousingKaggle.csv from Rattle

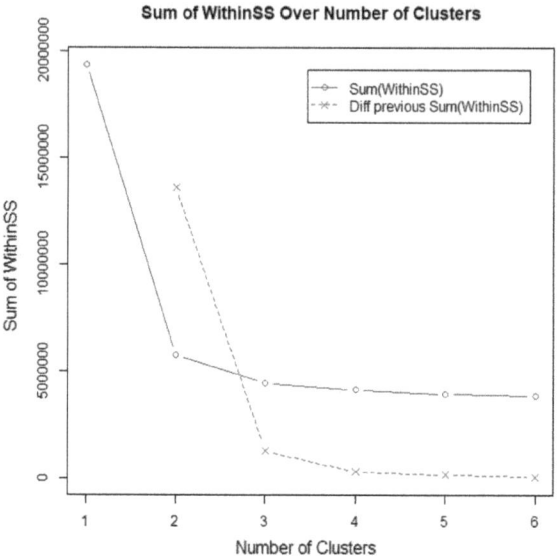

- TAX—full-value property-tax rate per $10,000
- PTRATIO—pupil-teacher ratio by town
- B—1000(Bk—0.63)^2 where Bk is the proportion of blacks by town
- LSTAT—% lower status of the population
- MEDV—Median value of owner-occupied homes in $1000's

The Rattle Elbow plot for this data is given in Fig. 5.10.

Here the elbow method indicates that K of 3 is appropriate.

K-means clustering analysis using the Euclidean distance metric assumes normal distributions in the data. Binary variables, such as CHAS here, violate that normality assumption. We will examine results with and without CHAS in Tables 5.10, 5.11, 5.12, and 5.13.

With respect to re-scaling or not, the output is very similar. Re-scaling is sounder statistically as scalar differences are washed out (although the algorithm does that anyway—re-scaling in effect washes out scale twice). Not re-scaling, however, is much more natural for humans—clusters are defined in nominal terms, not converted to 0–1 scales.

As to including the binary variable CHAS, in this case for this set of data it makes no difference. The re-scaled data had a slight difference in cluster counts, and very little difference in cluster center values. Not re-scaled data yielded identical cluster sets. The conclusion here is that the binary variable didn't hurt and including it might be valuable for the purpose of the study.

As to interpreting the cluster differences, all four permutations yield the same relative order. The cluster with the lowest median home value (MEDV) was the oldest as measured by proportion of owner-occupied units built prior to 1940, had the highest proportion of zoned residential land, as well as the highest proportion of

5.5 File BostonHousingKaggle.csv

Table 5.10 Cluster centers for K = 3 re-scaled including CHAS

n	CRIM	ZN	INDUS	CHAS	NOX	RM	AGE	DIS	RAD	TAX	PTRATIO	B	LSTAT	MEDV
1	136	**0.139**	*0.000*	**0.657**	0.059	**0.588**	0.469	**0.897**	*0.084*	**0.974**	**0.917**	**0.808**	*0.731*	**0.469**	*0.250*
2	185	0.007	0.019	0.415	0.114	0.394	0.509	0.835	0.170	0.158	0.281	0.573	0.939	0.325	0.386
3	185	*0.001*	**0.292**	*0.172*	0.032	*0.129*	0.574	*0.356*	**0.432**	0.142	0.200	0.536	0.981	*0.155*	**0.496**

Table 5.11 Cluster centers for K = 3 with no re-scale including CHAS

	n	CRIM	ZN	INDUS	CHAS	NOX	RM	AGE	DIS	RAD	TAX	PTRATIO	B	LSTAT	MEDV
1	137	**12.3**	*0.0*	**18.5**	0.058	**0.670**	6.0	**90.0**	*2.1*	**23.3**	**667.6**	**20.2**	*291.0*	**18.7**	*16.3*
2	101	0.8	9.7	13.1	0.069	0.587	6.2	73.7	3.3	4.8	405.8	17.6	363.1	12.8	22.2
3	268	*0.2*	**17.8**	*6.7*	0.075	*0.483*	6.5	55.7	**4.9**	*4.3*	*276.5*	17.9	387.8	*9.5*	**25.9**

5.5 File BostonHousingKaggle.csv

Table 5.12 Cluster centers for K = 3 re-scaled without CHAS

	n	CRIM	ZN	INDUS	NOX	RM	AGE	DIS	RAD	TAX	Pratio	B	LSTAT	MEDV
1	136	**0.139**	*0.000*	**0.657**	**0.588**	0.469	**0.897**	*0.084*	**0.974**	**0.917**	**0.808**	*0.731*	**0.469**	*0.250*
2	189	0.007	0.017	0.412	0.391	0.507	0.827	0.174	0.158	0.279	0.577	0.939	0.323	0.385
3	181	*0.001*	**0.300**	*0.170*	*0.126*	0.577	*0.353*	**0.433**	0.142	0.200	0.531	0.982	*0.153*	**0.500**

Table 5.13 Cluster centers for K = 3 with no re-scale without CHAS

	n	CRIM	ZN	INDUS	NOX	RM	AGE	DIS	RAD	TAX	PTRATIO	B	LSTAT	MEDV
1	137	*12.3*	*0.0*	*18.5*	*0.670*	*6.0*	*90.0*	*2.1*	*23.3*	*667.6*	*20.2*	*291.0*	*18.7*	*16.3*
2	101	0.8	9.7	13.1	0.587	6.2	73.7	3.3	4.8	405.8	17.6	363.1	12.8	22.2
3	268	0.2	*17.8*	6.7	0.483	6.5	55.7	*4.9*	4.3	276.5	17.9	387.8	9.5	*25.9*

5.5 File BostonHousingKaggle.csv

non-retail business acres. It also had the highest nitrous oxide concentration. It had higher accessibility to radial highways and higher property tax rates. It's pupil-teacher ratio was highest, and it had the highest percent of lower status population. The third cluster which had the highest median home value was pretty much the opposite, with the second cluster falling in between on every measure except pupil-teacher ratio.

5.5.1 R Code

```
boston <- read.csv("BostonHousingKaggle.csv")
row.names(boston) = 1:nrow(boston)
# Normalize data:
boston.norm <- sapply(boston, scale)
row.names(boston.norm) <- row.names(boston)

#kmeans algorithm
kmboston <- kmeans(boston.norm, 3) # the 3 tells R to run K=3 -
change for other sizes
kmboston$cluster # this tells which cluster each observation
belongs to
kmboston$size # this gives cluster size

kmboston <- kmeans(boston, centers = 3, nstart=30) # 30 is the
seed

#centroids plotting profile
plot(c(0), xaxt = 'n', ylab = "", type = 'l', ylim =
c(min(kmboston$centers),
           max(kmboston$centers)), xlim = c(0,14))
#label
axis(1, at = c(1:14), labels = names(boston))

#plot
for (i in c(1:6))
  lines(kmboston$centers[i, ], lty = i, lwd = 4, col = ifelse(i
%in% c(1, 3, 5), "red", "green"))
#name Clusters
text(x = 0.5, y = kmboston$centers[, 1], labels =
paste("Cluster", c(1:6)))

#Visualize clusters
library(factoextra)
fviz_cluster(kmboston, data = boston.norm)
fviz_cluster(kmboston, data = boston.norm, choose.vars =
c("PRICE", "DIS"))

#Optimal number of clusters
#Elbow method
fviz_nbclust(boston.norm, kmeans, method = "wss", k.max = 6)
#Silhouette method
```

```
fviz_nbclust(boston.norm, kmeans, method = "silhouette",
k.max = 6)

#Gap statistic method
fviz_nbclust(boston.norm, kmeans, method = "gap", k.max = 6)
```

The elbow output from R is given in Fig. 5.11, silhouette output Fig. 5.12, and Gap Statistic output in Fig. 5.13

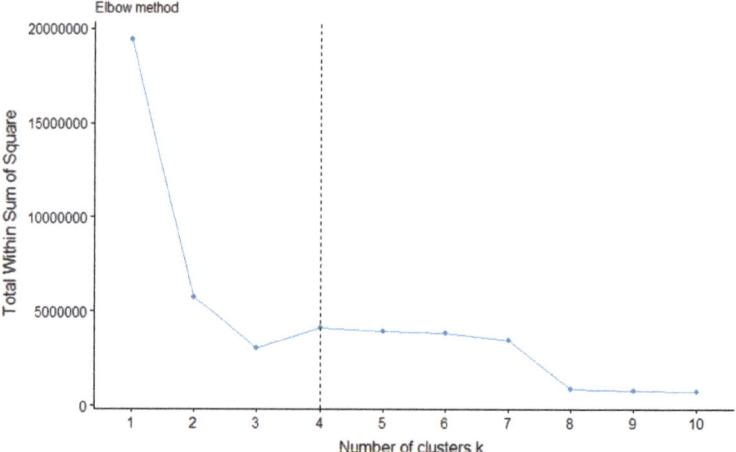

Fig. 5.11 R elbow for BankSegmentLuo.csv

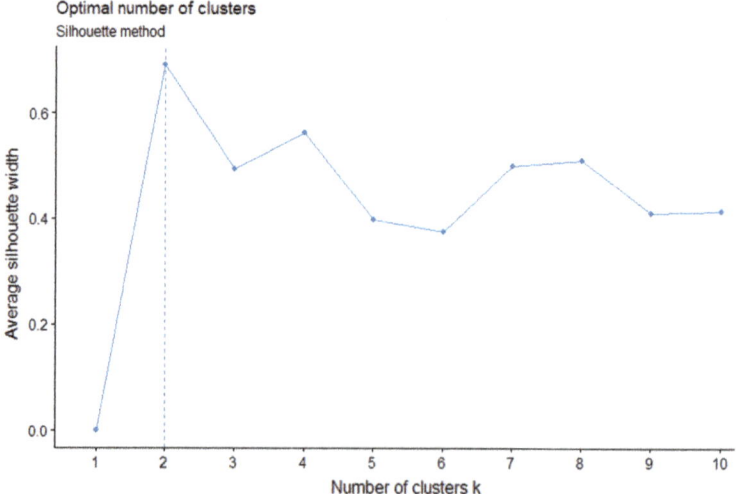

Fig. 5.12 R Silhoutte output for BankSegmentLuo.csv

5.5 File BostonHousingKaggle.csv

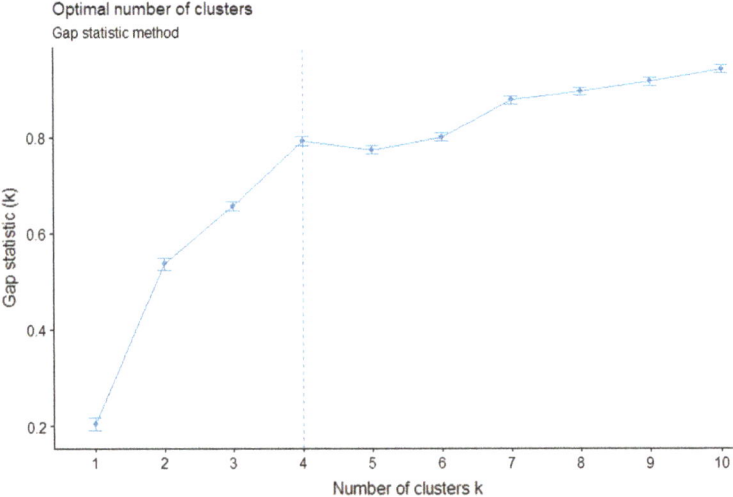

Fig. 5.13 Gap statistic output from R for BankSegmentLuo.csv

Note that Python has functionality to identify the silhouette score.

```
Sklearn.metrics.silhouette_score(,          labels,            *,
metric='Euclidean',  sample_size=None,  random_state=None,
**kwds)
```

The three tools to estimate the best K vary from 2 to 4. We will run K 2 through 6 with R. From R Studio we obtain the following cluster centers for K = 2 to 6 using data that is not re-scaled, sorting on Age and identifying the extreme values (larger in bold; smaller in italic) (Tables 5.14 and 5.15).

Note that this matches the Rattle output exactly for cluster 1, combining Rattle's clusters 2 and 3 from Table 5.11 into cluster 2 here

The R clusters with K = 3 vary from those obtained with Rattle (practically any change in clustering yields variances). But again, the higher value homes have lower crime rates, lower proportions of lower status, and lower tax rates as measured here. They also have lower access to radial highways, less nitric oxide concentrations and newer homes (none surprising). Table 5.16 gives clusters for K = 4.

These clusters are sorted by rising median home value. The same trends noted for the K = 3 clusters continues in Table 5.17 and 5.18.

Note that cluster 2 when K = 4 is the same as cluster 3 when K = 5. But while the count is the same, cluster 3 when K = 4 is not the same as cluster 4 when K = 5. There is little control in clustering—and different seeds yield different results

As K increased, differentiation increased, enabling focusing on extremes. Table 5.18 shows that higher priced homes had more zoning for larger lots and

Table 5.14 R Clusters for bank segment data K = 2

n	CRIM	ZN	INDUS	CHAS	NOX	RM	AGE	DIS	RAD	TAX	PTRATIO	B	LSTAT	MEDV
1	137	**12.3**	*0.0*	**18.5**	0.058	**0.670**	6.0	**90.0**	*2.1*	**23.3**	**667.6**	**20.2**	*291.0*	**18.7**	*16.3*
2	369	0.4	15.6	8.4	0.073	0.512	6.4	60.6	4.4	4.5	311.9	17.8	381.0	10.4	24.9

5.5 File BostonHousingKaggle.csv

Table 5.15 R Clusters for bank segment data K = 3

N	CRIM	ZN	INDUS	CHAS	NOX	RM	AGE	DIS	RAD	TAX	PTRATIO	B	LSTAT	MEDV
1	38	**15.2**	*0.0*	*17.9*	*0.026*	**0.674**	*6.1*	*89.9*	*2.0*	*22.5*	**644.7**	*19.9*	*57.8*	**20.4**	*13.1*
2	102	*10.9*	*0.0*	*18.6*	*0.078*	*0.671*	*6.0*	*89.9*	*2.1*	*23.0*	*668.2*	*20.2*	*371.8*	*17.9*	*17.4*
3	366	*0.4*	**15.7**	*8.4*	*0.071*	*0.510*	*6.4*	*60.4*	**4.5**	*4.5*	*311.2*	*17.8*	*383.5*	*10.4*	**24.9**

Table 5.16 R Clusters for bank segment data K = 4

	N	CRIM	ZN	INDUS	CHAS	NOX	RM	AGE	DIS	RAD	TAX	PTRATIO	B	LSTAT	MEDV
1	38	**15.2**	*0.0*	**17.9**	*0.026*	**0.673**	6.1	**89.9**	*2.0*	**22.5**	**644.7**	**19.9**	*57.8*	**20.4**	*13.1*
2	102	10.9	*0.0*	**18.6**	0.078	**0.671**	6.0	**89.9**	*2.1*	**23.0**	**668.2**	**20.2**	371.8	17.9	17.4
3	98	*0.7*	9.9	13.0	0.061	0.582	6.2	73.3	3.3	*4.8*	406.1	17.7	371.7	12.7	22.4
4	268	*0.2*	**17.8**	*6.7*	0.075	*0.483*	6.5	*55.7*	**4.9**	*4.3*	*276.5*	17.9	387.8	*9.5*	**25.8**

Table 5.17 R Clusters for bank segment data K = 5

	N	CRIM	ZN	INDUS	CHAS	NOX	RM	AGE	DIS	RAD	TAX	PTRATIO	B	LSTAT	MEDV
1	35	**16.3**	*0.0*	**18.1**	*0.000*	0.667	6.1	90.1	2.0	**24.0**	**666.0**	20.2	55.7	**21.0**	*12.9*
2	11	2.0	*0.0*	16.7	0.091	0.708	5.9	91.8	2.3	4.7	386.9	17.0	187.5	17.2	17.0
3	102	10.9	*0.0*	**18.6**	0.078	0.671	6.0	89.9	2.1	**23.0**	**668.2**	20.2	371.8	17.9	17.4
4	98	0.6	**12.9**	12.0	0.061	0.562	6.2	69.2	3.6	4.7	402.3	17.8	382.2	12.2	22.8
5	260	0.2	**17.3**	*6.7*	0.077	0.485	6.5	*56.1*	**4.8**	*4.3*	*274.7*	17.9	388.8	*9.5*	**26.0**

Table 5.18 R Clusters for bank segment data K = 6

N	CRIM	ZN	INDUS	CHAS	NOX	RM	AGE	DIS	RAD	TAX	PTRATIO	B	LSTAT	MEDV
1	35	**16.3**	*0.0*	**18.1**	*0.000*	0.667	6.1	90.1	2.0	**24.0**	**666.0**	20.2	55.7	**21.0**	*12.9*
2	11	2.0	*0.0*	16.7	0.091	0.708	5.9	91.8	2.3	4.7	386.9	17.0	187.5	17.2	*17.0*
3	102	10.9	*0.0*	**18.6**	0.078	0.671	6.0	89.9	2.1	**23.0**	**668.2**	20.2	371.8	17.9	*17.4*
4	87	*0.7*	**8.8**	13.1	0.069	0.581	6.2	74.0	3.2	4.9	408.8	17.9	381.7	12.7	*22.6*
5	191	*0.3*	**16.0**	6.7	0.068	0.489	6.4	57.5	**4.9**	4.6	299.7	17.8	387.6	9.8	*24.7*
6	80	*0.1*	**24.2**	17.9	0.088	0.465	6.6	49.2	**4.9**	3.6	225.5	17.9	391.4	8.5	***28.7***

more distance to employment centers. Wealthier people can afford to commute. The CHAS variable indicates that river-front property had higher median values as well.

5.6 Summary

Cluster analysis is a very attractive initial data examination tool. Once different clusters are identified, other methods are often used to discover rules and patterns. Outcome variables can be included but can also be dropped as they MAY influence cluster centers. They are treated just like any other variable in clustering, but it is convenient to include them to make interpretation of the differences in clusters easier. The intent of clustering, however, is to identify patterns rather than to predict.

Clustering is a task often used in text analysis, such as grouping online news to identify specific information. Term Frequency Inverse Document Frequency (TFIDF) is commonly used to represent textual data, but this method cannot consider the position of a word within a sentence nor context of its use. Bidirectional Encoder Representation from Transformers (BERT) can produce text representation incorporating word position and context. BERT has been found to usually outperform TFIDF.

Sometimes the median has been used rather than the mean as the basis for cluster centers. This is because outlier observations (radically different from the norm) do not affect the median but do influence the mean. It is very simple to implement the median rather than the mean in Excel (although not in packaged data mining software). In Excel all one does is use the formula " = MEDIAN(range)" rather than "AVERAGE(range)".

Some problems may not have an obvious set of clusters. There are a number of options for determining the number of clusters. Agglomeration is an approach where you start with the maximum number of clusters, and then merge clusters iteratively until there is only one cluster left. Then the cluster value that fits best (by whatever metric is selected and based upon the need for correct prediction—fewer clusters are better, along with the need for discrimination of difference—more clusters are better) is chosen. Commercial tools have a number of different parameters and methods. Some in fact use probability density rather than distance measures, which tends to work better when clusters overlap.

References

Jafari-Marandi R, Denton J, Idris A, Smith BK, Keramati A (2020) Optimum profit-driven churn decision making: Innovative artificial neural networks in telecom industry. Neural Comput Appl 32:14929–14962

Kohonen T (1997) Self-organizing maps. Springer-Verlag, Berlin

Moradi S, Mokhatab Rafiei F (2019) A dynamic credit risk assessment model with data mining techniques: evidence from Iranian banks. Financ Innov 5(15):1–27

Moro S, Cortez P, Rita P (2012) Bank marketing dataset, UCI Machine learning repository. https://archive.ics.uci.edu/dataset/222/bank+marketing

Moro S, Cortez P, Rita P (2014) A data-driven approach to predict the success of bank telemarketing. Decis Support Syst 62:22–31

Sarlin P (2013) Self-organizing time map: an abstraction of temporal multivariate patterns. Neurocomputing 99:496–508

Chapter 6
Regression Algorithms in Data Mining

Regression is a basic statistical tool. In data mining, it is one of the basic tools for analysis used in the classification applications through logistic regression and discriminant analysis, as well as the prediction of continuous data through ordinary least squares (OLS) and other forms. As such, regression is often taught in one (or more) three-hour courses. We cannot hope to cover all the basics of regression. However, we, here, present ways in which regression is used within the context of data mining.

Regression is used on a variety of data types. If data is time series, the output from regression models is often used for forecasting. Regression can be used to build predictive models for other types of data. Regression can be applied in several different forms. The class of regression models is a major class of tools available to support the Modeling phase of the data mining process.

Probably, the most widely used data mining algorithms are data fitting, in the sense of regression. Regression is a fundamental tool for statistical analysis to characterize relationships between a dependent variable and one or more independent variables. Regression models can be used for many purposes, to include explanation and prediction. *Linear* and *logistic* regression models are both primary tools in most general-purpose data mining software. Nonlinear data can sometimes be transformed into useful linear data and analyzed with linear regression. Some special forms of nonlinear regression also exist. *R*egression provides a formula that has a strong body of theory behind it for application and interpretation.

This chapter will present basic simple regression with one independent variable, time series modeling with ARIMA, multiple regression, stepwise regression, and logistic regression.

6.1 Regression Models

OLS regression is a model of the form:

$$Y = b_0 + b_1 X_1 + b_2 X_2 + \cdots + b_n X_n + e$$

> where, Y is the dependent variable (the one being forecast)
> X_n are the n independent (explanatory) variables
> b_0 is the intercept term
> b_n are the n coefficients for the independent variables
> e is the error term

OLS regression is a straight line (with intercept and slope coefficients b_n), which minimizes the sum of squared error terms e_i over all i observations. The idea is that you look at past data to determine the b coefficients that worked best. The model gives you the most likely future value of the dependent variable, given knowledge of the X_n for future observations. This approach assumes a linear relationship, and error terms that are normally distributed around zero without patterns. While these assumptions are often unrealistic, regression is highly attractive because of the existence of the widely available computer packages as well as highly developed statistical theory. The statistical packages provide the probability that estimated parameters differ from zero.

Establishing relationships is one thing—forecasting is another. For a model to perform well in forecasting, you have to know the future values of the independent variables. Measures such as r^2, assume absolutely no error in the values of the independent variables you use. The ideal way to overcome this limitation is to use independent variables whose future values are known.

Time is a very attractive independent variable in time series forecasting because you will not introduce additional error in estimating future values of time. About all we know for sure about next year's economic performance is that it will be next year. And models using time as the only independent variable have a different philosophical basis than causal models. With time, you do not try to explain the changes in the dependent variable. You assume that whatever has been causing changes in the past will continue to do so at the same rate in the future.

Another way to obtain known independent variable values is to lag them. For example, instead of regressing a dependent variable value for 2015 against the independent variable observation for 2015, regress the dependent variable value for 2015 against the 2014 value of independent variable. This would give you one year of known independent variable values with which to forecast. If the independent variable is a leading indicator of the dependent variable, r^2 of your model might actually go up. However, usually lagging an independent variable will lower r^2. Additionally, you will probably lose an observation, which in economic data may be a high price. But at least you have perfect knowledge of a future independent variable value for your forecast.

6.2 Forecasting S&P 500

We can demonstrate a simple regression model by forecasting the S&P 500 index. We have quarterly data from the first quarter of 2001 through the end of 2023. We run a regression of S&P Index versus time. The correlation between the index and time is 0.888, indicating a strong relationship. In Excel, the model we get is shown in Table 6.1. The r-squared measure is 0.789 based on the 277 observations. The model F statistic is 1027.494, highly significant.

This model indicates that the variable time is very good at explaining much of the change in the S&P index (it explained 78.9% of the change over the data period of 2001 through 2023). The trend is an increase of about 12 per year (there is a 95% probability that the trend is between 11.3 and 12.8).

The plot of this data is given in Fig. 6.1.

The Python code for this simple regression reads the same file (SPSAS.csv) used in Excel.

Table 6.1 S&P 500 regression model

Variable	Coefficients	StdError	t stat	p-value	Lower 95%	Upper 95%
Intercept	329.122	60.369	5.45	1.11E-7***	210.277	447.967
Time	12.067	0.376	32.05	7.24E-95***	11.326	12.809

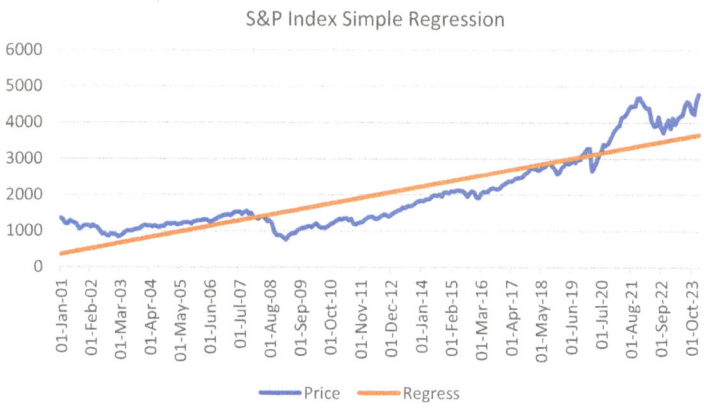

Fig. 6.1 Simple regression of S&P Index

6.2.1 R Code for Simple Regression

```
# import the necessary libraries
library(readr)
# input data
my_data <- read.csv('SPSAS.csv')
# Converts "Price" column to numeric type
my_data$Price <- as.numeric(gsub(",", "", my_data$Price))
# Check the converted data frame structure
str(my_data)

# Create the response variable y and the feature variable x
y <- my_data$Price
x <- my_data$Time
# Converts data to numeric type
y <- as.numeric(gsub(",", "", y))
x <- as.numeric(x)
# establish regression model
LR <- lm(y ~ x)
# output results
cat("coefficient(b1, b2, …, bn):", coef(LR), "\n")
```

Coefficient(b1, b2, …, bn): 12.06739

```
cat("intercept(b0):", coef(LR)[1], "\n")
```

Intercept(b0): 329.122

```
# predict with test set
y_prediction <- predict(LR, newdata = data.frame(x = x))
# R2
score <- cor(y, y_prediction)^2
cat("R2:", score, "\n")
```

R2: 0.7888666

```
# visualization
plot(x, y, col = "blue", type = "l", main = "Linear Regression", xlab = "Time", ylab = "Price")
abline(LR, col = "red")
legend("topleft", legend = c("Real", "Predicted"), col = c("blue", "red"), lty = 1)
```

6.2.2 Python Code for Simple Regression

```
import numpy as np
import pandas as pd
from sklearn.linear_model import LinearRegression
from sklearn import linear_model

df = pd.read_csv('SPSAS.csv')
df['Time'] = df['Time'].astype(float)
x = df[['Time']]
y = df['Price']
regr = linear_model.LinearRegression()
regr.fit(x.values, y)
R2 = regr.score(x.values, y)
print(f"coefficient of determination: {R2}")
#Coefficients
print(regr.coef_)
print(regr.intercept_)
res = predicted_Weekly_Sales = regr.predict([[270]])
print(res)
```

R-squared = 0.7889...
Intercept = 329.12198...
Coefficient(beta): 12.06739...

```
#Predict with testing set
res = predicted_Weekly_Sales = regr.predict([[270]])
print(res)
```

Prediction for Time = 270 is 3587.318...

Note that there is a slight difference in output—Excel's trend was 11.99 compared to Python's 12.08, the intercept from Excel was 337 versus 324 from Python. The last four lines of Python code provide a graph similar to Fig. 6.1.

6.3 ARIMA Modeling

Thus far we have only discussed linear relationships. Life usually consists of nonlinear relationships. Straight lines do not do well in fitting curves and explaining these nonlinearities. There is one trick to try when forecasting obviously nonlinear data. For certain types of curves, logarithmic transformations fall back into straight lines. When you make a log transform of the dependent variable, you will need to retransform the resulting forecasts to get useful information.

Most economic data is cyclical. Models with the single independent variable of time have some positive features. There is a statistical problem involved with OLS regressions on cyclical data. The error terms should be random, with no pattern. A straight line fit of cyclical data will have very predictable patterns of error (autocorrelation). This is a serious problem for OLS regression, warping all the statistical inferences.

Autocorrelation can occur in causal models as well, although not as often as in regressions versus time. When autocorrelation occurs in causal models, more advanced statistical techniques are utilized, such as second stage least squares. However, when autocorrelation occurs in regressions where time is the only independent variable, Box-Jenkins models are often very effective. Box-Jenkins forecasting takes advantage of the additional information of the pattern in error terms to give better forecasts. For the S&P data, we can start with:

```
proc arima data=A;
identify var=Price nlag=12;
run;
```

This yields Fig. 6.2 which shows the time series plot, autocorrelation function plot for lags given (ACF—here we asked for 12), partial autocorrelation factors (PACF) which shows that P of 1 is strong, and inverse autocorrelation function plot (IACF).

We infer that P of 1 or 2 might be useful. The second factor, D for differencing, we can judge from the time series plot. It is not linear, so D of 1 doesn't look promising. It does take something like a quadratic form, so D of 2 looks interesting. The third ARIMA parameter, Q, would be expected seasonality. For this monthly data, 12 looks interesting. So we can try an ARIMA model with $P = 2$, $D = 2$, $Q = 12$. SAS code for this is:

```
proc arima data=A;
identify var=Price nlag=12;
identify var=Price(2);
estimate p=2 q=12;
forecast lead=12 interval=month id=date out=results;
run;
quit;
```

6.3 ARIMA Modeling

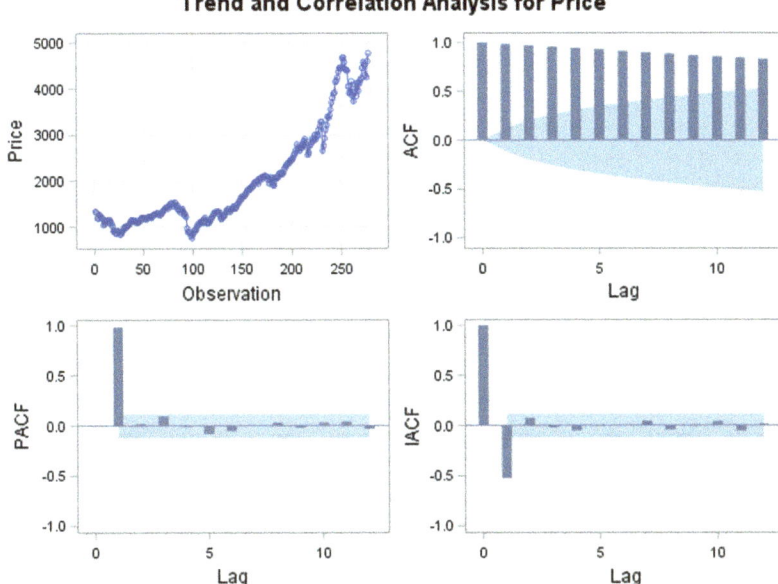

Fig. 6.2 Initial SAS ARIMA output

The AIC measure for this model was 3256.191. The forecasts obtained with this model are given in Table 6.2.

SAS provides a plot as shown in Fig. 6.3.

Figure 6.3 shows how ARIMA can pattern complex datasets.

Table 6.2 SAS ARIMA (2,2,12) forecasts for S&P

Forecasts for variable Price				
Obs	Forecast	Std error	95% Confidence Limits	
278	4837.91	87.79	4665.85	5009.97
279	4791.65	128.04	4540.70	5042.59
280	4773.52	155.36	4469.02	5078.01
281	4742.92	175.48	4398.97	5086.86
282	4796.19	198.24	4407.65	5184.73
283	4827.95	222.98	4390.91	5264.98
284	4938.34	248.89	4450.52	5426.15
285	4941.01	275.98	4400.11	5481.92
286	4932.57	304.93	4334.93	5530.22
287	4857.30	327.83	4214.77	5499.84
288	4912.00	347.62	4230.68	5593.32
289	4921.02	362.55	4210.44	5631.60

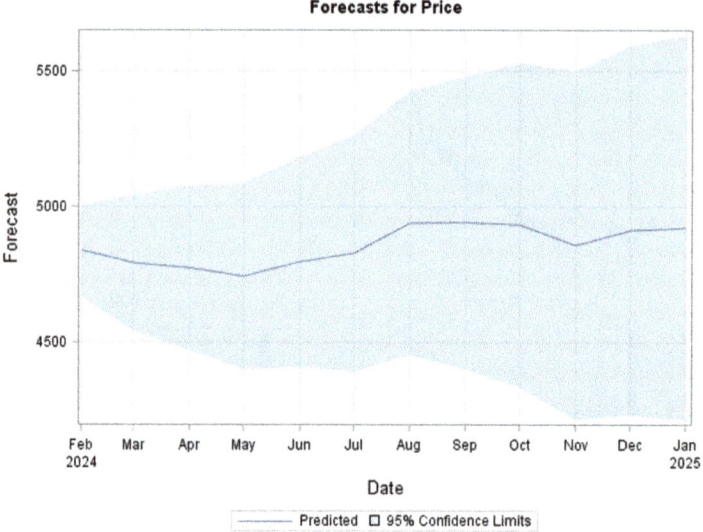

Fig. 6.3 SAS ARIMA (2,2,12) Model Forecasts

6.3.1 R Code for ARIMA

R includes an autoArima model that seeks to optimize the P, D & Q settings. The code follows.

```
library(readr)
library(forecast)

# input data
my_data <- read.csv("SPSAS.csv")
my_data.ts  <-   ts(my_data$Price,   start  =  c(2001,1),
end=c(2024, 1), freq = 12)

# fit a quadratic regression line to time series (quadratic)
my_data.lm <- tslm(my_data.ts ~ trend + I(trend^2))
summary(my_data.lm)

# seasonal check
my_data.season <- tslm(my_data.ts ~ season)
summary(my_data.season)

#Plot the time series and fit the overlay quadratic regression
line:
plot(my_data.ts, xlab = "Date", ylab = "Price", ylim = c(500,
5000))
lines(my_data.lm$fitted, lwd =2, col="blue")

# Rolling window for Autocorrelation and ARIMA
```

6.3 ARIMA Modeling

```
##my_data.ts.36 <- window(my_data.ts, start = c(2001, 1), end
= c(2004, 12))

## Rolling window for autocorrelation, covariance, and partial
correlation
##Acf(my_data.ts.36, lag.max = 48, type="correlation", main =
"Autocorrelation")
##Acf(my_data.ts.36, lag.max = 48, type="covariance", main =
"Covariance")
##Acf(my_data.ts.36, lag.max = 48, type="partial", main =
"Partial Autocorrelation")

#ACF of Monthly change graph in price. Auto correlation
ggAcf(my_data[,"Price"])
#Pacf of monthly change, partial autocorrelation
ggPacf(my_data[,"Price"])

##fit <- Arima(my_data[,"Price"], seasonal = TRUE)
##checkresiduals(fit)
##autoplot(forecast(fit))
##autoplot(fit)

# Seasonally differenced data:
my_data.ts %>% diff(lag = 12) %>% ggtsdisplay()

# auto.arima fpr best model selection:
fit <- auto.arima(my_data.ts, approximation = FALSE, stepwise
= FALSE, allowdrift = TRUE, allowmean = TRUE)
checkresiduals(fit)

#Plot the forecast:
fit %>% forecast(h=20) %>% autoplot()

#forecast:
spforecast <- forecast(fit)
spforecast

checkresiduals(spforecast)

#check accuracy:
accuracy(object = spforecast)
```

The code generated a model with $P = 2$, $D = 2$ and $Q = 3$. The results (Fig. 6.4) are quite similar to those using $Q = 12$, with AIC of 3254.237, slightly better fit.

There is relatively weak seasonality in this data, so while 12 made sense in that it is monthly data, that won't necessarily give the strongest fit. ARIMA models work well if the data has strong autocorrelation. The differencing (D) and moving average (Q) components are to try to make the data stationary and take advantage of the autocorrelation component. This sometimes works quite well but won't always provide the best forecast. It depends on the data.

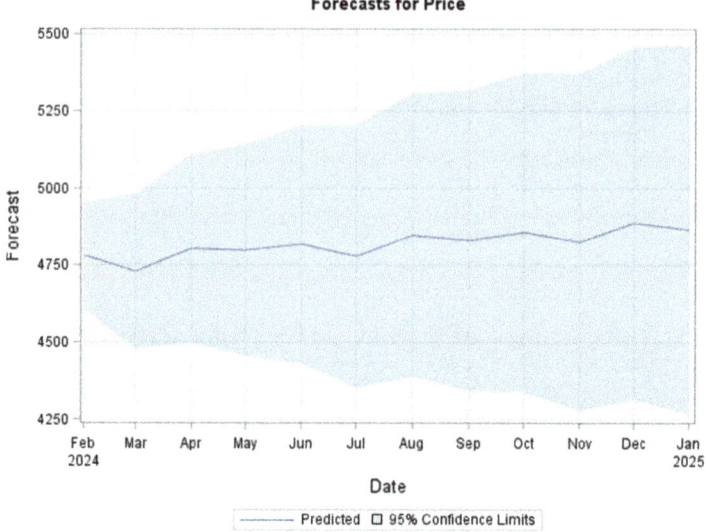

Fig. 6.4 S&P Forecast for ARIMA (2,2,3)

6.3.2 Python Code for ARIMA

```
import pandas as pd
from statsmodels.tsa.arima.model import ARIMA
import warnings
warnings.filterwarnings('ignore')
df = pd.read_csv("SPSAS.csv")
df['Date'] = pd.to_datetime(df['Date'])

df_arima = ARIMA(df.Price, order=(2, 2, 12))
model = df_arima.fit()
print(model.summary())
```

Python reported the AIC for this model as 3257.451, quite close to that obtained from SAS. The python model was rerun for (2,2,3), obtaining an AIC of 3254.424, practically the same as measured by SAS.

6.4 Multiple Regression

While simple regression has only one independent variable, multiple regression allows any number. We will use a dataset of Walmart sales data obtained from Kaggle at https://www.kaggle.com/datasets/mikhail1681/walmart-sales. The dataset has weekly sales over 143 weeks for 45 stores. The independent variables are:

6.4 Multiple Regression

Holiday Flag – a 0–1 variable with 1 indicating a holiday during that period.
Temperature – average temperature for the week.
Fuel price – average cost of fuel.
CPI – consumer price index (inflation indicator).
Unemployment – the unemployment rate.

The primary complication arising from the use of multiple independent variables is the potential for multicollinearity. What that means can be explained as two or more independent variables are likely to contain overlapping information, i.e., presenting high correlation. The effect of multicollinearity is that the t tests are drastically warped, and bias creeps into the model. This has the implication that as future information is obtained, the estimates of the ß coefficients will likely change drastically, because the model is unstable. Multicollinearity can be avoided by NOT including independent variables that are highly correlated with each other. How much correlation is too much is a matter of judgement. Note that the sign of correlation simply identifies if the relationship is positive or negative. In a positive relationship, if one variable goes up, the other variable tends to go up. A negative correlation indicates that as one variable goes up, the other variable tends to go down.

A variance inflation measure provides some measure of multicollinearity in a regression. In SAS, the option VIF can be included in the model line. If the variance inflation measure is below 10, the rule of thumb is that you don't reject the evidence of collinearity. However, this is a very easy test limit to pass. The first priority would be to select variables that would make sense. Secondly, it is best to design models without overlapping information.

The correlation for this data is given in Table 6.3.

The regression r-square was 0.025, indicating the vast majority of sales was explained by variables other than those included in the model. The adjusted r-square was also 0.025, indicating the there wasn't a great deal of overlapping information among the independent variables. The F test score was 33.57, highly significant (5.93E-34). The regression model from Excel is shown in Table 6.4.

The t-scores infer the given probabilities, showing that Unemployment, the consumer price index, and the holiday flag are significant at the 0.05 level. Temperature is near to that level of significance, implying that the colder it is, the more Walmart sells. Fuel price doesn't seem to matter, although if anything, the higher

Table 6.3 Correlation for Walmart sales data

Variable	WeeklySales	HolidayFlag	Temperature	FuelPrice	CPI
WeeklySales	1				
HolidayFlag	0.037	1			
Temperature	−0.064	−0.155	1		
FuelPrice	0.009	−0.078	0.145	1	
CPI	−0.073	−0.002	0.177	−0.171	1
Unemployment	−0.106	0.011	0.101	−0.035	−0.302

Table 6.4 Multiple regression of Walmart weekly sales

Variable	Coefficients	StdError	t stat	p-value	Lower 95%	Upper 95%
Intercept	1,726,523	79,763.46	21.65	2.4E-100***	1,570,160	1,882,886
HolidayFlag	74,891.66	27,639.35	2.71	0.007***	20,709	129,074
Temperature	−724.172	400.46	−1.81	0.071	−1509	61
FuelPrice	−10,167.9	15,762.78	−0.65	0.519	−41,068	20,732
CPI	−1598.87	195.13	−8.19	3.02E-16***	−1981	−1216
Unemployment	−41,552.3	3972.66	−10.46	2.12E-25***	−49,340	−33,764

fuel prices are, the less spent at Walmart. As unemployment increases, or the inflation level as measured by CPI increases, sales drop. Finally, holidays have higher sales. These all make sense. Nonetheless, we must remember that over 97% of sales change is explained by things not included in this regression model.

Discriminant analysis groups objects defined by a set of variables into a predetermined set of outcome classes. One example of this type of analysis is the classification of employees by their rated performance within an organization. The bank loan example could be divided into past cases sorted by the two distinct categories of repayment or default. The technical analysis is, thus, determining the combination of variables that best predict membership in one of the given output categories.

A number of methods can be used for discriminant analysis. Regression can be used for discriminant analysis. For the two-group case, this would require a cutoff between the groups, and if a new set of data yielded a functional value below the cutoff, the prediction would be that group, or conversely, if the value was above the cutoff, the prediction would be the other group. However, other techniques can be used for discriminant analysis. A discriminant function can be used in binary data to separate observations into two groups, with a cutoff limit used to divide the observations.

6.4.1 R Code for Multiple Regression

```
# install these packages
install.packages("caret")
install.packages("Metrics")
# load required libraries
library(readr)
library(caret)
library(Metrics)
# input data and preprocessing
df <- read.csv('Walmart_sales.csv')
y <- df[, "Weekly_Sales"]
```

6.4 Multiple Regression

```
x <- df[, c("Holiday_Flag","Temperature", "Fuel_Price",
"CPI", "Unemployment")]
# establish regression model
LR <- lm(Weekly_Sales ~ Holiday_Flag + Temperature + Fuel_
Price + CPI + Unemployment, data = df)
# output results
cat("Coefficients (b1, b2, …, bn):", coef(LR), "\n")
cat("Intercept (b0):", coef(LR)[1], "\n")
```

The output obtained is shown in Fig. 6.5.
To predict with this model, the following bit of code can be used:

```
# predict with test set
y_prediction <- predict(LR, newdata = x)
score <- R2(y_prediction, y)
cat("R2 Score:", score, "\n")
```

Fig. 6.5 R Walmart-Sales regression model

```
> summary(LR)

call:
lm(formula = Weekly_Sales ~ Holiday_Flag + Temperature +
Fuel_Price +
    CPI + Unemployment, data = df)

Residuals:
      Min       1Q   Median       3Q      Max
-1022429  -478555  -117266   397246  2800620

Coefficients:
              Estimate Std. Error t value Pr(>|t|)
(Intercept)  1726523.4    79763.5  21.646  < 2e-16
Holiday_Flag   74891.7    27639.3   2.710  0.00675
Temperature     -724.2      400.5  -1.808  0.07060
Fuel_Price    -10167.9    15762.8  -0.645  0.51891
CPI            -1598.9      195.1  -8.194  3.02e-16
Unemployment  -41552.3     3972.7 -10.460  < 2e-16

(Intercept)  ***
Holiday_Flag **
Temperature  .
Fuel_Price
CPI          ***
Unemployment ***
---
Signif. codes:
0 '***' 0.001 '**' 0.01 '*' 0.05 '.' 0.1 ' ' 1

Residual standard error: 557400 on 6429 degrees of freed
om
Multiple R-squared: 0.02544,  Adjusted R-squared: 0.0
2469
F-statistic: 33.57 on 5 and 6429 DF,  p-value: < 2.2e-16
```

6.4.2 Python Code for Multiple Regression

```
import numpy as np
import pandas as pd
from sklearn.linear_model import LinearRegression
from sklearn import linear_model
df = pd.read_csv('Walmart_sales.csv')
df['Holiday_Flag'] = df['Holiday_Flag'].astype(float)
x = df[['Holiday_Flag', 'Temperature', 'Fuel_Price', 'CPI',
'Unemployment']]
y = df['Weekly_Sales']
regr = linear_model.LinearRegression()
regr.fit(x.values, y)
res = predicted_Weekly_Sales = regr.predict([[0, 40, 3, 10
,7.9 ]])
print(res)
```

This last line shows how a prediction can be obtained. Here the example is Holiday_Flag 0, temperature 40 degrees, FuelPrice $3 per gallon, CPI 10, and Unemployment rate 7.9%. The resulting forecast generated by Python is 1322801.

To get r-squared:

```
R2 = regr.score(x.values, y)
print(f"coefficient of determination: {R2}")
```

This yields 0.02544366.... matching R and Rattle.
Model coefficients can be obtained with:

```
#Coefficients
print(regr.coef_)
print(regr.intercept_)
```

This gives the beta coefficients for the five independent variables in order:

74,891.661...   −724.172...   −10,167.878...   −1598.872...   −41,552.281...

Intercept is 1726523.3935....

6.5 Stepwise Regression

Regression can be applied by conventional software such as SAS, SPSS, or Excel. Additionally, there are many refinements to regression that can be accessed, such as stepwise linear regression. Stepwise regression uses partial correlations to select entering independent variables iteratively, providing some degree of automatic machine development of a regression model. Stepwise regression has its proponents and opponents but is a form of machine learning. Not all software supports stepwise regression. Rattle doesn't—Python is a programming language that could with a great deal of programming effort, but has no function to call as R has.

We demonstrate using the Walmart sales dataset.

```
proc glmselect data=A;
model Weekly_Sales=Holiday_Flag Temperature Fuel_Price CPI
Unemployment/selection=stepwise(SLENTRY=0.1 SLSTAY=0.08);
run;
```

The first variable entered was Unemployment, based on the greatest improvement in r-squared (at this stage, with that one variable, the r-squared is 0.0113). The algorithm will continue as long as the entry improvement is greater than 0.1 (the specified SLEntry). The algorithm checks at each iteration for deleting variables, but will not remove any unless the change is less than SLSTAY (here set at 0.08).

The second variable entered is CPI, which improves r-squared to 0.0233.

The third iteration enters Holiday_Flag, which improves r-squared to 0.0248.

The fourth iteration enters Temperature, improving r-squared to 0.0254.

No other variable (only Fuel_Price is left) can improve the model beyond the specified limit. The resulting model is given in Table 6.5.

This model's r-squared is 0.0254. Note that the stepwise regression has one less variable than the multiple regression model. R-squared will have to be lower, but not necessarily adjusted r-squared. In the full regression, not only Fuel_Price, but also Temperature had probabilities for beta coefficients below 0.05. Here Temperature barely passes that limit.

Table 6.5 Final stepwise regression model

Variable	Coefficient	Significance
Intercept	1,187,798	<0.0001
Holiday_Flag	75,760	0.0061
Temperature	−773.14736	0.0493
CPI	−1570.00529	<0.0001
Unemployment	−41,236	<0.0001

6.5.1 R Code for Stepwise Regression

```
library(readr)
walmart <- read.csv("Walmart.csv")

step_walmart <- lm(Weekly_Sales ~., data = walmart)
# Forward stepwise regression:
forward_walmart <- step(step_walmart, direction = "forward",
scope = formula(~.))

summary(forward_walmart)
#Backward stepwise regression:
backward_walmart <- step(step_walmart, direction = "back-
ward")
summary(backward_walmart)

# Both backward and forward model, starting with all predic-
tors:
both_walmart <- step(step_walmart, direction = "both")
summary(both_walmart)

# backward model returns slightly lower AIC and eliminates
fuel_price from the model

#Visualizing:
#Scatterplot Weekly_Sales VS Temperature:
plot(walmart$Weekly_Sales, walmart$Temperature, main =
"Sales VS Temperature",
   xlab = 'Weekly_Sales', ylab = 'Temperature', pch = 20)

#Scatterplot Weekly_Sales VS Fuel_price:
plot(walmart$Weekly_Sales, walmart$Fuel_price, main = "Sales
VS Fuel_price",
   xlab = 'Weekly_Sales', ylab = 'Fuel_price', pch = 20)

#Scatterplot Weekly_Sales VS CPI:

plot(walmart$Weekly_Sales, walmart$CPI, main = "CPI",
   xlab = 'Weekly_Sales', ylab = 'CPI', pch = 20)

#Scatterplot Weekly_Sales VS Unemployment:
plot(walmart$Weekly_Sales, walmart$Unemployment, main =
"Sales VS Unemployment",
   xlab = 'Weekly_Sales', ylab = 'Unemployment', pch = 20)

# Plot residuals
plot(both_walmart$residuals, main = "Model Residuals", ylab =
'Residuals')
```

6.5 Stepwise Regression

Python Code

```python
import numpy as np
import pandas as pd
from sklearn.linear_model import LinearRegression
from sklearn import linear_model
df = pd.read_csv('Walmart_Sales.csv')
df['Holiday_Flag'] = df['Holiday_Flag'].astype(float)
li = [ 'Unemployment', 'CPI' , 'Holiday_Flag', 'Temperature',
'Fuel_Price',]
x = df[li]
y = df['Weekly_Sales']
model = linear_model.LinearRegression()
list_choose = []
pri_R2=0
pre_x = [0, 40, 3, 10,7.9]
pre_x_choose = []
for i in range(len(li)):
    print("=============================")
    print("selected variables:")
    # select the first i variables
    list_choose.append(li[i])
    print(list_choose)
    input_x = x[list_choose]
    # training
    model.fit(input_x.values, y)

    #test data
    pre_x_choose.append(pre_x[i])
    forecast = predicted_Weekly_Sales = model.predict([pre_x_choose])

    # result
    print(f"Predicted Response:\n {forecast}")
    R2 = model.score(input_x.values, y)
    print(f"R2: {R2}")

    # judge if R2 satisfy the limitation
    if i == 0:
        continue

    else:
        # delete i-th variable if not satisfied
        if R2 - pri_R2 < 0.01:
            # delet the i-th variable
            list_choose.pop()
            pre_x_choose.pop()
print("==========Final===========")
print("final selected variables")
print(list_choose)
```

Fig. 6.6 Forward stepwise Python sequence

```
==============================
selected variables:
['Unemployment']
Predicted Response:
[1302485.39891258]
R2: 0.011273362015053912
==============================
selected variables:
['Unemployment', 'CPI']
Predicted Response:
[1603604.09182363]
R2: 0.023336073889825504
==============================
selected variables:
['Unemployment', 'CPI', 'Holiday_Flag']
Predicted Response:
[1852356.4341304]
R2: 0.024794495522624027
==============================
selected variables:
['Unemployment', 'CPI', 'Holiday_Flag', 'Temperature']
Predicted Response:
[1844546.99494078]
R2: 0.02538058955009337
==============================
selected variables:
['Unemployment', 'CPI', 'Holiday_Flag', 'Temperature', 'Fuel_Price']
Predicted Response:
[1799675.5548615]
R2: 0.025443664729580262
==========Final===========
final selected variables
['Unemployment', 'CPI', 'Holiday_Flag', 'Temperature', 'Fuel_Price']
```

The sequence of variables selected with current forecast and r-square value are shown in Fig. 6.6.

Python Code for Backwards Elimination.

```
import numpy as np
import pandas as pd
from sklearn.model_selection import train_test_split
from sklearn.linear_model import LinearRegression
import statsmodels.formula.api as sm
from dmba import regressionSummary, exhaustive_search
from dmba import backward_elimination, forward_selection,
stepwise_selection
from dmba import adjusted_r2_score, AIC_score, BIC_score

df = pd.read_csv("Walmart.csv")

df['Holiday_Flag'] = df['Holiday_Flag'].astype(float)
X = df.iloc[:,1:6]
y = df.iloc[:, 0]
X_train, X_test, y_train, y_test = train_test_split(X, y,
test_size = 0.2, random_state = 0)
walmart_lm = LinearRegression()
walmart_lm = walmart_lm.fit(X_train, y_train)
```

```
print(pd.DataFrame({'Predictor': X.columns, 'Coefficient':
walmart_lm.coef_}))
print('Intercept:', walmart_lm.intercept_)

regressionSummary(y_train, walmart_lm.predict(X_train))

walmart_lm_predict = walmart_lm.predict(X_test)

result = pd.DataFrame({'Predicted': walmart_lm_predict,
'Actual': y_test, 'Residual': y_test - walmart_lm_predict})
result

regressionSummary(y_test, walmart_lm_predict)

# Stepwise: Backward elimination
def train_model(variables):
  model = LinearRegression()
  model.fit(X_train[list(variables)], y_train)
  return model

def score_model(model, variables):
        return    AIC_score(y_train,   model.predict(X_
train[(variables)]), model)

allVariables = X_train.columns

best_model,      best_variables       =       backward_
elimination(allVariables, train_model, score_model, verbose
= True)
print(best_variables)
regressionSummary(y_test,  best_model.predict(X_test[best_
variables]))
```

6.6 Logistic Regression

Some data of interest in a regression study may be ordinal or nominal. The purpose of logistic regression is to classify cases into the most likely category. Logistic regression provides a set of β parameters for the intercept (or intercepts in the case of ordinal data with more than two categories) and independent variables, which can be applied to a logistic function to estimate the probability of belonging to a specified output class. The formula for probability of acceptance of a case i to a stated class j is:

$$P_j = \frac{1}{1 + e^{(-\beta_0 - \sum \beta_i X_i)}}$$

where, β coefficients are obtained from logistic regression.

The regression model provides a continuous formula. A cutoff needs to be determined to divide the value obtained from this formula, given independent variable values, which will divide the data into output categories in proportion to the population of cases.

6.6.1 Tests of the Regression Model

The universal test for classification models is the coincidence matrix that focuses on the ability of the model to categorize the data. There are a number of measures obtainable from the confusion matrix. Most are self-defining, such as:

True positive rate (TPR), which is equal to TP/(TP + FN) (also called *sensitivity* or *recall*)
True negative rate (TNR) equal to TN/(FP + TN) (also called *specificity*)
Positive predictive value (PPV) equal to TP/(TP + FP) (also called *precision*)
Negative predictive value (NPV) equal to TN/(TN + FN)
False positive rate (FPR) equal to FP/(FP + TN) (also called *fall-out*) *False discovery rate* (FDR) equal to FP/(FP + TP)
False negative rate (FNR) equal to FN/FN + TP) (also called *miss rate*). *Accuracy* is equal to (TP + TN)/(TP + TN + FP + FN)

A *receiver operating characteristic* (ROC) curve is obtained by plotting TPR versus FPR for various threshold settings. This is equivalent to plotting the cumulative distribution function of the detection probability on the y axis versus the cumulative distribution of the false-alarm probability on the x axis.

Note that recall, precision, and specificity depend upon definition of true positive and true negative.

For continuous regression, this requires identification of cutoffs between the classes. Data mining software doesn't do that, but we will demonstrate how it can be done. There are many other aspects to accuracy, just as there are many applications of different models, especially regression. The classical tests of regression models are based on the assumption that errors are normally distributed around the mean, with no patterns. The basis of regression accuracy is the residuals, or difference between the predicted and observed values. Residuals are then extended to a general measure of regression fit, R-squared.

Probit models are an alternative to logistic regression. Both estimate probabilities, usually with similar results, but probit models tend to have smaller coefficients and uses probit function instead of logit function.

6.6.2 Software Demonstrations of Logistic Regression

For OLS regression, we have used Excel. SAS is another widely used software, capable of logistic regression (which Excel can handle only with great difficulty). The other limitation we perceive to using Excel is that Excel regression is limited to 16 independent variables.

We demonstrate using the Portuguese bank credit card data used in Chapter 5 to demonstrate cluster analysis. The basic SAS has the ability to do OLS regression (so does Excel) and logistic regression. Rattle also has this function. We select the file BankSegmentLuo.csv in Fig. 6.7:

We Partitioned at 80% to build the model, 0 for intermediate testing, 20% for testing (validation is used when you have an intermediate step, which we will use in Chapter 8 when generating variable sets with classification models). Then, click on the *Execute* tab. Rattle has the full slate of data mining algorithms, to include regression models. They are attained under the *Model* tab as seen in Fig. 6.6, where you need to select the *Linear* button. Given that the data has a categorical outcome, the *Logistic* button will automatically be selected. Selecting *Execute* yields regression coefficients.

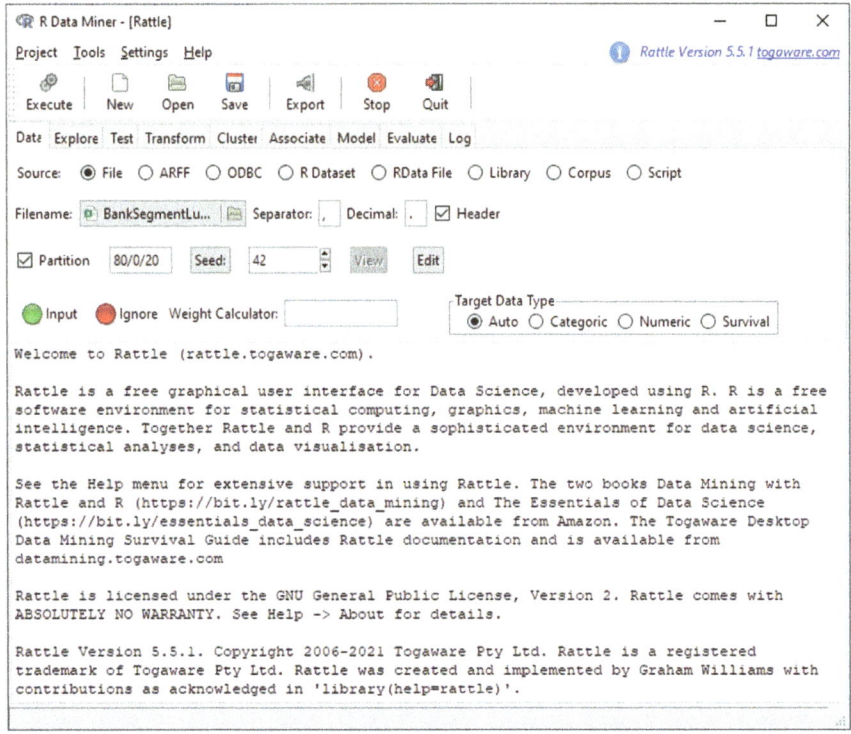

Fig. 6.7 Model tab in Rattle

The model for a logistic regression has b coefficients for continuous variables, which are multiplied by variable values. For categorical variables, the intercept contains the contribution for the case of amber credit and high risk, which is adjusted if other categories are present. Significance is as in linear regression. The calculation for the dependent variable is on a logistic scale, which the software adjusts. Figure 6.8 gives the Rattle input screen:

This yields the model displayed in Table 6.6.

Aic: 2137.6

Model significance by Chi-square p-value 0.0000000

Pseudo R-Square (optimistic): 0.40979070

Area under the curve was 0.856. Using the 20% held out of the data for testing, the coincidence matrix obtained is given in Table 6.7.

Overall error (accuracy): 9.3%, Averaged class error: 38.55%

Recall $= 23/(23 + 71) = 0.245$.

Precision $= 23/(23 + 13) = 0.639$.

Specificity $= 798/(798 + 13) = 0.984$.

Accuracy $= (798 + 23)/905 = 0.907$.

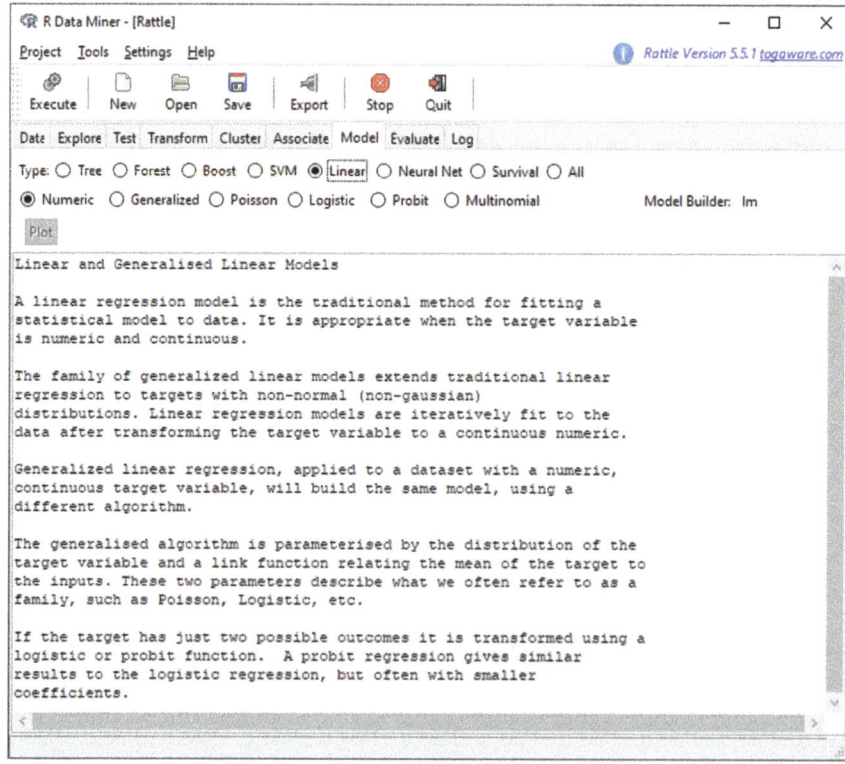

Fig. 6.8 Rattle linear regression screen

6.6 Logistic Regression

Table 6.6 Logistic regression model

Variable	Estimate	Std. Error	z-value	Prob{>|z|
Intercept	−4.52233137	0.33569	−13.472	<2E-16***
Age	0.01795129	0.00533	3.368	0.000756***
Ed	0.25744679	0.07759	3.319	0.000905***
Balance	0.00001585	0.00001830	0.866	0.386414
Duration	0.00364682	0.00019822	18.398	<2E-16***
Campaign	−0.09075801	0.028259	−3.235	0.001218**
Pdays	0.00194383	0.00054489	3.567	0.000361***
Previous	0.10133593	0.02783773	3.640	0.000272***

Significances: *** 0.001; ** 0.01; * 0.05

Table 6.7 Rattle Coincidence matrix for BankSegmentLuo.csv

	Model 0	Model 1 (subscribed)	Totals
Actual 0 (no subscribe)	(tn) 798	(fp) 13	811
Actual 1 (subscribed)	(fn) 71	(tp) 23	94
Totals	869	36	905

6.6.3 R Code

```
library(caret)
library(pROC)

# Read data.
df <- read_csv('BankSegmentLuo.csv')

# Extract features and labels
features <- as.matrix(df[, 1:8])
labels <- df[[8]] # Use the labels directly without one-hot
encoding

# Split the dataset into training and testing sets
set.seed(123)
list_indexes <- createDataPartition(labels, p = 0.8, list =
TRUE)
train_indexes <- list_indexes[[1]]
X_train <- features[train_indexes, ]
Y_train <- labels[train_indexes]
X_test <- features[-train_indexes, ]
Y_test <- labels[-train_indexes]

# Assuming the 'method' variable is also set
method <- "Logistic"

if (method == "Logistic") {
```

```
cat(sprintf("method: %s\n", method))

# Use the 'glm' function to initialize and train a logistic
regression model
logistic_model <- glm(as.factor(Y_train) ~ ., data =
as.data.frame(X_train), family = binomial(link = "logit"))

# Use the model to make predictions on the test set to obtain
categorical predictions
predictions          <-          ifelse(predict(logistic_model,
as.data.frame(X_test), type = "response") > 0.5, 1, 0)

# Convert both predictions and true labels to factors in order
to calculate the confusion matrix and performance metrics
predictions_factor <- as.factor(predictions)
Y_test_factor <- as.factor(Y_test)

# Calculate the confusion matrix
confusion_matrix <- confusionMatrix(predictions_factor, Y_
test_factor)
cat("Confusion matrix:\n")
print(confusion_matrix$table)

# Calculate the evaluation metrics
recall <- confusion_matrix$byClass['Sensitivity']
precision <- confusion_matrix$byClass['Precision']
f1_macro <- 2 * (recall * precision) / (recall + precision) #
Manually calculate the F1 score

# Calculate GMean
gmean <- sqrt(recall * confusion_matrix$byClass['Specificity'])

# Calculate AUC. Here, use the original labels and predicted
probabilities.
roc_result <- roc(response = as.numeric(Y_test_factor),
predictor = predict(logistic_model, as.data.frame(X_test),
type = "response"))
auc_value <- auc(roc_result)

# Print the results
cat(sprintf("F1 Macro: %f, AUC: %f, GMean: %f, Recall: %f,
Precision: %f\n", f1_macro, auc_value, gmean, recall, preci-
sion))
}
```

Drawing different samples, this run managed a perfect prediction of the test set (Table 6.8).

Overall error (accuracy): 0%, Averaged class error: 0%
Recall = 107/(0 + 107) = 1.0
Precision = 107/(107 + 0) = 1.0
Specificity = 797/(797 + 0) = 1.0
Accuracy = (797 + 107)/904 = 1.0

6.6 Logistic Regression

Table 6.8 R coincidence matrix for BankSegmentLuo.csv

	Model 0	Model 1 (subscribed)	Totals
Actual 0 (no subscribe)	(tn) 797	(fp) 0	797
Actual 1 (subscribed)	(fn) 0	(tp) 107	107
Totals	797	107	904

6.6.4 Python Code

```python
import numpy as np
import pandas as pd
from sklearn.linear_model import LogisticRegression as LR
from sklearn.model_selection import train_test_split
from sklearn.metrics import confusion_matrix
from sklearn.metrics import recall_score
from sklearn.metrics import f1_score
from sklearn.metrics import roc_auc_score
from sklearn.metrics import precision_score
from sklearn.metrics import classification_report

df = pd.read_csv('BankSegmentLuo.csv')

X = df.iloc[:,0:7]
y = df.iloc[:, 7]
X_train, X_test, y_train, y_test = train_test_split(X, y,
test_size = 0.2, random_state = 0)

# initialize model
lrl1    =    LR(penalty='l1',solver='liblinear',C=0.5,max_iter=1000)
# model training
lrl1.fit(X_train, y_train)
# model test
logits = lrl1.predict(X_test)

# metrics
def conf_gmean(conf):
  tn, fp, fn, tp = conf.ravel()
  return (tp*tn/((tp+fn)*(tn+fp)))**0.5
def evaluate(labels, logits):
  conf = confusion_matrix(labels, logits)
  recall = recall_score(labels, logits)
  f1_macro = f1_score(labels, logits, average='macro')
  auc = roc_auc_score(labels, logits)
  gmean = conf_gmean(conf)
  precision = precision_score(labels, logits)
  return f1_macro, auc, gmean, recall, precision
# compute metrics
f1_macro, auc, gmean, recall, precision = evaluate(y_test,
logits)
```

Table 6.9 Python coincidence matrix for BankSegmentLuo.csv

	Model 0	Model 1 (subscribed)	Totals
Actual 0 (no subscribe)	(tn) 775	(fp) 18	793
Actual 1 (subscribed)	(fn) 82	(tp) 30	112
Totals	857	48	905

```
print(f"fi_macro:{f1_macro},AUC:{auc},GMean:{gmean},Recall:{recal
Precision:{precision}")
#y_pred = logits.predict(X_test)
confusion_matrix = confusion_matrix(y_test, logits)
print(confusion_matrix)
print(classification_report(y_test, logits))
```

Table 6.9 gives output.
AuC is 0.6226. Overall error (accuracy): 11.0%.
Recall = 30/(30 + 82) = 0.268.
Precision = 30/(30 + 18) = 0.625.
Specificity = 775/(775 + 18) = 0.977.
Accuracy = (775 + 30)/905 = 0.890.

6.7 Summary

Regression models have been widely used in classical modeling. They continue to be very useful in data mining environments, which differ primarily in the scale of observations and the number of variables used. Classical regression (usually OLS) can be applied to continuous data. If the output variables (or input variables) are categorical, logistic regression can be applied. Regression can also be applied to identify a discriminant function, separating observations into groups. If this is done, the cutoff limits to separate the observations based on the discriminant function score need to be identified. While discriminant analysis can be applied to multiple groups, it is much more complicated if there are more than two groups. Thus, other discriminant methods, such as the centroid method demonstrated in this chapter, are often used.

Regression can be applied by conventional software such as SAS, SPSS, or Excel. Additionally, there are many refinements to regression that can be accessed, such as stepwise linear regression. Stepwise regression uses partial correlations to select entering independent variables iteratively, providing some degree of automatic machine development of a regression model. Stepwise regression has its proponents and opponents but is a form of machine learning.

Chapter 7
Classification Tools

This chapter will look at classification tools, beginning with logistic regression, moving on to support vector machines, neural networks, and decision trees (to include random forests). We will demonstrate with Rattle, which also includes boosting. Classification uses a training data set to identify classes or clusters, which then are used to categorize data. Typical applications include categorizing risk and return characteristics of investments, and credit risk of loan applicants. We will use a bankruptcy data file.

7.1 Classification Models

7.1.1 Regression

As covered in Chapter 6, Regression models fit a function through the data minimizing some error metric. You can include as many independent variables as you want, but in traditional regression analysis, there are good reasons to limit the number of variables. The spirit of exploratory data mining, however, encourages examining a large number of independent variables. In data mining applications, the assumption is that you have very many observations, so that there is no technical limit on the number of independent variables.

7.1.2 Decision Trees

Decision trees are models that process data to split it in strategic places to divide the data into groups with high probabilities of one outcome or another. They are widely used because the resulting model is easy to understand. Decision trees consist of nodes, or splits in the data defined as particular cutoffs for a particular independent variable, and leaves, which are the outcome. It is especially effective at data with finite categorical outcomes, but can also be applied to continuous data, such as time series (but the results are limited as it can only predict a finite number of continuous outcomes). For categorical data, the outcome is a class. For continuous data, the outcome is a continuous number, usually some average measure of the dependent variable. Application of decision tree models to continuous data is referred to as regression trees.

7.1.3 Random Forest

Random forest models are an ensemble of un-pruned decision trees. Essentially they consist of a melding of many decision tree runs. They are often used when there are large training datasets available with many input variables. They tend to be robust to variance and bias, and thus more reliable than single decision trees.

7.1.4 Extreme Boosting

Extreme boosting builds a series of decision tree models, and associates a weight with each dataset observation. Weights are increased (boosted) if a model incorrectly classifies the observation. Along with random forests, they tend to fit data quite well.

7.1.5 Support Vector Machines

Support vector machines (SVMs) are supervised learning methods that generate input–output mapping functions from a set of labeled training data. The mapping function can be either a classification function (used to categorize the input data) or a regression function (used to estimation of the desired output). For classification, nonlinear kernel functions are often used to transform the input data (inherently representing resenting highly complex nonlinear relationships) to a high dimensional feature space in which the input data becomes more separable (i.e., linearly separable) compared to the original input space. Then, the maximum-margin hyperplanes are constructed to optimally separate the classes in the training data. Two parallel hyperplanes are constructed on each side of the hyperplane that separates the data by maximizing the distance between the two parallel hyperplanes. An assumption is made that the larger the margin or distance between these parallel hyperplanes the better the generalization error of the classifier will be.

7.1.6 Neural Networks

Neural network models are applied to data that can be analyzed by alternative models. The normal data mining process is to try all alternative models and see which works best for a specific type of data over time. But there are some types of data where neural network models usually outperform alternatives, such as regression or decision trees. Neural networks tend to work better when there are complicated relationships in the data, such as high degrees of nonlinearity. Thus, they tend to be viable models in problem domains where there are high levels of unpredictability. Each node is connected by an arc to nodes in the next layer. These arcs have weights, which are multiplied by the value of incoming nodes and summed. The input node values are determined by variable values in the data set. Middle layer node values are the sum of incoming node values multiplied by the arc weights. These middle node values in turn are multiplied by the outgoing arc weights to successor nodes. Neural networks "learn" through feedback loops. For a given input, the output for starting weights is calculated. Output is compared to target values, and the difference between attained and target output is fed beck to the system to adjust the weights on arcs. This process is repeated until the network correctly classifies the proportion of learning data specified by the user (tolerance level). Ultimately a set of weights might be encountered that explain the learning (training) data set very well. The better the fit that is specified, the longer the neural network will take to train, although there is really no way to accurately predict how long a specific model will take to learn. The resulting set of weights from a model that satisfies the set tolerance level is retained within the system for application to future data. The neural network model is a black box. Output is there, but it is too complex to analyze.

There are other models that have been applied to classification. Clustering has been used but is not really appropriate for classification—it is better at initial analysis trying to identify distinct groups.

Clustering requires numeric data. Naïve Bayes models have also been applied, but only apply to categorical data.

Tests of classification models are based on the coincidence matrix discussed in Chapter 6. In addition to comparing accuracy, a common measure is the Akaike information criterion (AIC), which estimates prediction error of a model and is intended to compare with other models. AIC estimates the relative amount of information lost by a given model trading off goodness of fit and model simplicity. Given k is the number of estimated model parameters and L is the maximized value of the likelihood function of the model:

$$\text{AIC} = 2k - 2\ln(L)$$

7.2 Bankruptcy Data Set

This data concerns 100 US firms that underwent bankruptcy (Olson et al., 2012). All of the sample data are from the USA companies. About 400 bankrupt company names were obtained using google.com, and the next step is to find out the Ticker name of each company using Compustat database. This data set includes companies bankrupted during Jan. 2006 and June 2010. This overlaps the 2008 financial crisis, and 99 companies left after that period. After getting the company Ticker code list, the Ticker list was submitted to the Compustat database to get the financial data ratios during Jan. 2005–June 2010. Those financial data and ratios are factors that we can predict the company bankruptcy. The factors we collected are based on the literature, which contain total asset, book value per share, inventories, liabilities, receivables, cost of goods sold, total dividends, earnings before interest and taxes, gross profit (loss), net income (loss), operating income after depreciation, total revenue, sales, dividends per share, and total market value. The LexisNexis database was used to find the company SEC filling after June 2010, which means that companies are still active today, and then we selected 200 companies from the results and got the company CIK code list. The CIK code list was submitted to the Compustat database to obtain financial data and ratios during Jan. 2005-June 2010, the same period for failed companies.

The data set consists of 1,321 records with full data over 19 attributes. The outcome attribute in bankruptcy, which has a value of 1 if the firm went bankrupt by 2011 (746 cases), and a value of 0 if it did not (575 cases). We divided this data set into records prior to 2008 for training (1030 cases—454 not bankrupt, 576 bankrupt), holding out the newer 2008–2010 cases for testing (291 cases, 170 no (not bankrupt) and 121 yes (suffered bankruptcy). Note that it is better if data sets are balanced, as most models are more reliable if the data have roughly equal numbers of outcomes. In severe cases, models will predict all cases to be the majority, which could be considered degenerate, and which provides little useful prediction. This data is relatively well balanced. Were it not, means to rectify the situation include replicating the rarer outcome, or if there is a very large data set, even deleting some of the larger set. Care must be taken to not introduce bias during balancing operations. Table 7.1 displays variables in our data set, with the outcome variable No. 17.

In the data mining process using R, we need to first link the data. Figure 7.1 shows the variables in the data file.

Figure 7.2 displays the Rattle screen to partition the data into training, validation, and test sets. The default is 70 percent for training, 15 percent for validation (if used), 15 percent for testing. We will change that to 80 percent training, 0 for validation, 20 percent testing.

Because variable number 17 is categorical, R presumes (appropriately) that it is the variable to be predicted (target).

Table 7.1 Attributes in bankruptcy data

No	Short Name	Long Name
1.	Year	Data Year—Fiscal
2.	At	Assets—Total
3.	Bkvlps	Book Value Per Share
4.	Invt	Inventories—Total
5.	Lt	Liabilities—Total
6.	Rectr	Receivables—Trade
7.	Cogs	Cost of Goods Sold
8.	Dvt	Dividends—Total
9.	Ebit	Earnings Before Interest and Taxes
10.	Gp	Gross Profit (Loss)
11.	Ni	Net Income (Loss)
12.	revt	Revenue—total
13.	dvpsx_f	Dividends per Share—Ex-Date—Fiscal
14.	Mkvalt	Market Value—Total—Fiscal
15.	prch_f	Price High—Annual—Fiscal
16.	Bankruptcy	bankruptcy (output variable)

7.3 Logistic Regression

Figure 7.3 displays Rattle's logistic regression output.

Note that variable revt was found to be a complex combination of other variables, leading to a singularity. Using the 20 percent held-out test data, the coincidence matrix obtained is shown in Table 7.2.

AIC is reported as 966.45; Overall error (1—accuracy): 11.3%

Recall = 112/(112 + 24) = 0.824	True positive rate
Precision = 112/(112 + 6) = 0.949	Positive predictive rate
Specificity = 123/(123 + 6) = 0.953	True negative rate
Accuracy = (123 + 112)/265 = 0.887	Correct predictive rate

In Rattle, note that revt is shown as singular (denoted by the NAs), and thus excluded from the model. The three most significant variables were rectr (receivables from trade), gp (gross profit), and fyear (year). Fyear has a negative coefficient, indicating a negative trend in bankruptcy risk. Both of the other highly significant beta coefficients are positive, indicating that as these variables increase, probability of bankruptcy increases. Here the pseudo r-square is 0.645, indicating a relative good fit, but is potentially unstable due to overlapping information content among variables. This model was quite good at predicting firms that did not go bankrupt ($114/129 = 0.884$ correct). It was poor at predicting bankruptcy ($94/136 = 0.691$), for an overall correct classification rate of 0.785.

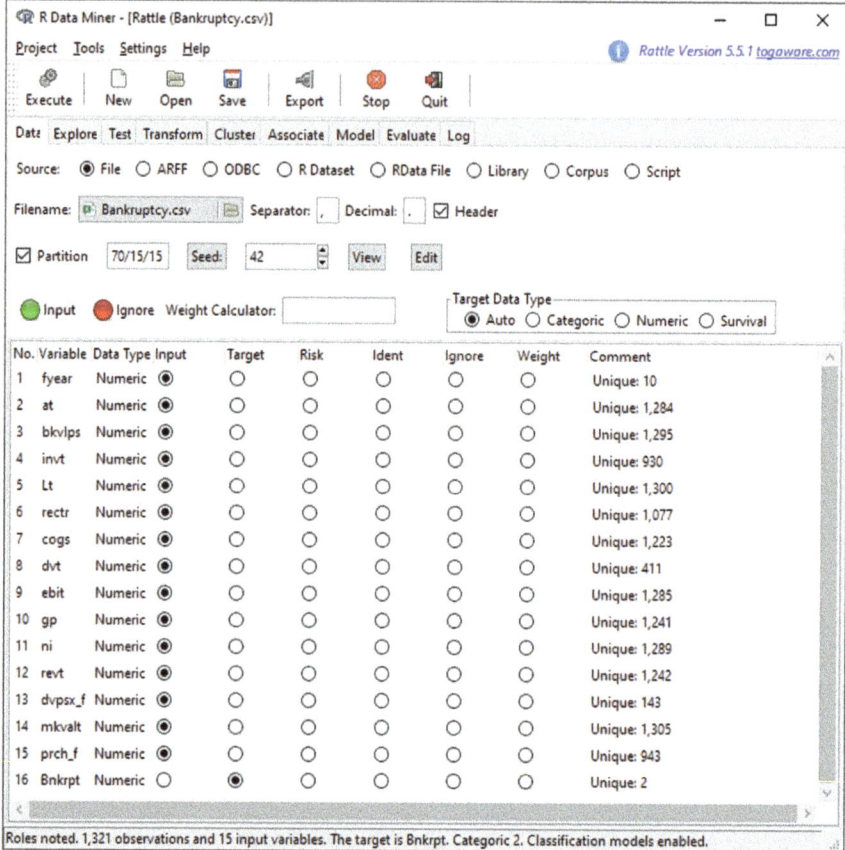

Fig. 7.1 Loading Bankruptcy.csv in R

Fig. 7.2 Partitioning option

7.3 Logistic Regression

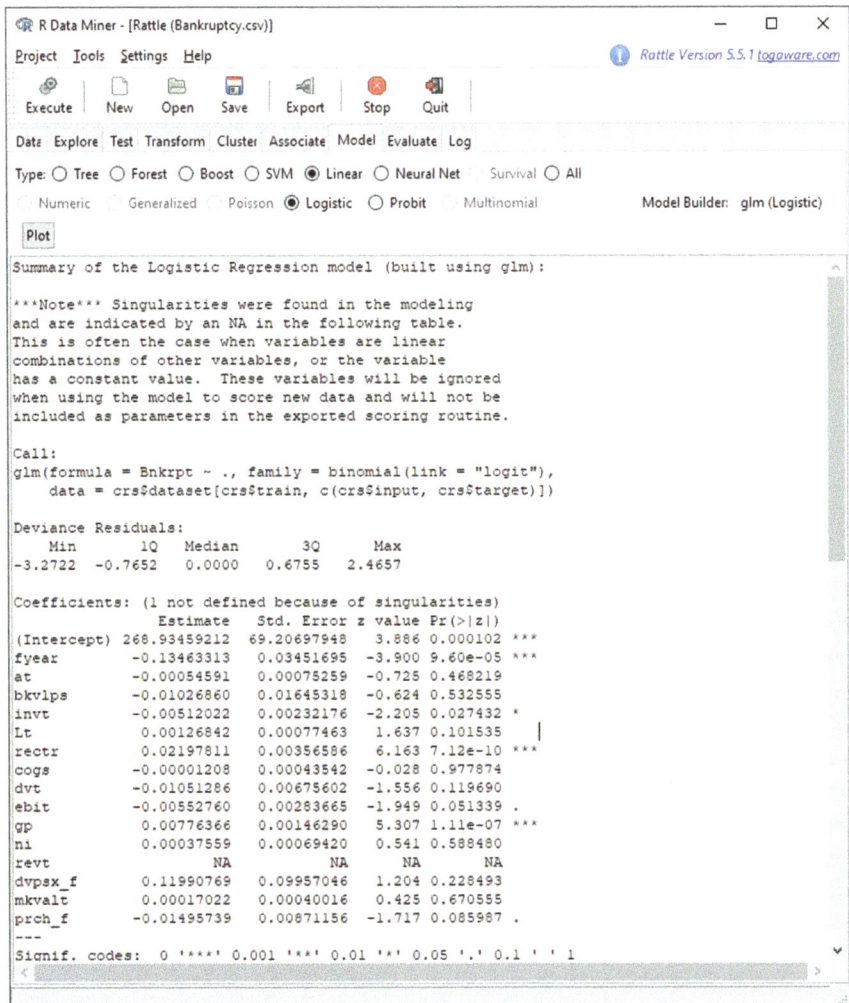

Fig. 7.3 Rattle Logistic Regression model for Bankruptcy.csv

Table 7.2 Rattle logistic regression coincidence matrix

	Model 0	Model 1 (subscribed)	Totals
Actual 0 (no subscribe)	(tn) 123	(fp) 6	129
Actual 1 (subscribed)	(fn) 24	(tp) 112	136
Totals	147	118	265

7.3.1 R Code Logistic Regression

```r
library(caret)
library(pROC)

# Read data.
df <- read.csv('Bankruptcy.csv')

# Extract features and labels
features <- as.matrix(df[, 1:15])
labels <- df[[16]] # Use the labels directly without one-hot encoding

# Split the dataset into training and testing sets
set.seed(123)
list_indexes <- createDataPartition(labels, p = 0.8, list = TRUE)
train_indexes <- list_indexes[[1]]
X_train <- features[train_indexes, ]
Y_train <- labels[train_indexes]
X_test <- features[-train_indexes, ]
Y_test <- labels[-train_indexes]

# Assuming the 'method' variable is also set
method <- "Logistic"

if (method == "Logistic") {
cat(sprintf("method: %s\n", method))

# Use the 'glm' function to initialize and train a logistic regression model
  logistic_model <- glm(as.factor(Y_train) ~ ., data = as.data.frame(X_train), family = binomial(link = "logit"))

# Use the model to make predictions on the test set to obtain categorical predictions
    predictions      <-     ifelse(predict(logistic_model, as.data.frame(X_test), type = "response") > 0.5, 1, 0)

# Convert both predictions and true labels to factors in order to calculate the coincidence matrix and performance metrics
predictions_factor <- as.factor(predictions)
Y_test_factor <- as.factor(Y_test)

# Calculate the coincidence matrix
coincidence_matrix <- confusionMatrix(predictions_factor, Y_test_factor)
cat("Coincidence matrix:\n")
print(coincidence_matrix$table)

# Calculate the evaluation metrics
specificity <- coincidence_matrix$byClass['Specificity']
recall <- coincidence_matrix$byClass['Recall']
precision <- coincidence_matrix$byClass['Precision']
```

7.3 Logistic Regression

Table 7.3 Coincidence matrix for the R logistic regression model

	Model no	Model yes	
Actual no	109	41	150
Actual yes	14	100	114
	123	141	264

```
f1_macro <- 2 * (recall * precision) / (recall + precision) #
Manually calculate the F1 score

# Calculate GMean
gmean <- sqrt(recall * coincidence_matrix$byClass['Specificity'])

# Calculate AUC. Here, use the original labels and predicted
probabilities.
roc_result <- roc(response = as.numeric(Y_test_factor),
predictor = predict(logistic_model, as.data.frame(X_test),
type = "response"))
auc_value <- auc(roc_result)

# Print the results
cat(sprintf("F1 Macro: %f, AUC: %f, GMean: %f, Specificity:
%f, Recall: %f, Precision: %f\n", f1_macro, auc_value, gmean,
specificity, recall, precision))
}
```

Table 7.3 shows results.

Area under the curve is 0.891, recall 0.877, precision 0.709, specificity 0.727 and accuracy 0.792.

7.3.2 Python Code Logistic Regression

```
import numpy as np
import pandas as pd
from sklearn.tree import LogisticRegression as LR
from sklearn.model_selection import train_test_split
from sklearn.metrics import confusion_matrix
from sklearn.metrics import recall_score
from sklearn.metrics import f1_score
from sklearn.metrics import roc_auc_score
from sklearn.metrics import precision_score
from sklearn.metrics import classification_report

df = pd.read_csv('Bankruptcy.csv')

X = df.iloc[:,0:15]
y = df.iloc[:, 15]
```

```
X_train, X_test, y_train, y_test = train_test_split(X, y,
test_size = 0.2, random_state = 0)
# initialize model
lrl1    =    LR(penalty='l1',solver='liblinear',C=0.5,max_
iter=1000)
# model training
lrl1.fit(X_train, y_train)
# model test
logits = lrl1.predict(X_test)

# metrics
def conf_gmean(conf):
   tn, fp, fn, tp = conf.ravel()
   return (tp*tn/((tp+fn)*(tn+fp)))**0.5
def evaluate(labels, logits):
   conf = confusion_matrix(labels, logits)
   recall = recall_score(labels, logits)
   f1_macro = f1_score(labels, logits, average='macro')
   auc = roc_auc_score(labels, logits)
   gmean = conf_gmean(conf)
   precision = precision_score(labels, logits)
   return f1_macro, auc, gmean, recall, precision
# compute metrics
f1_macro, auc, gmean, recall, precision = evaluate(y_test,
logits)
print(f"fi_macro:{f1_macro},AUC:{auc},GMean:{gmean},Recall:{recal
Precision:{precision}")

#y_pred = logits.predict(X_test)
confusion_matrix = confusion_matrix(y_test, logits)
print(confusion_matrix)

print(classification_report(y_test, logits))
```

Table 7.4 gives the resulting coincidence matrix.

Area under the curve is 0.804, recall 0.660, precision 0.943, specificity 0.948 and accuracy 0.785.

Three different codes were used on the data with different random number seeds. Drawing random numbers for the test sets yielded essentially the same but slightly different results (Table 7.5).

Our purpose is to demonstrate how models can be accessed in the different software systems. Relative accuracies are unimportant here, although these results

Table 7.4 Coincidence matrix for the python logistic regression model

	Model no	Model yes	
Actual no	109	6	115
Actual yes	51	99	150
	160	105	265

Table 7.5 Comparative logistic regression results

Metric	Rattle	R	Python
Area under curve	0.923	0.891	0.804
Recall	0.824	0.877	0.660
Precision	0.949	0.709	0.943
Specificity	0.953	0.727	0.948
Accuracy	0.887	0.792	0.785

demonstrate that data mining results are variable. Here the Python output drew different random test sets for each model, introducing some additional variance in output. We do not expect any essential relative accuracy of one system over the others. But we would like to demonstrate the measures that are important in assessing models.

7.4 Support Vector Machines

Support vector machines (SVMs) are supervised learning methods that generate input–output mapping functions from a set of labeled training data. The mapping function can be either a classification function (used to categorize the input data) or a regression function (used to estimation of the desired output). For classification, nonlinear kernel functions are often used to transform the input data (inherently representing highly complex nonlinear relationships) to a high dimensional feature space in which the input data becomes more separable (i.e., linearly separable) compared to the original input space. Then, the maximum-margin hyperplanes are constructed to optimally separate the classes in the training data. Two parallel hyperplanes are constructed on each side of the hyperplane that separates the data by maximizing the distance between the two parallel hyperplanes. An assumption is made that the larger the margin or distance between these parallel hyperplanes the better the generalization error of the classifier will be.

SVMs belong to a family of generalized linear models which achieves a classification or regression decision based on the value of the linear combination of features. They are also said to belong to "kernel methods". In addition to its solid mathematical foundation in statistical learning theory, SVMs have demonstrated highly competitive performance in numerous real-world applications, such as medical diagnosis, bioinformatics, face recognition, image processing and text mining, which has established SVMs as one of the most popular, state-of-the-art tools for knowledge discovery and data mining. Similar to artificial neural networks, SVMs possess the well-known ability of being universal approximators of any multivariate function to any desired degree of accuracy. Therefore, they are of particular interest to modeling highly nonlinear, complex systems and processes.

Generally, many linear classifiers (hyperplanes) are able to separate data into multiple classes. However, only one hyperplane achieves maximum separation.

SVMs classify data as a part of a machine-learning process, which "learns" from the historic cases represented as data points. These data points may have more than two dimensions. Ultimately we are interested in whether we can separate data by an $n - 1$ dimensional hyperplane. This may be seen as a typical form of linear classifier. We are interested in finding if we can achieve maximum separation (margin) between the two (or more) classes. By this we mean that we pick the hyperplane so that the distance from the hyperplane to the nearest data point is maximized. Now, if such a hyperplane exists, the hyperplane is clearly of interest and is known as the maximum-margin hyperplane and such a linear classifier is known as a maximum margin classifier.

In Rattle, an SVM model can be selected from the Model tab as shown in Fig. 7.4. Clicking on Execute yielded a model with 724 support vectors (Table 7.6).

The SVM model correctly classified 114 of 129 cases where firms did not go bankrupt (0.884—specificity), and 94 of 136 cases where firms did go bankrupt (0.691—recall). Overall correct classification was 0.785. Precision was 0.862.

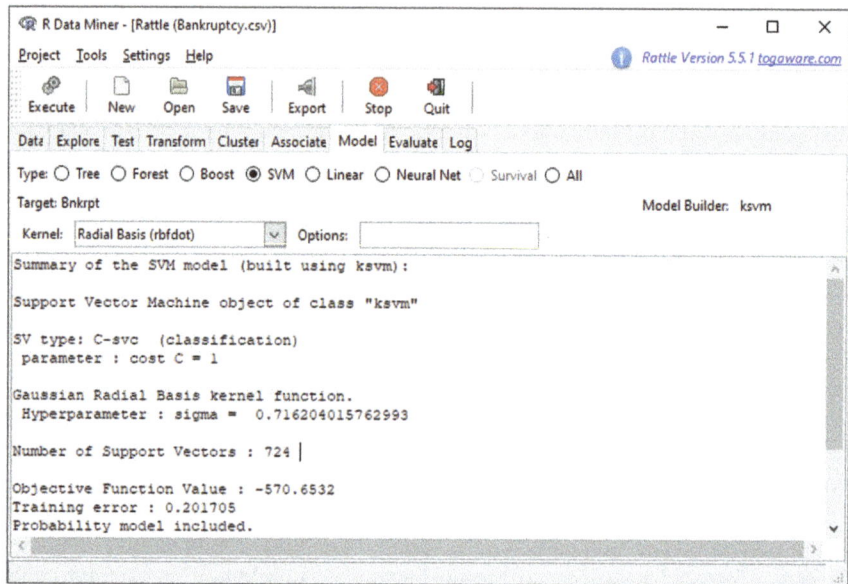

Fig. 7.4 Rattle SVM model

Table 7.6 Coincidence matrix for the rattle SVM model

	Model no	Model yes	
Actual no	114	15	129
Actual yes	42	94	136
	156	109	265

7.4 Support Vector Machines

7.4.1 R Code SVM

```r
library(readr)
library(e1071)
library(caret)
library(pROC)

# Read data
df <- read.csv('Bankruptcy.csv')

# Extract features and labels
features <- as.matrix(df[, 1:15])
labels <- df[[16]] # Use the labels directly without one-hot encoding

# Split the dataset into training and testing sets
set.seed(123)
list_indexes <- createDataPartition(labels, p = 0.8, list = TRUE)
train_indexes <- list_indexes[[1]]
X_train <- features[train_indexes, ]
Y_train <- labels[train_indexes] # Use the original labels directly
X_test <- features[-train_indexes, ]
Y_test <- labels[-train_indexes] # Use the original labels directly

method <- "SVM"

if (method == "SVM") {
cat(sprintf("method: %s\n", method))

# Initialize and train an SVM model
svm_model <- svm(x = X_train, y = as.factor(Y_train), kernel = "linear", cost = 1e9)

# Use the model to make predictions on the test set
predictions <- predict(svm_model, X_test)

# Convert both predictions and true labels to factors in order
to calculate the coincidence matrix and performance metrics
predictions_factor <- as.factor(predictions)
Y_test_factor <- as.factor(Y_test)

# Calculate the coincidence matrix
coincidence_matrix <- confusionMatrix(predictions_factor, Y_test_factor)

# Print the table of the confusion matrix
  print(coincidence_matrix$table)

# Calculate the evaluation metrics
specificity <- coincidence_matrix$byClass['Specificity']
recall <- coincidence_matrix$byClass['Recall']
precision <- coincidence_matrix$byClass['Precision']
```

Table 7.7 Coincidence matrix for the R SVM model

	Model no	Model yes	
Actual no	99	79	178
Actual yes	24	62	86
	123	141	264

```
f1_macro <- 2 * (recall * precision) / (recall + precision) #
Manually calculate the F1 score

# Calculate GMean
gmean <- sqrt(recall * coincidence_matrix$byClass['Specificity'])

# Calculate AUC
roc_result <- roc(response = as.numeric(as.factor(Y_test)),
predictor = as.numeric(as.factor(predictions)))
auc_value <- auc(roc_result)

# Print the results
cat(sprintf("F1 Macro: %f, AUC: %f, GMean: %f, Specificity:
%f, Recall: %f, Precision: %f\n", f1_macro, auc_value, gmean,
specificity, recall, precision))
}
```

Table 7.7 gives the resulting coincidence matrix.

This yields AUC = 0.622, Recall = 0.721, Precision = 0.440, Specificity 0.556 and Accuracy 0.610.

7.4.2 Python Code SVM

```
import numpy as np
import pandas as pd
from sklearn.svm import LinearSVC
from sklearn.model_selection import train_test_split
from sklearn.metrics import confusion_matrix
from sklearn.metrics import recall_score
from sklearn.metrics import f1_score
from sklearn.metrics import roc_auc_score
from sklearn.metrics import precision_score
from sklearn.metrics import classification_report

df = pd.read_csv('Bankruptcy.csv')

X = df.iloc[:,0:15]
y = df.iloc[:, 15]
X_train, X_test, y_train, y_test = train_test_split(X, y,
test_size = 0.2, random_state = 0)
```

Table 7.8 Coincidence matrix for the Python SVM model

	Model no	Model yes	
Actual no	109	6	115
Actual yes	56	94	150
	165	100	265

```
# initialize model
linearSVC = LinearSVC(C=1e9)
# model training
linearSVC.fit(X_train, y_train)
# model test
logits = linearSVC.predict(X_test)

# metrics
def conf_gmean(conf):
    tn, fp, fn, tp = conf.ravel()
    return (tp*tn/((tp+fn)*(tn+fp)))**0.5
def evaluate(labels, logits):
    conf = confusion_matrix(labels, logits)
    recall = recall_score(labels, logits)
    f1_macro = f1_score(labels, logits, average='macro')
    auc = roc_auc_score(labels, logits)
    gmean = conf_gmean(conf)
    precision = precision_score(labels, logits)
    return f1_macro, auc, gmean, recall, precision
# compute metrics
f1_macro, auc, gmean, recall, precision = evaluate(y_test,
logits)
print(f"fi_macro:{f1_macro},AUC:{auc},GMean:{gmean},Recall:{recall},
Precision:{precision}")

#y_pred = logits.predict(X_test)
confusion_matrix = confusion_matrix(y_test, logits)
print(confusion_matrix)

print(classification_report(y_test, logits))
```

Table 7.8 gives the resulting coincidence matrix.

AuC was 0.787, recall 0.627, precision 0.940, specificity 0.948 and accuracy 0.766.

7.5 Neural Networks

Neural network models are applied to data that can be analyzed by alternative models. The normal data mining process is to try all alternative models and see which works best for a specific type of data over time. But there are some types of data where neural

Table 7.9 Rattle neural network model coincidence matrix

	Model no	Model yes	
Actual no	122	7	129
Actual yes	29	107	136
	151	114	265

network models usually outperform alternatives, such as regression or decision trees. Neural networks tend to work better when there are complicated relationships in the data, such as high degrees of nonlinearity. Thus they tend to be viable models in problem domains where there are high levels of unpredictability.

Each node is connected by an arc to nodes in the next layer. These arcs have weights, which are multiplied by the value of incoming nodes and summed. The input node values are determined by variable values in the data set. Middle layer node values are the sum of incoming node values multiplied by the arc weights. These middle node values in turn are multiplied by the outgoing arc weights to successor nodes. Neural networks "learn" through feedback loops. For a given input, the output for starting weights is calculated. Output is compared to target values, and the difference between attained and target output is fed beck to the system to adjust the weights on arcs.

This process is repeated until the network correctly classifies the proportion of learning data specified by the user (tolerance level). Ultimately, a set of weights might be encountered that explain the learning (training) data set very well. The better the fit that is specified, the longer the neural network will take to train, although there is really no way to accurately predict how long a specific model will take to learn. The resulting set of weights from a model that satisfies the set tolerance level is retained within the system for application to future data.

The neural network model is a black box. Output is there, but it is too complex to analyze. We ran the model, which generated a model with the 16 inputs, 10 intermediate nodes, and 197 weights which were reported in an output too long to show. Testing this model on the test set obtained the coincidence matrix shown in Table 7.9.

The neural network model correctly classified 122 of 129 cases where firms did not go bankrupt (0.946), and 107 of 136 cases where firms did go bankrupt (0.787). Overall correct classification was thus 0.864. Precision was 0.939.

7.5.1 R Code Neural Network

```
library(class)
library(caret)
library(pROC)

# Read the data
```

7.5 Neural Networks

```r
df <- read_csv('Bankruptcy.csv')

# Extract features and labels
features <- as.matrix(df[, 1:15])
labels <- df[[16]]

# Split the dataset into training and testing sets
set.seed(123)
list_indexes <- createDataPartition(labels, p = 0.8, list = TRUE)
train_indexes <- list_indexes[[1]]
X_train <- features[train_indexes, ]
Y_train <- labels[train_indexes]
X_test <- features[-train_indexes, ]
Y_test <- labels[-train_indexes]

method <- "KNN"

if (method == "KNN") {
 cat(sprintf("method: %s\n", method))

 # Initialize and train a KNN model
 # Note: The `knn` function from the `class` package in R uses the entire dataset directly for prediction, without a separate fitting step
  knn_predictions <- knn(train = as.data.frame(X_train), test = as.data.frame(X_test), cl = Y_train, k = 1)

 # Calculate the evaluation metrics
    confusion_matrix <- confusionMatrix(knn_predictions, as.factor(Y_test))
  cat("Confusion matrix:\n")
  print(confusion_matrix$table)

 # Calculate performance metrics
  recall <- confusion_matrix$byClass['Sensitivity']
  precision <- confusion_matrix$byClass['Precision']
  f1_score <- 2 * (precision * recall) / (precision + recall)

 # Calculate GMean
  gmean <- sqrt(recall * confusion_matrix$byClass['Specificity'])

 # Calculate AUC
  # Note: For KNN models, we typically do not directly obtain predicted probabilities, so the calculation of AUC may require additional steps or assumptions.
  # Here, we will not calculate the AUC as probability outputs are not provided.

 # Print the results
  cat(sprintf("F1 Macro: %f, GMean: %f, Recall: %f, Precision: %f\n", f1_score, gmean, recall, precision))
}
```

Table 7.10 R neural network model coincidence matrix

	Model no	Model yes	
Actual no	127	12	139
Actual yes	7	118	125
	134	130	264

For neural networks, the knn function in R does not directly provide predicted probabilities, so the calculation of AUC would require extra steps or assumptions and we do not calculate AUC. Table 7.10 gives the resulting the coincidence table:

The other metrics obtained are Recall = 0.944, Precision = 0.908, Specificity 0.914 and Accuracy 0.928.

7.5.2 Python Code Neural Network

```
import numpy as np
import pandas as pd
from sklearn.ensemble import RandomForestClassifier as RF
from sklearn.model_selection import train_test_split
from sklearn.metrics import confusion_matrix
from sklearn.metrics import recall_score
from sklearn.metrics import f1_score
from sklearn.metrics import roc_auc_score
from sklearn.metrics import precision_score
from sklearn.metrics import classification_report

df = pd.read_csv('Bankruptcy.csv')

X = df.iloc[:,0:15]
y = df.iloc[:, 15]
X_train, X_test, y_train, y_test = train_test_split(X, y,
test_size = 0.2, random_state = 0)

from sklearn.neighbors import KNeighborsClassifier as KN
# initialize model
knn = KN(n_neighbors=1)
# model training
knn.fit(X_train, y_train)
# model test
logits = knn.predict(X_test)

# metrics
def conf_gmean(conf):
    tn, fp, fn, tp = conf.ravel()
    return (tp*tn/((tp+fn)*(tn+fp)))**0.5
def evaluate(labels, logits):
    conf = confusion_matrix(labels, logits)
    recall = recall_score(labels, logits)
```

7.6 Decision Trees

Table 7.11 Python neural network model coincidence matrix

	Model no	Model yes	
Actual no	107	8	125
Actual yes	6	144	150
	113	152	265

```
    f1_macro = f1_score(labels, logits, average='macro')
    auc = roc_auc_score(labels, logits)
    gmean = conf_gmean(conf)
    precision = precision_score(labels, logits)
    return f1_macro, auc, gmean, recall, precision
# compute metrics
f1_macro, auc, gmean, recall, precision = evaluate(y_test,
logits)
print(f"fi_macro:{f1_macro},AUC:{auc},GMean:{gmean},Recall:{recall},
Precision:{precision}")

#y_pred = logits.predict(X_test)
confusion_matrix = confusion_matrix(y_test, logits)
print(confusion_matrix)

print(classification_report(y_test, logits))
```

Table 7.11 gives the resulting the coincidence table.

Area under the curve was 0.945. The other metrics obtained are Recall = 0.960, Precision = 0.947, Specificity 0.930 and Accuracy 0.947.

7.6 Decision Trees

Decision trees provide a means to obtain product-specific forecasting models in the form of rules that are easy to implement. These rules have an IF-THEN form, which is easy for users to implement. This data mining approach can be used by groceries in a number of policy decisions, to include ordering inventory replenishment, as well as evaluation of alternative promotion campaigns.

As was the case with regression models and neural networks, decision tree models support the data mining process of modeling. Decision trees in the context of data mining refer to the tree structure of rules (often referred to as association rules). The data mining decision tree process involves collecting those variables that the analyst thinks might bear on the decision at issue, and analyzing these variables for their ability to predict outcome. Decision trees are useful to gain further insight into customer behavior, as well as lead to ways to profitably act on results. The algorithm automatically determines which variables are most important, based on their ability to sort the data into the correct output category. The method has relative advantage over neural network and genetic algorithms in that a reusable set of rules are provided, thus explaining model conclusions. There are many examples where decision trees have been applied to business data mining, including classifying loan applicants, screening potential consumers, and rating job applicants.

Decision trees provide a way to implement rule-based system approaches. All objects in the training set are classified into these branches. If all objects in a branch belong to the same output class, the node is labeled and this branch is terminated. If there are multiple classes on a branch, another attribute is selected as a node, with all possible attribute values branched. An entropy heuristic is used to select the attributes with the highest information. In other data mining tools, other bases for selecting branches are often used.

The decision tree output is shown in Fig. 7.5.

Table 7.12 shows Rattle Decision tree in tabular form.

Figure 7.6 displays this tree graphically.

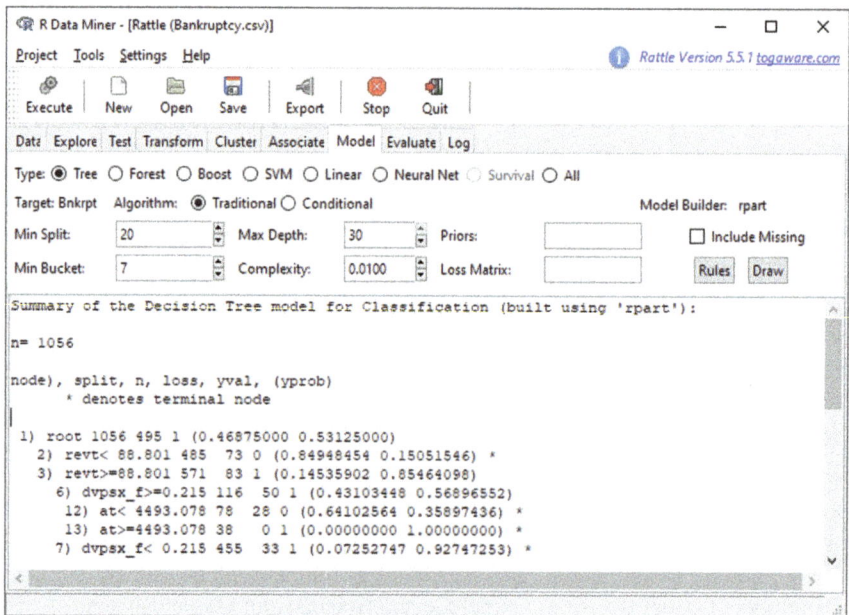

Fig. 7.5 Rattle decision tree results

Table 7.12 Rattle decision tree

			Result	Total	Wrong
Revt<88.801			No	485	73
Revt≥88.801	Dvpsx_f≥0.215	At<4493.078	No	78	28
		At≥4493.078	Yes	38	0
	Dvpsx_f<0.215		Yes	455	33

7.6 Decision Trees

Fig. 7.6 Rattle decision tree

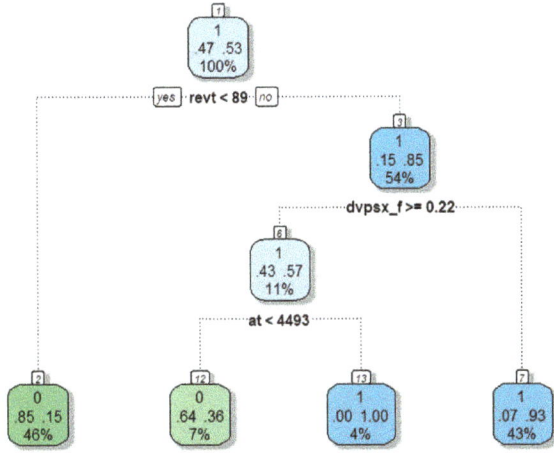

Table 7.13 Rattle decision tree coincidence matrix

	Model no	Model yes	
Actual no	123	6	129
Actual yes	24	112	136
	147	118	265

The top rule is that if revt (total revenue) is <88.801, the model predicts no bankruptcy at a probability of 0.849. Other variables considered are dvpsx_f (dividends per share). If this value is less than 0.215, the model predicts bankruptcy with a confidence of 0.927. If this figure is greater than or equal to 0.215, then the tree continues by looking at At (total assets). If total assets are less than 4493.078 the model predicts no bankruptcy. Otherwise it predicts bankruptcy. Table 7.13 gives the coincidence matrix.

The decision tree model correctly classified 123 of 129 cases (0.953) where firms did not go bankrupt and 112 of 136 cases where firms did go bankrupt (0.824) for an overall correct classification rate of 0.887. Precision was 0.949.

7.6.1 R Code Decision Tree

```
library(readr)
library(rpart)
library(caret)
library(pROC)

# Read the data
```

```r
df <- read_csv('Bankruptcy.csv')

# Extract features and labels
features <- as.matrix(df[, 1:15])
labels <- df[[16]]

# Split the dataset into training and testing sets
set.seed(123)
list_indexes <- createDataPartition(labels, p = 0.8, list = TRUE)
train_indexes <- list_indexes[[1]]
X_train <- features[train_indexes, ]
Y_train <- labels[train_indexes]
X_test <- features[-train_indexes, ]
Y_test <- labels[-train_indexes]

method <- "DecisionTree"

if (method == "DecisionTree") {
 cat(sprintf("method: %s\n", method))

  # Initialize and train a decision tree model
    dt_model <- rpart(as.factor(Y_train) ~ ., data = as.data.frame(X_train), method = "class")

rpart.plot(dt_model, type =1)
rpart.rules(dt_model, cover = TRUE)
rpart.rules(dt_model, clip.facs = TRUE)

# Use the model to make predictions on the test set
predictions <- predict(dt_model, newdata = as.data.frame(X_test), type = "class")

# Evaluate the model performance
coincidence_matrix <- confusionMatrix(predictions, as.factor(Y_test))
cat("Confusion matrix:\n")
print(coincidence_matrix$table)

recall <- confusion_matrix$byClass['Sensitivity']
precision <- confusion_matrix$byClass['Precision']
f1_macro <- 2 * (recall * precision) / (recall + precision)
gmean <- sqrt(recall * confusion_matrix$byClass['Specificity'])

# Calculate AUC
roc_result <- roc(response = as.numeric(as.factor(Y_test)), predictor = as.numeric(predictions))
auc_value <- auc(roc_result)

cat(sprintf("F1 Macro: %f, AUC: %f, GMean: %f, Recall: %f, Precision: %f\n", f1_macro, auc_value, gmean, recall, precision))
}
```

This code yields the coincidence matrix given in Table 7.14.

7.6 Decision Trees

Table 7.14 R decision tree coincidence matrix

	Model no	Model yes	
Actual no	108	29	137
Actual yes	15	112	127
	123	141	264

This yields AUC = 0.836, Recall = 0.882, Precision = 0.794, Specificity 0.788 and Accuracy 0.833.

7.6.2 Python Code Decision Tree

```
import numpy as np
import pandas as pd
from sklearn.linear_model import DecisionTreeClassifier as DT
from sklearn.model_selection import train_test_split
from sklearn.metrics import confusion_matrix
from sklearn.metrics import recall_score
from sklearn.metrics import f1_score
from sklearn.metrics import roc_auc_score
from sklearn.metrics import precision_score
from sklearn.metrics import classification_report

df = pd.read_csv('Bankruptcy.csv')

X = df.iloc[:,0:15]
y = df.iloc[:, 15]
X_train, X_test, y_train, y_test = train_test_split(X, y,
test_size = 0.2, random_state = 0)

# initialize model
lrl1    =    DT(penalty='l1',solver='liblinear',C=0.5,max_
iter=1000)
# model training
lrl1.fit(X_train, y_train)
# model test
logits = lrl1.predict(X_test)

# metrics
def conf_gmean(conf):
   tn, fp, fn, tp = conf.ravel()
   return (tp*tn/((tp+fn)*(tn+fp)))**0.5
def evaluate(labels, logits):
   conf = confusion_matrix(labels, logits)
   recall = recall_score(labels, logits)
   f1_macro = f1_score(labels, logits, average='macro')
   auc = roc_auc_score(labels, logits)
   gmean = conf_gmean(conf)
   precision = precision_score(labels, logits)
```

Table 7.15 Python decision tree coincidence matrix

	Model no	Model yes	
Actual no	99	16	115
Actual yes	13	137	150
	112	153	265

```
    return f1_macro, auc, gmean, recall, precision
# compute metrics
f1_macro, auc, gmean, recall, precision = evaluate(y_test,
logits)
print(f"fi_macro:{f1_macro},AUC:{auc},GMean:{gmean},Recall:{recal
Precision:{precision}")

#y_pred = logits.predict(X_test)
confusion_matrix = confusion_matrix(y_test, logits)
print(confusion_matrix)

print(classification_report(y_test, logits))
```

This code yields the coincidence matrix given in Table 7.15.

AuC was 0.887, recall 0.913, precision 0.895, specificity 0.861 and accuracy 0.891.

7.7 Random Forests

Rattle provides a description of random forests (see Fig. 7.7), which are essentially multiple decision trees.

The random forest for this full set of variables is called as shown in Fig. 7.8.

Asking for the OOB ROC curve gave the learning displayed in Fig. 7.9.

ROC, for historical reasons, stands for "receiver operating characteristics" (from World War II, actually) where it was used to display the area under the curve for true hits versus misses. OOB stands for Out-of-Bag, reflecting a sampling method. Here in the full model we might be interested in variable importance, shown in Fig. 7.10.

Table 7.16 gives test results for the Rattle Random Forest model.

The random forest model correctly classified 126 of 129 cases (0.977) where firms did not go bankrupt. It did nearly as well for the cases where firms did go bankrupt with 131 of 136 correct (0.963) for an overall correct classification rate of 0.970. Precision was 0.978.

7.7 Random Forests

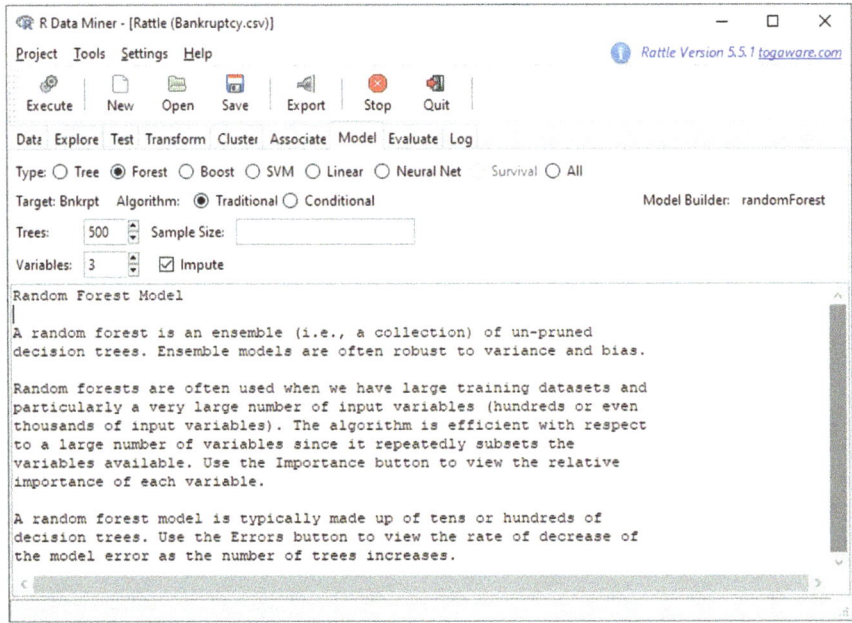

Fig. 7.7 Rattle description of random forests

7.7.1 R Code Random Forest

```
library(gbm)
library(caret)
library(pROC)
library(randomForest)

# Read the data
df <- read.csv('Bankruptcy.csv')

# Extract features and labels
features <- as.matrix(df[, 1:15])
labels <- df[[16]]

# Split the dataset into training and testing sets
set.seed(123)
list_indexes <- createDataPartition(labels, p = 0.8, list =
TRUE)
train_indexes <- list_indexes[[1]]
X_train <- features[train_indexes, ]
Y_train <- as.factor(labels[train_indexes])   # Convert to
factor
X_test <- features[-train_indexes, ]
Y_test <- labels[-train_indexes]
```

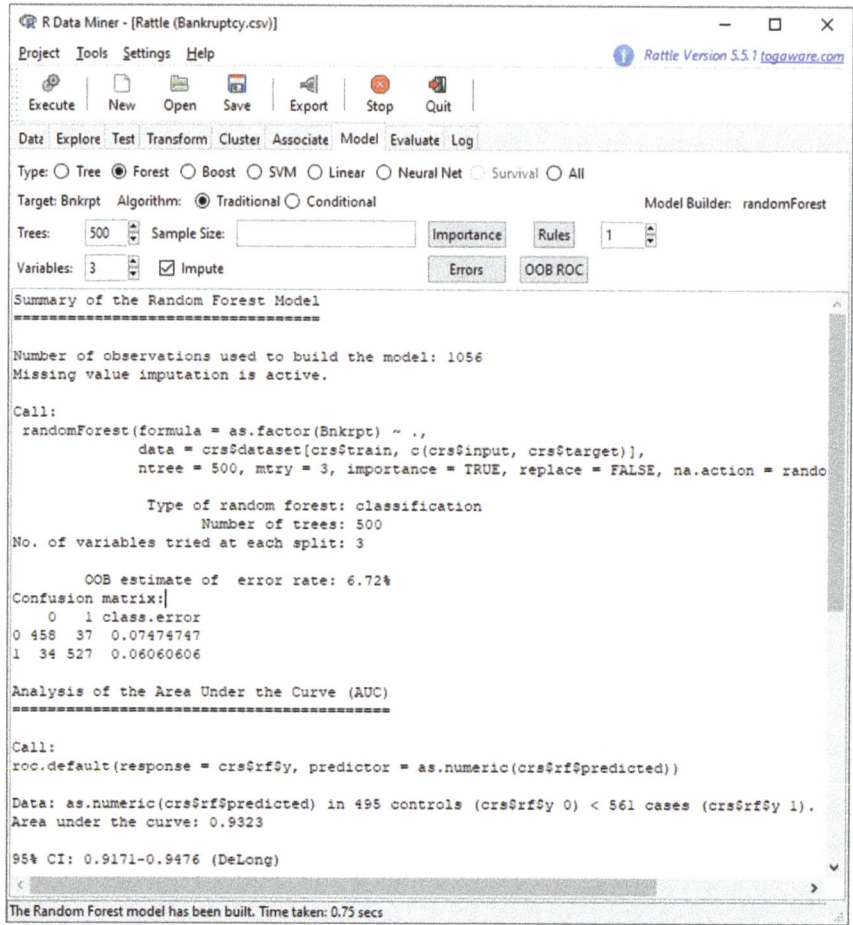

Fig. 7.8 Call for rattle random forest

```
# Initialize and train a random forest model
set.seed(1) # Set a random seed for reproducibility
rf_model <- randomForest(x = X_train, y = Y_train, ntree = 500)

# Use the model to make predictions on the test set
predictions <- predict(rf_model, newdata = as.data.frame(X_
test))

# Calculate the evaluation metrics.
coincidence_matrix      <-      confusionMatrix(predictions,
as.factor(Y_test))
cat("Coincidence matrix:\n")
print(coincidence_matrix$table)
```

7.7 Random Forests

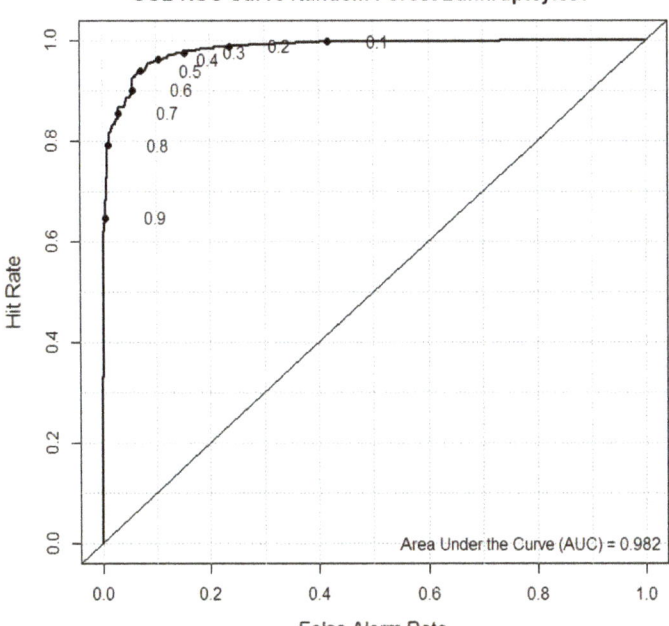

Fig. 7.9 Random forest OOB ROC curve

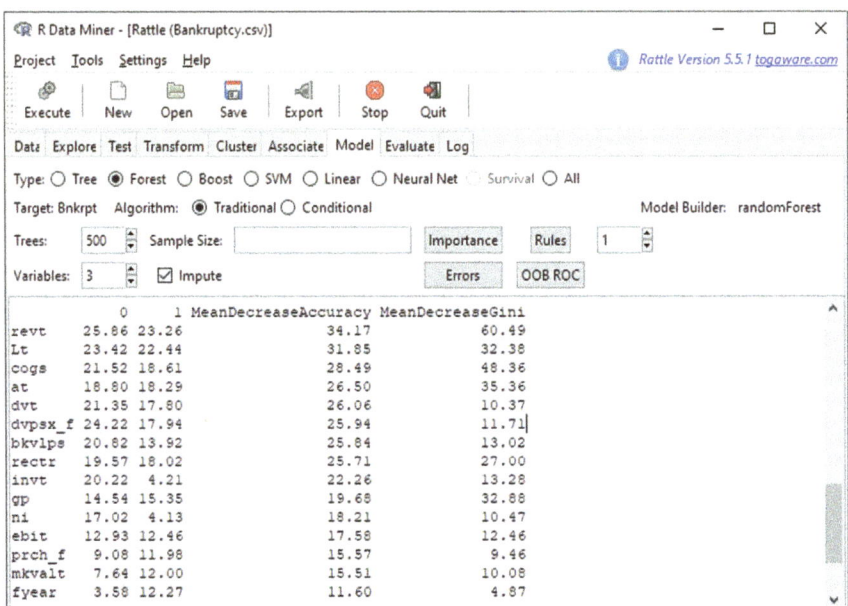

Fig. 7.10 Variable relative importance in random forest model

Table 7.16 Coincidence matrix—Rattle Random Forest Model

	Model no	Model yes	
Actual no	126	3	129
Actual yes	5	131	136
	131	134	265

Table 7.17 R random forest model coincidence matrix

	Model no	Model yes	
Actual no	116	12	128
Actual yes	7	129	136
	123	141	264

```
recall <- coincidence_matrix$byClass['Sensitivity']
precision <- coincidence_matrix$byClass['Precision']
f1_score <- 2 * (precision * recall) / (precision + recall)

# Calculate GMean
gmean <- sqrt(recall * coincidence_matrix$byClass['Specificity'])

# Calculate the AUC value
auc_value <- roc(response = as.factor(Y_test), predictor =
as.numeric(predictions))$auc

# Print the results
cat(sprintf("F1 Macro: %f, AUC: %f, GMean: %f, Recall: %f,
Precision: %f\n", f1_score, auc_value, gmean, recall, preci-
sion))
```

Table 7.17 gives the resulting the coincidence table.

The area under the curve was 0.929. The other metrics obtained are Recall = 0.949, Precision = 0.915, Specificity 0.906 and Accuracy 0.928.

7.7.2 Python Code Random Forest

```
import numpy as np
import pandas as pd
from sklearn.ensemble import RandomForestClassifier as RF
from sklearn.model_selection import train_test_split
from sklearn.metrics import confusion_matrix
from sklearn.metrics import recall_score
from sklearn.metrics import f1_score
from sklearn.metrics import roc_auc_score
from sklearn.metrics import precision_score
```

7.7 Random Forests

```
from sklearn.metrics import classification_report

df = pd.read_csv('Bankruptcy.csv')

X = df.iloc[:,0:15]
y = df.iloc[:, 15]
X_train, X_test, y_train, y_test = train_test_split(X, y,
test_size = 0.2, random_state = 0)

# initialize model
rf = RF(random_state=0)
# model training
rf.fit(X_train, y_train)
# model test
logits = rf.predict(X_test)

# metrics
def conf_gmean(conf):
   tn, fp, fn, tp = conf.ravel()
   return (tp*tn/((tp+fn)*(tn+fp)))**0.5
def evaluate(labels, logits):
   conf = confusion_matrix(labels, logits)
   recall = recall_score(labels, logits)
   f1_macro = f1_score(labels, logits, average='macro')
   auc = roc_auc_score(labels, logits)
   gmean = conf_gmean(conf)
   precision = precision_score(labels, logits)
   return f1_macro, auc, gmean, recall, precision
# compute metrics
f1_macro, auc, gmean, recall, precision = evaluate(y_test,
logits)
print(f"fi_macro:{f1_macro},AUC:{auc},GMean:{gmean},Recall:{recall},
Precision:{precision}")

#y_pred = logits.predict(X_test)
confusion_matrix = confusion_matrix(y_test, logits)
print(confusion_matrix)

print(classification_report(y_test, logits))
```

This code yields the coincidence matrix given in Table 7.18.

AuC is 0.932, Recall 0.933, precision 0.946, specificity 0.930 and accuracy 0.932.

Random forest models consist of multiple (often many) decision trees. They will almost always provide much better fit than single decision tree models.

Table 7.18 Python random forest coincidence matrix

	Model no	Model yes	
Actual no	107	8	115
Actual yes	10	140	150
	117	148	265

7.8 Boosting

Boosting is a means to run multiple models with different weights to reduce error, much in the spirit of neural networks, or as we have just seen, random forests. All involve intense computation searching for reduced error over the training set. Figure 7.11 gives R's short description of Adaptive Boosting.

The area under the curve for the boosting model was 0.952. Table 7.19 gives the coincidence matrix.

The boosted model correctly classified 126 of 129 cases (0.977) where firms did not go bankrupt and 130 of 136 cases where firms did go bankrupt (0.956) for an overall correct classification rate of 0.966. Precision was 0.977.

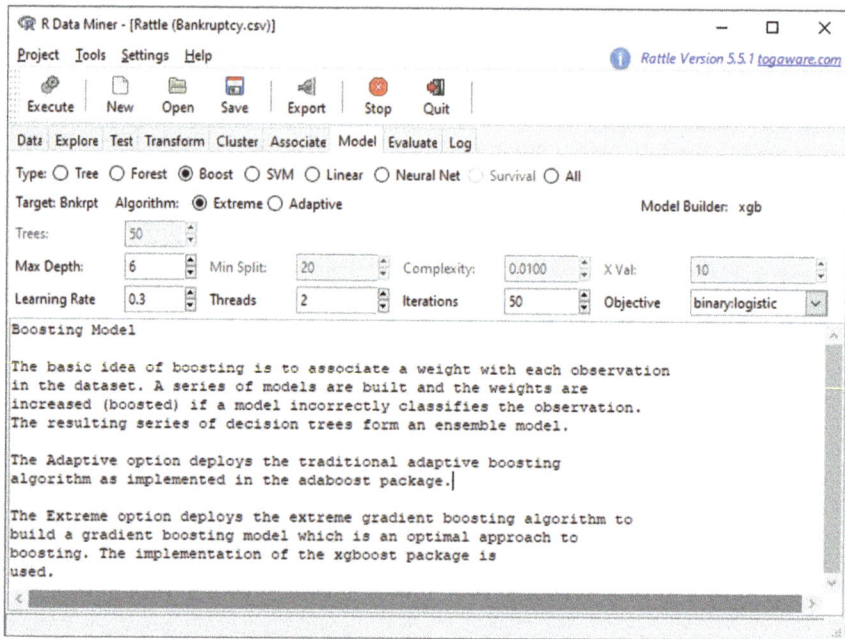

Fig. 7.11 Rattle boosting selection

Table 7.19 Coincidence matrix—Rattle Extreme Boosting

	Model no	Model yes	
Actual no	126	3	129
Actual yes	6	130	136
	132	133	265

7.8.1 R Code XGBoost

```
library(xgboost)
library(caTools)
library(dplyr)
library(caret)
library(pROC)

df <- read.csv('Bankruptcy.csv')
df$Bnkrpt <- as.factor(df$Bnkrpt)

set.seed(123)
sample_split <- sample.split(Y = df$Bnkrpt, SplitRatio = 0.8)
train_set <- subset(x = df, sample_split == TRUE)
test_set <- subset(x = df, sample_split == FALSE)

y_train <- as.integer(train_set$Bnkrpt) - 1
y_test <- as.integer(test_set$Bnkrpt) - 1
X_train <- train_set %>% select(-Bnkrpt)
X_test <- test_set %>% select(-Bnkrpt)

xgb_train <- xgb.DMatrix(data = as.matrix(X_train), label = y_train)
xgb_test <- xgb.DMatrix(data = as.matrix(X_test), label = y_test)

xgb_params <- list(
  booster = "gbtree",
  eta = 0.3,
  max_depth = 6,
  gamma = 4,
  subsample = 0.5,
  colsample_bytree = 1,
  objective = "multi:softprob",
  eval_metric = "auc",
  num_class = length(levels(df$Bnkrpt))
)
#eval_metric = "mlogloss",

xgb_model <- xgb.train(
  params = xgb_params,
  data = xgb_train,
  nrounds = 2000,
  verbose = 1
)
xgb_model

xgb_preds <- predict(xgb_model, as.matrix(X_test), reshape = TRUE)
xgb_preds <- as.data.frame(xgb_preds)
colnames(xgb_preds) <- levels(df$Bnkrpt)
xgb_preds
```

Table 7.20 R Extreme Boosting Model Coincidence Matrix

	Model no	Model yes	
Actual no	118	7	125
Actual yes	11	128	139
	129	135	264

```
xgb_preds$PredictedClass <- apply(xgb_preds, 1, function(y)
colnames(xgb_preds)[which.max(y)])
xgb_preds$ActualClass <- levels(df$Bnkrpt)[y_test + 1]
xgb_preds

accuracy    <-    sum(xgb_preds$PredictedClass    ==    xgb_
preds$ActualClass) / nrow(xgb_preds)
accuracy

confusionMatrix(factor(xgb_preds$ActualClass), factor(xgb_
preds$PredictedClass))

roc_test    <-    roc(factor(xgb_preds$PredictedClass),
as.numeric(xgb_preds$ActualClass), algorithm =2)
#plot(roc_test)
auc(roc_test)
}
```

Table 7.20 gives the resulting the coincidence table.

Area under the curve was 0.931. The other metrics obtained are Recall = 0.921, Precision = 0.948, Specificity 0.944 and Accuracy 0.932.

7.8.2 Python Code Gradient Boosting

```
import pandas as pd
import numpy as np
from sklearn.model_selection import train_test_split
import argparse
from sklearn.metrics import f1_score, roc_auc_score, confu-
sion_matrix, recall_score, precision_score
import warnings
# import the original data
df = pd.read_csv('Bankruptcy.csv')
inp = []
label = []
# Traverse the original data row by row
for index, row in df.iterrows():
    # get the data for each row and turn it to list type
    temp = list(row)
```

7.8 Boosting

```python
    # features generation
    inp.append(temp[:15])
    # labels generation
    label.append(temp[15])
X = np.array(inp)
Y = np.array(label)
# split the samples into train set and test set
X_train, X_test, Y_train, Y_test = train_test_split(X, Y,
train_size=0.8, test_size=0.2, shuffle=True)
from sklearn.ensemble import GradientBoostingClassifier as GB
# initialize model
gb = GB(n_estimators=10, random_state=1)
# model training
gb.fit(X_train, Y_train)
# model test
logits = gb.predict(X_test) # metrics
def conf_gmean(conf):
    tn, fp, fn, tp = conf.ravel()
    return (tp*tn/((tp+fn)*(tn+fp)))**0.5
def evaluate(labels, logits):
    conf = confusion_matrix(labels, logits)
    print("conf matrix:")
    print(conf)
    recall = recall_score(labels, logits)
    f1_macro = f1_score(labels, logits, average='macro')
    auc = roc_auc_score(labels, logits)
    gmean = conf_gmean(conf)
    precision = precision_score(labels, logits)
    return f1_macro, auc, gmean, recall, precision
# compute metrics
f1_macro, auc, gmean, recall, precision = evaluate(Y_test,
logits)
print(f"fi_macro:{f1_macro},AUC:{auc},GMean:{gmean},Recall:{recall},
Precision:{precision}")
```

Table 7.21 gives the resulting the coincidence table.

Area under the curve was 0.902. The other metrics obtained are Recall = 0.889, Precision = 0.916, Specificity 0.915 and Accuracy 0.902.

Table 7.21 Python gradient boosting model coincidence matrix

	Model no	Model yes	
Actual no	119	11	130
Actual yes	15	120	135
	134	131	265

7.9 Comparison

Running all of these models gives a flavor for the R toolbox of classification models. Table 7.22 compares test results for these models for the trimmed data set with 3 input variables (selected based upon correlation) as well as all of the models run with the full set of input variables.

The best overall fit tends to be the Random Forest and Boosting models, although the neural network models did reasonable well in R and Python (note that the parameters for neural networks were not optimized, which expert users can refine to get better results). Results should not be taken blindly, and judgment withheld considering expected stability and ease of implementation. More complex models, such as neural networks, random forests, and boosting, will usually provide better fit on past data. However, part of that is because the more basic models (like logistic regression and decision trees) are subsets of these more complex models. Here the simpler models have the benefit of being easier for users to understand, and we would also contend that they are more stable as new data is encountered.

Table 7.22 Comparisons

Rattle Model	AIC	AuC	Recall	Precision	Specificity	Accuracy
Log Reg	966.45	0.910	0.711	0.924	0.938	0.827
SVM		0.882	0.691	0.862	0.884	0.785
Neural Net		0.925	0.801	0.939	0.946	0.864
Decision Tree		0.923	0.824	0.949	0.953	0.887
Random Forest		**0.994**	**0.963**	**0.978**	**0.977**	**0.970**
XBoosting		**0.992**	**0.956**	**0.977**	**0.977**	**0.966**
R Model	AuC	Recall	Precision	Specificity	Accuracy	
Log Reg	0.891	0.877	0.709	0.727	0.792	
SVM	0.622	0.721	0.440	0.556	0.610	
Neural Net		**0.944**	0.908	0.914	**0.928**	
Decision Tree	0.836	0.882	0.794	0.788	0.833	
Random Forest	**0.929**	0.949	0.915	0.906	**0.928**	
XBoosting	**0.931**	0.921	**0.948**	**0.944**	**0.932**	
Python Model	AuC	Recall	Precision	Specificity	Accuracy	
Log Reg	0.804	0.660	0.943	0.948	0.785	
SVM	0.787	0.627	0.940	0.948	0.766	
Neural Net	**0.945**	**0.960**	**0.947**	**0.930**	**0.947**	
Decision Tree	0.887	0.913	0.895	0.861	0.891	
Random Forest	**0.932**	0.933	**0.946**	**0.930**	**0.932**	
XBoosting	0.902	0.889	0.916	0.915	0.902	

7.9 Comparison

Usually relative cost matters a lot. If each case that the model predicted to be bankrupt that actually wasn't, business would have been lost—the expected profit of that investment. The other type of error would be to invest in a firm that actually went bankrupt. If the cost of this case was 5 times that of the first type of error, we could compare relative costs (Table 7.23).

Considering weighted costs, we get pretty much the same outcome—the Random Forest model came out best, with decision trees very close. Note that it is usually best practice to run multiple models and see which fit your particular dataset best, realizing that the results can change with new data.

We now can show how to apply these models. Given a set of new cases, shown in Table 7.24.

After all of the models are run, we can select Score on the Evaluate tab (see Fig. 7.12):

Note that we selected the Probability button, which yields the probability of being bankrupt. If you select the Class button, Rattle will use a cutoff of 0.5 and categorize cases as Yes or No. The Probability button gives the user the option of setting whatever cutoff they want. Note that Rattle will create a.csv file with the output. If you select the All button, all of the input values are shown. If the Identifiers button is selected, just the answers are shown. We don't have space to repeat the All inputs (they are shown in Fig. 7.1 anyway). The output we obtain is shown in Table 7.25:

Rattle's nomenclature for logistic regression is glm, support vector machine is ksvm, neural network is nnet, decision tree is rpart, random forest is rf, and boosting is ada. The boosting model didn't forecast. It is sensitive. The support vector machine model is suspect, the only model to predict cases 1 and 2 to be bankrupt. The other models are clear—cases 1 and 2 look OK, cases 3, 4 and 5 look risky. The value of running multiple models is to see which may be more believable.

Table 7.23 Comparison—errors weighted by cost

Model	Actual no Model yes Cost 1	Actual yes Model no Cost 5	Total Cost
Log Reg	6	24	126
SVM	15	42	225
Neural Net	7	29	152
Decision Tree	6	24	126
Random For	3	5	28
XBoosting	3	6	33

Table 7.24 New cases

	Case1	Case2	Case3	Case4	Case5
fyear	2011	2011	2011	2011	2011
at	0.001	0	312,061	410,063	1,856,646
bkvlps	−1.1581	−0.0218	45.4816	57.8366	5.3501
invt	0	0	137,040	182,413	283,894
Lt	0.376	13.91	298,887	393,269	1,701,673
rectr	0	0	65,080	98,796	705,958
cogs	0	4.677	5719	9375	95,740
dvt	0	0	178	302	7674
ebit	−0.821	−4.625	11,253	22,619	5566
gp	0	−4.625	11,568	23,045	8419
ni	−0.815	−5.361	1699	3260	−1606
oiadp	−0.821	−4.625	11,253	22,619	5566
revt	0	0.052	17,287	32,420	104,159
dvpsx_f	0	0	0.48	0.8	0.01
mkvalt	0.3605	58.9719	19,256.89	34,201.06	5,820,729
prch_f	1.75	0.155	76.25	133.16	7.585

7.10 Loan Default Prediction Model

Credit risk assessment is one of the major applications of business data mining. We give an example study of loan default prediction. The risk of loss due to borrowers not fulfilling their debt contract obligations is the definition of default risk. Banks and other lending institutions face economic loss from non-repayment, but also face the risk of churn of high-quality borrowers should those applicants be denied loans. Yuan et al. (2022) gave a prediction model using k-means clustering to partition data, and support vector machine modeling for classification.

The first step of their analysis was to determine the optimal number of clusters. Too few clusters led to ineffective classification of cases. Too many clusters risked over-fitting the data (the model would be very good with the training dataset, but much less effective on the test set and on future cases). Instead of the elbow method or the silhouette method, this study used a Bayesian-Kullback Ying-Yang selection procedure.

Credit scoring of clusters was then obtained through support vector domain description (SVDD) to predict defaults. SVDD differs from support vector machines in that the training data belongs to only one class. A hyper-sphere is identified with minimum volume surrounding the target clas samples.

Feature selection was a pre-processing activity to select those variables that would give better learning accuracy and computational efficiency. Four feature selection methods were considered. Filter methods select features based on some ranking of

7.10 Loan Default Prediction Model

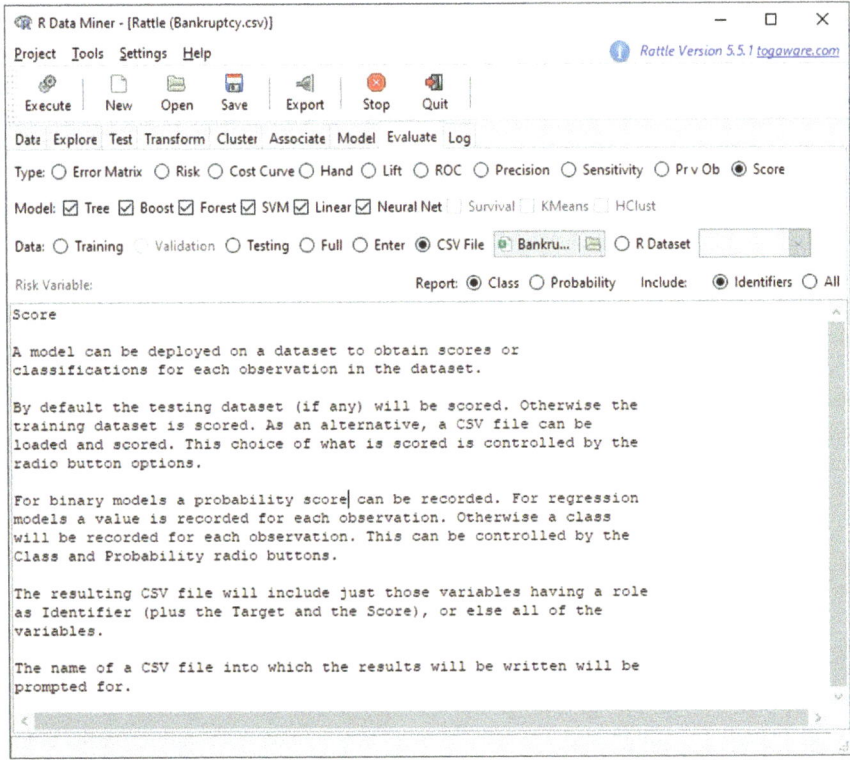

Fig. 7.12 Scoring Window

Table 7.25 Rattle Model Predictions

Case	Full glm	ksvm	nnet	rpart	Rf
1	0.153	0.840	0	0.150	0.264
2	0.165	0.840	0	0.150	0.098
3	1	0.860	1	1	1
4	1	0.860	1	1	1
5	1	0.860	1	0.942	0.984

importance in explanatory power as well as elimination of redundancy. However, they may not attain the best performance due to lack of an optimization procedure. Wrapper methods select those features providing the highest accuracy of all possible subsets of features. This approach can have a high computational cost. Embedded methods focus on model-based modifications, such as eliminating those features with zero beta coefficients. Hybrid methods combine different feature selection methods. Yuan et al. utilized a hybrid method combining filtering with a wrapper-based method.

The process applied was to obtain data. The original data consisted of 396 features (198 financial, 85 non-financial, 112 macro, and defaulter status, obtained from the Wind Financial database, the CSMAR database, and the National Bureau of Statistics of China) of 3425 Chinese listed companies over the period 2000 to 2019. This data was then divided into training data (80 percent) and testing data (20 percent). Then two-stage feature selection was applied to select variables. In the next stage, k-means clustering identified clusters (k ranging form 2 through 52), followed by application of SVDD to classify cases and predict those expected to default. Kernel functions for SVDD used were linear, radial-basis function, sigmoid, and polynomial. Evaluation measures used were area under the curve, G-mean, and Type-II error. These were measured on all 208 combinations of K and kernel. The best fit for time horizons of 2 years forward, 3 years forward, 4 years forward, and 5 years forward were obtained, finding widely different K values and kernel functions for each time horizon. The optimal number of clusters one year ahead was 12 with a radial basis kernel function. Overall the radial basis and polynomial kernel functions were found preferable.

7.11 Summary

We recap the essential points in classification modeling:

1. The process of training, testing, and applying the model is best done if you have independent training and test sets. In this case, you do not want to partition the data. If you need to skip the test set, you can partition, selecting the proportion of the dataset you want the software to hold out for testing.
2. Classification if for categorical target variables. Prior chapters have covered techniques for continuous target variables. Ordinary least squares is the common regression model for continuous variables. Logistic regression works for categorical targets. Decision trees work best for categorical targets. You can run regression trees on continuous targets, but as we discussed in that chapter, the finite number of possible predictions make regression trees less believable.
3. Models can be controlled. Regression is controlled primarily through variable selection. Using all available input variables will always yield a higher r-squared, but will usually involve overlapping information that makes the beta coefficients unstable. Predicting isn't a problem as long as you have inputs for all independent variables, but trimmed models are stabler. Decision trees are controlled by setting minimum support and minimum confidence. An easier control within Rattle is to use the Complexity parameter. A lower complexity will yield models with fewer rules, which are easier to implement. Neural network models can be controlled by adjusting hidden layers, although "control" is probably too clear a term in this case.
4. There are alternative softwares available. Commercial softwares are very good, but often very expensive. Rattle and WEKA are open source. There are quite a few other open source softwares. WEKA is very interesting from a research

perspective, with many optional modeling techniques. Rattle is a GUI for R, which makes it commercially viable and scalable.

References

Olson DL, Delen D, Meng Y (2012) Comparative analysis of data mining methods for bankruptcy prediction. Decis Support Syst 52:464–473

Yuan K, Chi G, Zhou Y, Yin H (2022) A novel two-stage hybrid default prediction model with k-means clustering and support vector domain description. Res Int Bus Financ 59:101536. https://doi.org/10.1016/j.ribaf.2021.101536

Chapter 8
Variable Selection

Frequently, data mining analysis involves data with a large number of variables. Often some variables contribute more noise than value in predicting the dependent variable. Irrelevant and redundant information can adversely affect model performance. (Chan et al. 2007) identified several applications where too many features generated noise, and ignoring redundant variables improved organizational failure prediction, and reducing the set of independent variables can result in better prediction.

The best approach to variable selection is expert knowledge of subject matter. But there are machine learning tools as well. There are three basic approaches for variable selection in data mining. Filter methods preprocess the data, considering correlation or other metrics to select a subset of likely candidate variables. Wrapper methods train a model using a selected subset of variables and apply either forward selection or backward elimination (as in stepwise regression). Embedded models are more complex, embedding selection techniques within an algorithm as is done with least absolute shrinkage and selection operator (LASSO). Boruta is a wrapper method using random forests to identify important features.

Tsai (2009) discussed feature selection methods such as stepwise regression and correlation matrix for bankruptcy prediction. We will consider four simple and easy-to-apply approaches on bankruptcy data:

1. Correlation analysis
2. Stepwise regression
3. Entropy using decision tree models
4. Information gain obtained from random forest models

Often independent variables may be highly correlated, containing overlapping information which may distort regression coefficients. Usually, a small subset of these explanatory (independent) variables provide the bulk of the predictive power of a model. It would be beneficial to identify the kernel of explanatory variables that give most if not all of a model's accurate prediction. The reasons to be able to trim larger sets of variables in data mining to smaller subsets include:

1. Easier analysis
2. Shorter training time
3. Avoiding the curse of dimensionality, which makes problems more complex
4. Reducing overfitting, by reducing variance

Analysts of financial modeling seem to be able to come up with a plethora of ratios to measure firm performance. This creates some problems for regression, in that the correlation across these variables makes it difficult to assess relative contribution of each variable. Stepwise regression is a means to apply machine learning characteristics to logistic regression (which is used in bankruptcy analysis, with a binary output variable). Primarily, however, most of the predictive power comes from a subset of available variables. Ideally a parsimonious model with good predictive power that is easy to implement is preferable.

The ideal way to select variables is based on deep understanding of the problem. This is the approach of classical statistics, where the ideal regression model is based on selecting variables known to have strong relationships with the dependent variable. This amounts to understanding the system and selecting independent variables the human analyst expects to have a strong relationship with the dependent variable. Machine learning, conversely, uses statistical measures to select variables. Zeng et al. (2009) gave the general idea of attribute relevance analysis to quantify attribute relevance for a given class. Information gain, as reported by random forest in Rattle, is a commonly used measure. Zeng (2017) conversely suggested using boosting to select relevant variables. Both random forest and boosting can be based on decision trees. Thus, a machine learning method to select variables is to apply a decision tree, which has a complexity parameter based on entropy levels to select variables.

The traditional regression method of variable reduction is stepwise, adding variables by their contribution to explaining variance in the dependent variable (Foster 2004). This is done with partial correlation, which considers overlapping content of potential independent variables. The process can start with selecting that independent variable with the highest correlation with the dependent variable. Then, given use of that variable, the partial contribution of independent variables are analyzed to iteratively proceed until added improvement in fit falls below some stated level.

We will apply both the decision tree approach based on entropy as well as stepwise regression as machine learning tools to select explanatory variables. The number of variables selected can be controlled in decision trees through the complexity parameter the minimum improvement in the model needed at each node. We used three levels of this complexity parameter.

8.1 Taiwan Bankruptcy Data

Liang et al. (2016) presented 6819 observations over 95 available explanatory variables for firm bankruptcy in Taiwan. This dataset was also highly imbalanced, with 220 bankrupt and 6599 not. They used three filtering methods (stepwise discriminant

8.1 Taiwan Bankruptcy Data

analysis, stepwise logistic regression, and t-testing as well as two wrapper methods (genetic algorithm and recursive feature elimination). Here we will use correlation, variable significance from logistic regression, entropy from decision trees, and variable information from random forest models. We will divide the dataset into 20% for variable identification (the validation set), 60% for training models, and 20% for testing.

The 95 independent variables are given in Table 8.1.

8.1.1 Correlation

Correlation analysis of the dataset yields results given in Table 8.2 (showing those correlations greater than 0.05). Variables can be selected at whatever cutoff desired. For instance, with a cutoff of 0.10, the first ten variables listed would be selected.

Using a cutoff of 0.10, we would use all 12 variables to develop models using the training set. Results are given in Table 8.3.

A smaller set of 7 variables would be obtained if we used a cutoff of 0.10. For the models with correlation of at least 0.10, all of the models were very good at predicting cases not going bankrupt (specificity). But all were very bad at predicting bankrupt cases (recall). If models predicted bankruptcy, precision varied a great deal due to the small numbers involved. Accuracy was quite similar for all models.

Increasing the number of variables to 12 (correlation of 0.05 or more) yielded the results in Table 8.4.

Increasing the number of variables did not result in great improvement. Recall continued to be bad, and specificity very good. Accuracy for neural networks was terrible, but otherwise all were quite good.

8.1.2 Logistic Regression Variable Significance

Table 8.5 gives the validation dataset logistic regression output for probability of measure greater than Chi-squared using a cutoff of 0.05.

Using a probability cutoff of less than 0.01, we would select 7 variables. Table 8.6 gives results.

Using a cutoff of 0.05, we would use all 14 variables to develop models using the training set. A smaller set of 7 variables would be obtained if we used a cutoff of 0.10. Results are given in Table 8.7.

Accuracy was quite similar for all models except that the neural network model was very bad (neural network models take some design).

Increasing the number of variables did not result in great improvement. Recall continued to be bad, and specificity very good. Accuracy for neural networks was terrible, but otherwise all were quite good.

Table 8.1 Taiwan bankruptcy variables

1 ROA(C) before interest and depreciation before interest	25 Operating Profit Growth Rate
2 ROA(A) before interest and % after tax	26 After-tax Net Profit Growth Rate
3 ROA(B) before interest and depreciation after tax	27 Regular Net Profit Growth Rate
4 Operating Gross Margin	28 Continuous Net Profit Growth Rate
5 Realized Sales Gross Margin	29 Total Asset Growth Rate
6 Operating Profit Rate	30 Net Value Growth Rate
7 Pre-tax net Interest Rate	31 Total Asset Return Growth Rate Ratio
8 After-tax net Interest Rate	32 Cash Reinvestment %
9 Non-industry income and expenditure/revenue	33 Current Ratio
10 Continuous interest rate (after tax)	34 Quick Ratio
11 Operating Expense Rate	35 Interest Expense Ratio
12 Research and development expense rate	36 Total debt/Total net worth
13 Cash flow rate	37 Debt ratio %
14 Interest-bearing debt interest rate	38 Net worth/Assets
15 Tax rate (A)	39 Long-term fund suitability ratio (A)
16 Net Value Per Share (B)	40 Borrowing dependency
17 Net Value Per Share (A)	41 Contingent liabilities/Net worth
18 Net Value Per Share (C)	42 Operating profit/Paid-in capital
19 Persistent EPS in the Last Four Seasons	43 Net profit before tax/Paid-in capital
20 Cash Flow Per Share	44 Inventory and accounts receivable/Net value
21 Revenue Per Share (Yuan ¥)	45 Total Asset Turnover
22 Operating Profit Per Share (Yuan ¥)	46 Accounts Receivable Turnover
23 Per Share Net profit before tax (Yuan ¥)	47 Average Collection Days
24 Realized Sales Gross Profit Growth Rate	48 Inventory Turnover Rate (times)
49 Fixed Assets Turnover Frequency	73 Working capital Turnover Rate
50 Net Worth Turnover Rate (times)	73 Cash Turnover Rate
51 Revenue per person	75 Cash Flow to Sales
52 Operating profit per person	76 Fixed Assets to Assets
53 Allocation rate per person	77 Current Liability to Liability
54 Working Capital to Total Assets	78 Current Liability to Equity
55 Quick Assets/Total Assets	79 Equity to Long-term Liability
56 Current Assets/Total Assets	80 Cash Flow to Total Assets
57 Cash/Total Assets	81 Cash Flow to Liability
58 Quick Assets/Current Liability	82 CFO to Assets
59 Cash/Current Liability	83 Cash Flow to Equity
60 Current Liability to Assets	84 Current Liability to Current Assets

(continued)

8.1 Taiwan Bankruptcy Data

Table 8.1 (continued)

61 Operating Funds to Liability	85 Liability-Assets Flag
62 Inventory/Working Capital	86 Net Income to Total Assets
63 Inventory/Current Liability	87 Total assets to GNP price
64 Current Liabilities/Liability	88 No-credit Interval
65 Working Capital/Equity	89 Gross Profit to Sales
66 Current Liabilities/Equity	90 Net Income to Stockholder's Equity
67 Long-term Liability to Current Assets	91 Liability to Equity
68 Retained Earnings to Total Assets	92 Interest Coverage Ratio (Interest expense to EBIT)
69 Total income/Total expense	93 Net Income Flag
70 Total expense/Assets	94 Equity to Liability
71 Current Asset Turnover Rate	95 Degree of Financial Leverage (DFL)
72 Quick Asset Turnover Rate	

Table 8.2 Correlation

70 Total expense/Assets	0.207939
84 Current Liability to Current Assets	0.207637
37 Debt ratio %	0.155172
87 Total assets to GNP price	0.146062
60 Current Liability to Assets	0.128766
66 Current Liabilities/Equity	0.101552
78 Current Liability to Equity	0.101552
49 Fixed Assets Turnover Frequency	0.093655
72 Quick Asset Turnover Rate	0.071761
91 Liability to Equity	0.069751
40 Borrowing dependency	0.058440
92 Degree of Financial Leverage (DFL)	0.051981

Table 8.3 Metrics for models with variables selected by correlation > 0.10

Correlation 7 variables	Random forest	Extreme boosting	Decision tree	Logistic regression	SVM	Neural network
Area under ROC	0.8882	0.9005	0.8978	0.9362	0.7144	0.9150
Recall	0.045	0.091	0	0.136	0	0
Specificity	0.985	0.985	0.984	0.986	0.984	0.984
Precision	0.500	0.333	0	0.750	0	0
Accuracy	0.9839	0.9824	0.9809	0.9853	0.9831	0.9809

Table 8.4 Metrics for models with variables selected by correlation > 0.05

Correlation 12 variables	Random forest	Extreme boosting	Decision tree	Logistic regression	SVM	Neural network
Area under ROC	0.9620	0.9543	0.8647	0.9495	0.7295	0.5137
Recall	0.136	0.091	0	0.091	0.045	0.455
Specificity	0.986	0.985	0.984	0.985	0.985	0.982
Precision	0.500	0.400	0	0.667	1	0.014
Accuracy	0.9839	0.9831	0.9824	0.9846	0.9846	0.4975

Table 8.5 Validation set variable significance using logistic regression

Variable	Pr(>Chi)
X1ROA.C..before.interest.and.depreciation.before.interest	1.20E-11
X63Inventory.Current.Liability	9.18E-11
X2ROA.A..before.interest.and…after.tax	0.000525
X48Inventory.Turnover.Rate..times	0.000661
X33Current.Ratio	0.002745
X40Borrowing.dependency	0.003320
X3ROA.B..before.interest.and.depreciation.after.tax	0.007919
X44Inventory.and.accounts.receivable.Net.value	0.010830
X49Fixed.Assets.Turnover.Frequency	0.014456
X34Quick.Ratio	0.015322
X41Contingent.liabilities.Net.worth	0.016013
X6Operating.Profit.Rate	0.020383
X30Net.Value.Growth.Rate	0.026537
X13Cash.flow.rate	0.048058

Table 8.6 Metrics for models with variables selected by logistic regression probability < 0.01

Log Reg 7 variables	Random forest	Extreme boosting	Decision tree	Logistic regression	SVM	Neural network
Area under ROC	0.9447	0.9601	0.8684	0.9568	0.7551	0.2299
Recall	0.136	0.227	0.091	0.182	0.045	0
Specificity	0.986	0.983	0.984	0.985	0.984	0.951
Precision	1	0.455	0.500	0.667	0.500	0
Accuracy	0.9861	0.9831	0.9839	0.9853	0.9839	0.9509

8.1 Taiwan Bankruptcy Data

Table 8.7 Metrics for models with variables selected by logistic regression probability < 0.05

Log reg 14 variables	Random forest	Extreme boosting	Decision tree	Logistic regression	SVM	Neural network
Area under ROC	0.9743	0.9667	0.8493	0.9547	0.8716	0.3859
Recall	0.318	0.364	0.682	0.182	0	0.864
Specificity	0.989	0.990	0.995	0.987	0.984	0.971
Precision	1	0.800	0.600	0.667	0	0.015
Accuracy	0.9890	0.9883	0.9875	0.9853	0.9831	0.0872

Table 8.8 Entropy variables

X25Operating.Profit.Growth.Rate
X36Total.debt.Total.net.worth
X52Operating.profit.per.person
X83Cash.Flow.to.Equity
X90Net.Income.to.Stockholder.s.Equity

Table 8.9 Metrics for models with variables selected by entropy complexity 0.01

DTree 5 variables	Random forest	Extreme boosting	Decision tree	Logistic regression	SVM	Neural network
Area under ROC	0.9133	0.9468	0.8716	0.9048	0.8660	0.5786
Recall	0.136	0.273	0.136	0.091	0	0
Specificity	0.986	0.988	0.986	0.985	0.984	0.984
Precision	0.375	0.286	0.273	1	0	Degenerate
Accuracy	0.9824	0.9773	0.9802	0.9853	0.9824	0.9839

8.1.3 Entropy

Running a decision tree on the validation data with complexity set at 0.01 yielded the five variables given in Table 8.8.

Running this variable set on the training data set and testing on the test set gave the measures shown in Table 8.9.

8.1.4 Information Content from Random Forest Models

Running a random forest model on the validation data yielded the 81 variables, all except those given in Table 8.10.

Table 8.10 Information content variables failing the cutoff of 0

Variables	Information content
X72Quick.Asset.Turnover.Rate	0
X29Total.Asset.Growth.Rate	−1.80E-01
X67Long.term.Liability.to.Current.Assets	−2.90E-01
X82CFO.to.Assets	−0.37
X62Inventory.Working.Capital	−0.38
X49Fixed.Assets.Turnover.Frequency	−0.44
X53Allocation.rate.per.person	−0.58
X63Inventory.Current.Liability	−0.65
X57Cash.Total.Assets	−1.03
X35Interest.Expense.Ratio	−1.29
X88No.credit.Interval	−1.55
X81Cash.Flow.to.Liability	−1.64
X92Degree.of.Financial.Leverage..DFL	−1.96
X87Total.assets.to.GNP.price	−2.25

Table 8.11 Metrics for models with variables selected by information content > 0

	Random forest 14 variables	Random forest	Extreme boosting	Decision tree	Logistic regression	SVM	Neural network
Area under ROC	0.9721	0.9624	0.9301	0.9569	0.9305		0.4597
Recall	0.181	0.318	0.364	0.318	0		0.318
Specificity	0.987	0.989	0.990	0.989	0.984		0.981
Precision	0.667	0.438	0.471	0.538	0		0.012
Accuracy	0.9853	0.9824	0.9831	0.9846	0.9683		0.5770

Running this variable set on the training data set and testing on the test set gave the measures shown in Table 8.11.

8.1.5 Control Models Using All 94 Variables

As a control, we ran the full model using all 94 explanatory variables. We ran the two ensemble models, which consistently were among the best in the other runs. The resulting coincidence matrix for the random forest is shown in Table 8.12.

Area under the ROCurve 0.9699; Accuracy 0.9846; Recall 0.136; Precision 0.600; Specificity 0.986.

The coincidence matrix for the Extreme Boosting Model is shown in Table 8.13.

Table 8.12 Coincidence matrix—Full random forest model

	Model no	Model yes	Totals
Actual no	1340	2	1342
Actual yes	19	3	22
	1359	5	1364

Table 8.13 Coincidence matrix—Full model

	Model no	Model yes	Totals
Actual no	1334	8	1342
Actual yes	13	9	22
	1347	17	1364

Area under the ROCurve 0.9739; Accuracy 0.9846; Recall 0.409; Precision 0.529; Specificity 0.990.

8.2 Example Variable Selection Case

Financial statement fraud causes problems by inducing excessive hiring during fraud schemes, as well as long-term costs to society through reducing confidence in financial systems. Many business decisions rely on financial statement accuracy, which is difficult to accurately assess. Penalties to fraud perpetrators are insufficient to deter negative actions. Auditors have a hard time detecting financial statement fraud. Further, perpetrators are becoming more proficient in evading regulatory oversight.

Gepp et al. (2021) conducted a literature review of financial statement fraud detection academic papers. Key drivers of fraud are opportunity, pressure, and rationalization. Data widely used in prior studies was obtained on 34 financial variables, 6 non-financial variables, and 3 variables comparing financial and non-financial information. There were four control variables and three new variables to include macroeconomic indicators, corporate governance index, and accounting complexity of the industry. Gepp et al. found that model performance is overestimated if they are tested on training data. It is better to test on holdout test data, ideally partitioned chronologically. However, if the dataset is too small for a separate holdout test set, cross-validation can be used.

They also found that it is important to consider the relative cost of errors. Missing fraud misleads stakeholders into making decisions by investing in fraudulent companies. Falsely alleging fraud Also costs through losing investment opportunities. Thus a cost model of errors is desirable.

The Gepp et al. study used 590 cases through 2002 and earlier as a training set. This data was balanced at 295 cases for both fraud and not fraud. Data 2003 and later was used for testing (338 cases, 169 in each category of fraud and not fraud).

Models considered included standard regression-based models, neural networks, support vector machines, decision trees and their ensembles, and ensembles involving multiple models. The best at detecting financial statement fraud was found to be an average between a CART decision tree, a TreeNet ensemble with 1184 trees, a random forest model with 1000 trees and 8 variables, a linear regression using all variables, and a stepwise regression using all variables.

While this complex model provided the best fit, it also was quite complex and difficult to interpret. The authors found greater fraud when there were lower levels of debt to equity, return on equity, sales to total assets, and company age. They found higher levels of fraud with higher levels of inventory to sales, total accruals to total assets, the percentage of directors who were also executives, positive total accruals, new equity or long-term debt, demand for financing, use of operating leases, and return on average prior assets.

8.3 Value of Variable Reduction

In the bankrupty.csv data set, there are many variables, which probably contain overlapping information. One of the first activities we should apply with regression is to look at correlation, to determine if some variables could be eliminated without losing predictive power. In correlation, we would like high correlation with Bankrupt, but low correlation across candidate independent variables. Table 8.14 shows the correlation matrix obtained in Excel for the training data.

From Table 8.14, we can see that the strongest correlation with BankR in order is with revt, cogs, prch_f, and gp. The others are all below 0.1. The variables revt and cogs have correlation of 0,0.95, meaning we should only use one of the pair. Thus a safe set of regression variables would be revt, prch_f, and gp. We can deselect the other variables on the Data tab, as shown in Fig. 8.1. Note that we have a test set, so we do not want to partition. After executing, we double check to make sure Rattle didn't partition the data.

Some data of interest in a regression study may be ordinal or nominal. For instance, in our example job application model, sex and college degree are nominal. In the loan application data, the outcome is nominal, while credit rating is ordinal. Since regression analysis requires numerical data, we included them by *coding* the variables. Here, each of these variables is dichotomous; therefore, we can code them as either 0 or 1 (as we did in the regression model for loan applicants). For example, a male is assigned a code of 0, while a female is assigned a code of 1. The employees with a college degree can be assigned a code of 1, and those without a degree a code of 0. Figure 8.2 shows the logistic regression modeling screen.

You have the option to use Logistic regression, or Probit. Figure 8.3 gives the logistic regression output for a dataset trimmed to the three variables selected above:

The output indicates that revt (total revenue) is the most significant independent variable. This implies that firms with higher revenues are more apt to go bankrupt. Gross profit (gp) is also highly significant and makes more intuitive sense—the more

8.3 Value of Variable Reduction

Table 8.14 Correlation matrix—BankruptcyTrain.csv

	fyear	at	bkvlps	invt	Lt	Rectr	cogs	Dvt	ebit	gp	ni	oiadp	revt	dvpsx_f	mkvalt	prch_f
Year	1.00															
At	0.06	1.00														
bkvlps	0.05	0.06	1.00													
invt	0.05	0.93	0.09	1.00												
Lt	0.06	1.00	0.06	0.94	1.00											
rectr	0.05	0.99	0.05	0.89	0.99	1.00										
cogs	0.09	0.87	0.01	0.74	0.87	0.87	1.00									
Dvt	0.06	0.95	0.04	0.82	0.95	0.98	0.86	1.00								
ebit	0.04	0.74	0.10	0.90	0.75	0.71	0.53	0.67	1.00							
Gp	0.06	0.75	0.09	0.88	0.75	0.71	0.60	0.68	0.98	1.00						
Ni	−0.04	0.01	0.11	0.15	0.01	0.02	−0.17	0.05	0.44	0.40	1.00					
oiadp	0.04	0.74	0.10	0.90	0.75	0.71	0.53	0.67	1.00	0.98	0.44	1.00				
revt	0.09	0.92	0.04	0.88	0.92	0.90	0.95	0.88	0.77	0.82	0.04	0.77	1.00			
dvpsx_f	−0.01	0.02	0.07	0.02	0.02	0.02	0.02	0.04	0.02	0.02	0.01	0.02	0.02	1.00		
mkvalt	0.07	0.97	0.07	0.87	0.97	0.98	0.87	0.98	0.73	0.75	0.09	0.73	0.91	0.02	1.00	
prch_f	0.12	0.14	0.26	0.18	0.14	0.11	0.13	0.11	0.20	0.22	0.10	0.20	0.18	0.27	0.16	1.00
BankR	−0.05	0.07	−0.01	0.07	0.07	0.06	0.18	0.06	0.07	0.13	−0.02	0.07	0.18	0.03	0.09	0.17

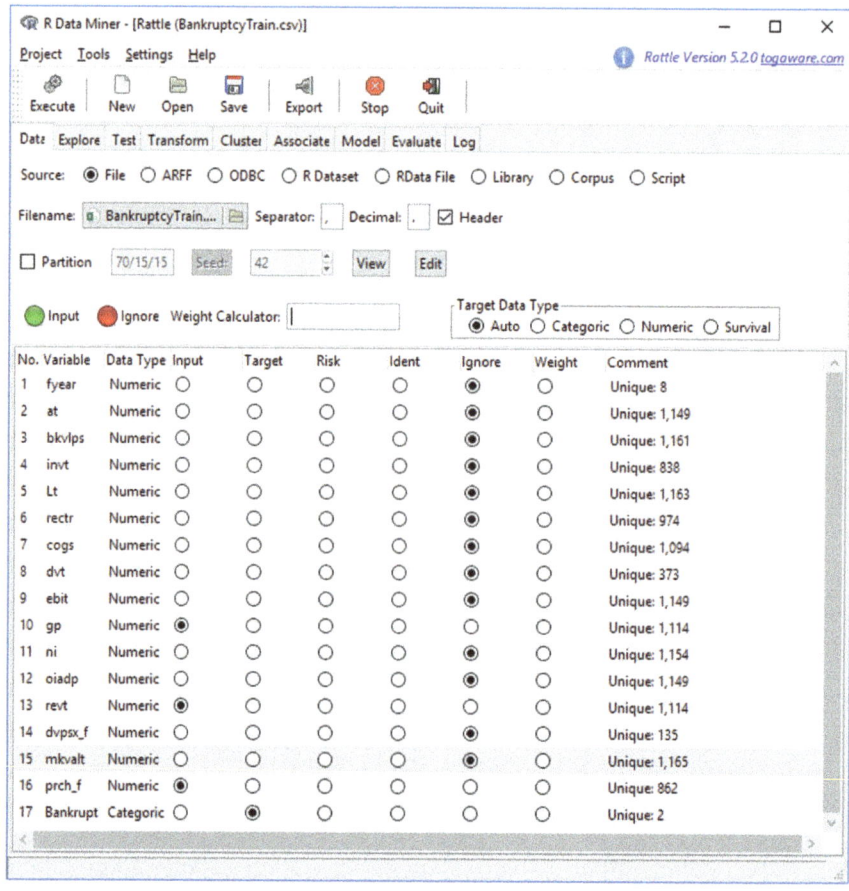

Fig. 8.1 Selecting independent variables

gross profit, the less likely the firm will go bankrupt. The third variable, prch_f (high stock price over the year) indicates that the higher the maximum stock price, the less likely the firm would go bankrupt (although this isn't significant). We can test this model on our test set by selecting the Evaluate tab, as shown in Fig. 8.4.

Clicking on the Execute button yields a coincidence matrix as shown in Table 8.15.

There are a number of standard metrics related to such a coincidence matrix. Sensitivity is the true positive rate—the true positive count (39) over total actual positive (53). Specitificity is the true negative rate—the true negative count (83) over total actual negative (90). Accuracy is total correctly classified (83 + 39) over total possible (143). Note that positive and negative are arbitrary—depending on how the outcomes are defined. Here the logistic regression model correctly classified 83 of 90 cases where firms did not go bankrupt (0.922), and 39 of 53 cases where firms did go bankrupt (0.736) for an overall correct classification rate of 0.853.

8.3 Value of Variable Reduction

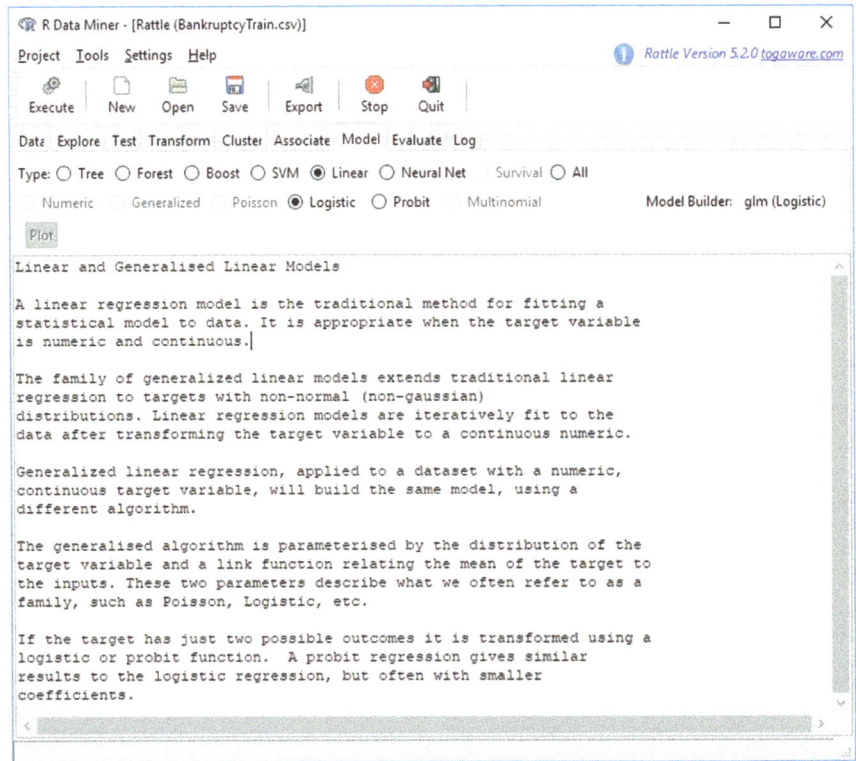

Fig. 8.2 Logistic regression modeling screen

Variable selection has some benefit, although there is a slight cost in reduced accuracy. The smaller number of variables reduced from stepwise variable selection improved accuracy slightly. The benefits of trimming datasets is that results are much more focused and clearer to apply, at a small cost in accuracy.

For this type of data, with many variables, ensemble models such as random forests or gradient boosting are supposed to do better. For balanced data, they clearly did. In general, as the number of bankrupt cases increased with balancing, logistic regression and neural network results had more errors. The type of error varied—sometimes type I getting worse, sometimes type II. SVM models were relatively accurate, in line with single decision trees. But random forest and gradient boosting models clearly were better.

Random forests and boosting ensembles were clearly better than the other algorithms. The gradient boosting method had a slight advantage over random forests in AuC with no balancing, but these algorithms performed nearly identically with balanced data sets. They were also usually better on specific error measures. Support vector machines was a clear third in average error, both for of type I and type II as well as overall average error. Logistic regression and neural networks were less

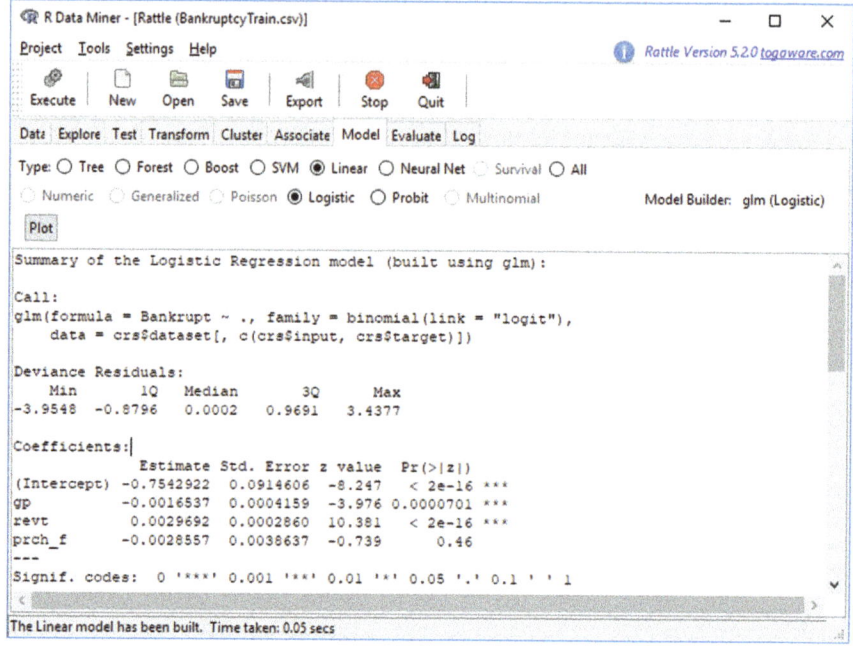

Fig. 8.3 R Logistic regression output

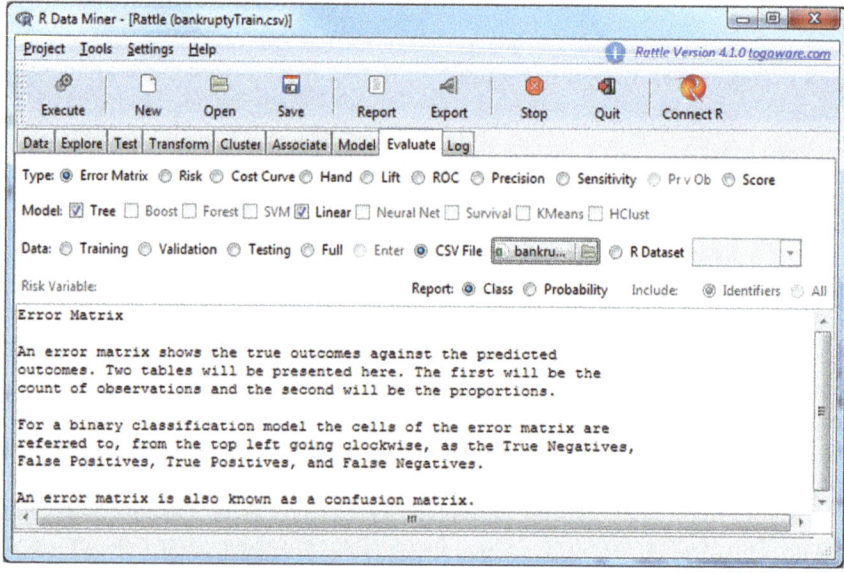

Fig. 8.4 Linking test data set in R

Table 8.15 Coincidence matrix—Trimmed logistic regression model

	Model no	Model yes	Totals
Actual no	83	7	90
Actual yes	14	39	53
	97	46	143

accurate as measured by errors on holdout data. We understand that these last three algorithms include parameters that can be adjusted so that they can perform much better, but that takes quite a bit of searching. It seems more efficient to go to extreme boosting and random forests, which in effect do some of that parameter searching automatically (a form of machine learning).

References

Chan AB, Vasconcelos N, Lanckriet GR (2007) Direct convex relaxations of sparse SVM. Proceedings of the twenty-fourth international conference on machine learning, 145–153
Foster DP (2004) Variable selection in data mining: Building a predictive model for bankruptcy. J Am Stat Assoc 99(466):303–313
Gepp A, Kumar K, Bhattacharya S (2021) Lifting the numbers game: Identifying key input variables and a best-performing model to detect financial statement fraud. Account Financ 61:4601–4638
Liang D, Lu C-C, Tsai C-F, Shih G-A (2016) Financial ratios and corporate governance indicators in bankruptcy prediction: A comprehensive study. Eur J Oper Res 252:561–572
Olson DL, Chae B (2022) A study of data mine balancing and variable reduction. J Supply Chain Manag Sci 3(1–2):3–15
Tsai C-F (2009) Feature selection in bankruptcy prediction. Knowl-Based Syst 22(2):120–127
Zeng J (2017) Forecasting aggregates with disaggregate variables: Does boosting help to select the most relevant predictors? J Forecast 36(1):74–90
Zeng F, Li L, Li J, Wang X (2009) Research on test suite reduction using attribute relevance analysis. Eighth IEEE/ACIS international conference on computer and information science, 961–966

Chapter 9
Dataset Balancing

Predictive data mining is a common tool for predicting bankruptcy. Bankruptcy often involves highly imbalanced datasets with a large number of potential variables, with bankrupt firms being by far the minority case. This chapter uses data from four studies of firm bankruptcy and examines the impact of data balancing on model accuracy. The models used are random forest and gradient boosting based on decision trees, logistic regression, neural networks, and support vector machines. Error metrics used were type I and type II error (sensitivity and specificity), overall average error (accuracy), and area under the recall curve (AuC). The experiments into balancing found that unbalanced data had high error rates, which dropped a great deal with even 10 percent balancing, but balancing beyond 10 percent was found to provide little additional accuracy.

9.1 Bankruptcy Datasets

Bankruptcy is important for any business, including supply chain contexts. The interrelationship of supply chain members creates interdependencies where the bankruptcy of one supply chain member can create problems for its supply chain partners. Financially distressed companies are highly likely to reorganize with few spillover costs. Economically distressed firms can suffer large losses in market value costs of replacing bankrupt customers.

Should a supply chain member undergo financial distress, three effects that could change firm behavior. The predation effect would result in increased competition prior to potential bankruptcy as the non-distressed competitor would seek first-mover advantage to increase pressure on the distressed firm. In a more cooperative environment, a supplier might react to bail out the distressed firm through concessions to preserve competition and improve supply chain efficiency. The abatement effect would find a supplier deliberately abetting the competitor's predation, placing increased pressure on the distressed firm. Overall, these effects lead to conditions where a firm's bankruptcy potential can hurt its competitors and benefit its suppliers as well as customers.

Thus, financial risk is important to supply chain networks. Data mining classification provides a tool to aid in firm financial bankruptcy. If extremely imbalanced data is not balanced, the minority cases (usually bankrupt firms) are disregarded as a very high accuracy rate is obtained by defaulting to assigning all cases to the non-bankrupt category. Such models are degenerate, providing no help in analyzing cases. We will review basic balancing methods, and our experiments seek to identify the impact of various levels of balancing.

Data mining is widely applied to classification problems. One area that has received a great deal of study is bankruptcy prediction. We examine the impact of balancing datasets. Financial failure hopefully is rare within such datasets, leading to imbalanced outcomes. We find that even low levels of balancing help a great deal in improving model accuracy.

9.2 Balancing

In many real applications, imbalanced class distributions are present, confusing many machine learning algorithms because data is often skewed. For instance, insurance companies hope that only a small portion of claims are fraudulent. Physicians hope that only a small portion of tested patients have cancerous tumors. Banks hope that only a small portion of their loans will turn out to have repayment problems. Imbalanced datasets negatively impact classifier learning. The most common method to deal with imbalanced data is resampling. Learning algorithms include ensemble classifiers, cost-sensitive learning, and one-class learning. Preprocessing techniques include undersampling (which makes computation easier, but reduces data content), oversampling (which increases computational burden). One oversampling method is SMOTE (synthetic minority over-sampling technique). SMOTE randomly draws observations from the smaller set of outcomes, which can provide exactly the degree of balance desired, but risks some unintentional bias. We prefer to replicate the entire minority set multiple times to roughly attain the level of balance desired. In our experiments we us 10%, 20%, 30%, 40% and 50% levels measuring the proportion of failed cases to total cases for balancing with the intention of looking at relative elimination of data problems, and relative accuracy performance.

9.3 Process

Because financial failure is heavily weighted with failing firms usually in the minority, dataset balancing is important, and we use five levels reflecting the proportion of failed firms. Every data mining application involves selecting a training set and applying it to a test set. We used a common test set for each of the four national datasets. The third step of our process was to select independent variables. We used stepwise regression as one method, and used single decision tree models with three levels of the complexity parameter as another means to select variables. Single decision trees were not included as they were used to select variables, and random forests and extreme gradient boosting are ensembles of decision tree algorithms. We then applied the five classification algorithms studied. Neural network and support vector machine models can be refined for specific datasets, but that involves a complex and time-consuming process. The last step of our process was to measure errors. Thus, the four steps of our process:

1. Generate balanced datasets (five levels: 10%, 20%, 30%, 40%, 50%)
2. Partition data (80% training, 0 validation, 20% testing)
3. Run algorithms (random forest, gradient boosting, logistic regression, neural network, SVM)
4. Measure errors (sensitivity, specificity, overall error, AuC)

9.4 Data

We utilized four datasets related to firm bankruptcy.

9.4.1 Poland Data

Zięba et al. (2016) provided a database of 10,000 observations over 64 financial measures related to firms in Poland. This dataset was highly imbalanced, with 203 bankrupt and 9797 not. Due to data availability, they obtained data on the bankrupt firms over the period 2007–2013 and 2000–2012 for those firms still operating. The 64 financial indicators they selected were determined by availability of data and intensity of occurrence. They tested 16 algorithms, with multiple versions of decision trees, logistic regression, boosting, support vector machines, and random forests.

9.4.2 Taiwan Data

Liang et al. (2016) presented 6819 observations over 95 explanatory variables for firm bankruptcy in Taiwan. This dataset was also highly imbalanced, with 220 bankrupt and 6599 not. The prediction models used were decision trees, neural networks, support vector machines, naïve Bayes, and K-means clustering.

9.4.3 Slovak Data

Drotár et al. (2019) presented bankruptcy prediction data for 2013–2016 for Slovak companies in agriculture, construction, manufacturing and retail. This dataset was extremely imbalanced, with 63 bankrupt and 25,932 not. The dataset contained 21 distinct financial ratios, along with other variables yielding a total of 63 variables.

9.4.4 U.S. Data

Olson et al. (2012) used data over the period 2005–2009 of US firms, balancing bankrupt with not bankrupt. This data involved 100 U.S. firms that underwent bankruptcy. All of the sample data are from U.S. companies. About 400 bankrupt company names were obtained using google.com. The companies bankrupted during January 2006 and December 2009 were retained, since it was expected that different results would be obtained after that economic crisis. Financial data ratios during January 2005 to December 2009 were obtained from the Compustat database, yielding the explanatory variables available to predict company bankruptcy. The factors collected were based on the literature. The dataset consists of 1,321 records with full data over 19 attributes. The outcome attribute in bankruptcy has a value of 1 if the firm went bankrupt by 2011 (697 cases) and a value of 0 if it did not (624 cases).

9.5 Results

Table 9.1 recaps the three datasets showing the ratio of bankrupt to total firms. The ratio of bankrupt to total changes as when more bankrupt cases are added, the total number of variables increases.

Balancing yielded different models.

Table 9.2 gives the proportion of variables (relative to the full model) by balancing level.

Balancing level tended to increase the number of variables selected initially, but with little consistent trend.

The algorithms used in addition to decision trees were random forests, gradient boosting, logistic regression, neural networks, and support vector machines. Anzanello et al. (2012) addressed the accuracy measures of sensitivity, specificity, and overall accuracy. Dag et al. (2016) applied sensitivity analysis in comparing classification models using accuracy, sensitivity, specificity, and information gain measures. We compared relative overall accuracy, as well as the maximum of sensitivity (type I) and specificity (type II) errors over the five algorithms. Table 9.3 gives average errors obtained by algorithm.

9.5 Results

Table 9.1 Dataset parameters

Dataset	Explanatory variables	OK	Bankrupt	Ratio bankrupt/total
Poland	64	9797	203	0.020
		,,	1015	0.094
		,,	2436	0.199
		,,	4263	0.303
		,,	6496	0.399
		,,	9684	0.497
Taiwan	95	6599	220	0.032
		,,	660	0.091
		,,	1760	0.211
		,,	2860	0.302
		,,	4500	0.405
		,,	6700	0.504
Slovak	63	25,932	189	0.007
		,,	2835	0.098
		,,	6426	0.199
		,,	11,151	0.304
		,,	17,199	0.399
		,,	25,893	0.500
US	14	624	697	0.528

Table 9.2 Relative number of variables by balancing level and variable generation method

Balancing level	Step	Entropy.01	Entropy.02	Entropy.03
Base	0.329	0.176	0.109	0.065
10%	0.673	0.212	0.105	0.072
20%	0.504	0.130	0.067	0.045
30%	0.585	0.122	0.049	0.021
40%	0.498	0.134	0.031	0.028
50%	0.367	0.086	0.040	0.033

Figures 9.1 through 9.4 display this data visually.

Degeneracy was identified when models assigned all forecasts to the majority class. This occurred in the Poland dataset for SVM models with the base model, as well as balancing at 10%, 20%, and 30%. Degeneracy occurred in the Taiwan dataset for neural network models balanced at 20% when complexity was set at 0.01 and 0.03 (but not of 0.02). In the Slovak data, there was degeneracy for the logistic regression model for data balanced at 10% with complexity set at 0.02, and for SVM models in the unbalanced dataset for the base (unbalanced) data, and data balanced

Table 9.3 Average errors—Balancing level versus algorithm

sensitivity	Random forest	Gradient boost	Log Regression	Neural net	SVM
Base	0.237	0.457	0.694	0.625	0.722
10%	0.018	0.016	0.695	0.628	0.538
20%	0.016	0.002	0.620	0.461	0.328
30%	0.002	0.007	0.488	0.473	0.202
40%	0.003	0.003	0.339	0.254	0.117
50%	0.002	0.002	0.315	0.369	0.061
Specificity	Random forest	Gradient boost	Log Regression	Neural net	SVM
Base	0.073	0.023	0.058	0.129	0.035
0.1	0.059	0.010	0.045	0.043	0.014
0.2	0.002	0.007	0.115	0.127	0.036
0.3	0.004	0.013	0.163	0.142	0.064
0.4	0.007	0.016	0.194	0.214	0.104
0.5	0.004	0.024	0.194	0.182	0.161
Overall	Random forest	Gradient boost	Log Regression	Neural net	SVM
Base	0.035	0.033	0.081	0.129	0.048
0.1	0.008	0.004	0.058	0.054	0.025
0.2	0.003	0.010	0.121	0.129	0.040
0.3	0.006	0.013	0.164	0.096	0.066
0.4	0.055	0.015	0.212	0.214	0.100
0.5	0.028	0.021	0.195	0.186	0.121
AuC	Random forest	Gradient boost	Log Regression	Neural net	SVM
Base	0.949	0.957	0.832	0.745	0.828
0.1	0.998	0.999	0.803	0.804	0.904
0.2	0.999	0.999	0.851	0.781	0.929
0.3	0.999	0.998	0.827	0.790	0.919
0.4	0.999	0.999	0.825	0.776	0.888
0.5	1.000	0.999	0.799	0.856	0.956

at 10%, 20%, and 30%. Thus SVM models had degeneracy occur 8 times out of 95, neural networks twice, and logistic regression once. Random forest and extreme boosting models had no degenerate models. Average performance by balancing is given in Table 9.4.

This information is shown graphically in Figs. 9.5 through 9.8:

Viewing Figs. 9.5 and 9.6, we see that the bias in bankruptcy data gets more extreme with smaller datasets. Sensitivity (type II error) improved with smaller datasets, while specificity (type I error) got worse. Overall error (Fig. 9.7) was best with the Step datasets, but got worse as datasets were further trimmed. The results

9.5 Results

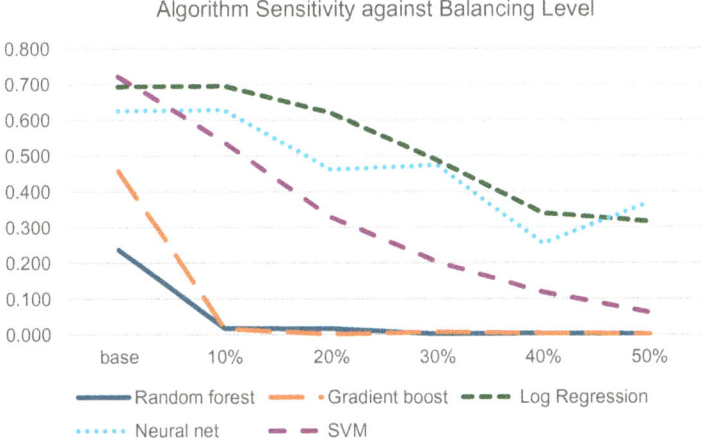

Fig. 9.1 Sensitivity by algorithm

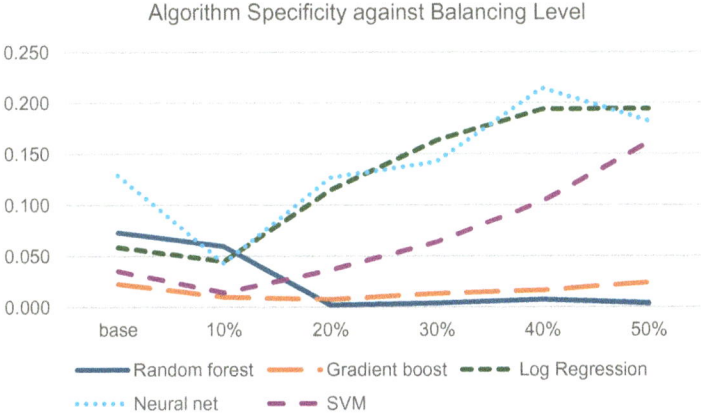

Fig. 9.2 Specificity by algorithm

for Area under the curve were best for Step data, with full datasets next, and generally decreasing accuracy with smaller datasets. We conclude that some trimming of variables is beneficial, but too much is counterproductive.

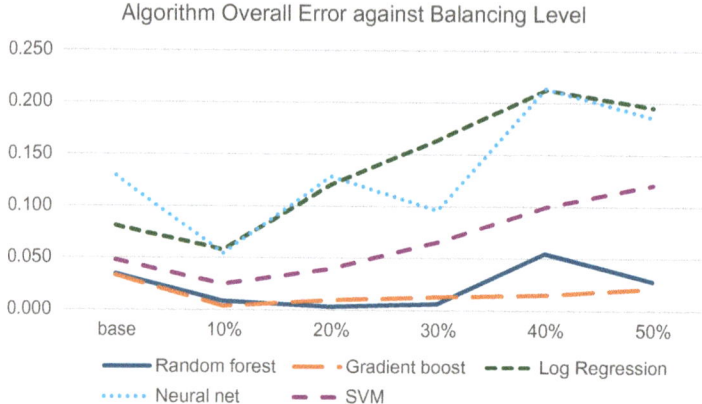

Fig. 9.3 Overall error by algorithm

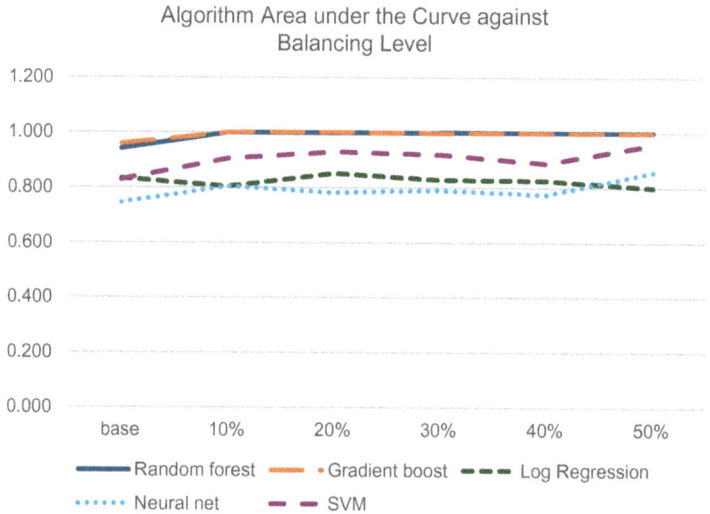

Fig. 9.4 Area under the curve by algorithm

9.6 Example Credit Card Fraud Detection Case

Credit cards are endemic in the United States, and are becoming do around the world. Credit card fraud has increased along with the growth of their use. E-commerce firms work very hard to data mine the logs of their servers to better detect fraudulent purchases of their products.

Karthik et al. (2022) proposed an improved credit card fraud detection model based on a hybrid ensemble model utilizing random forest models. Data is obtained

9.6 Example Credit Card Fraud Detection Case

Table 9.4 Scores by balancing level

Sens	Full	Step	Ent.01	Ent.02	Ent.03
Base	0.4797	0.6668	0.6039	0.6287	0.65205
10%	0.400579	0.432632	0.397842	0.488053	0.478947
20%	0.173579	0.236684	0.384684	0.369263	0.448842
30%	0.173684	0.250684	0.222526	0.302211	0.419632
40%	0.148	0.138421	0.151526	0.288632	0.241579
50%	0.145474	0.21	0.075526	0.232737	0.135579
Spec	Full	Step	Ent.01	Ent.02	Ent.03
Base	0.0924	0.07345	0.0455	0.02405	0.08235
10%	0.029421	0.094368	0.029316	0.008789	0.062842
20%	0.086211	0.074789	0.019053	0.072053	0.023263
30%	0.061895	0.102684	0.061737	0.094	0.089632
40%	0.110632	0.102947	0.079421	0.082053	0.173211
50%	0.093105	0.105421	0.138842	0.130684	0.167158
Overall	Full	Step	Ent.01	Ent.02	Ent.03
Base	0.0697	0.04795	0.06265	0.0435	0.1019
10%	0.037211	0.061895	0.037526	0.016632	0.070421
20%	0.089316	0.074053	0.026158	0.076526	0.026579
30%	0.063842	0.102895	0.063158	0.098	0.056421
40%	0.123789	0.102474	0.083947	0.099526	0.151474
50%	0.095053	0.105316	0.138211	0.101526	0.181895
AuC	Full	Step	Ent.01	Ent.02	Ent.03
Base	0.88315	0.86845	0.8828	0.8487	0.82895
10%	0.859737	0.885	0.873	0.882895	0.822105
20%	0.901579	0.919263	0.912105	0.891316	0.844737
30%	0.899632	0.915737	0.894842	0.863105	0.879789
40%	0.888684	0.935579	0.828895	0.873263	0.885158
50%	0.891789	0.932684	0.897263	0.885842	0.890684

from point of sale transactions, which e-commerce firms accept or reject on a case-by-case basis. This data is thus streamed. Identifying fraudulent purchases is challenging. Such data is highly imbalanced (hopefully) with a great deal of noise and massive scale. The noise and presence of outliers seriously impact classifier performance. Pre-processing is needed to clean data for analysis.

The process is to first pre-process data to detect outliers and reduce noise. Then an Adaboost algorithm is applied to select variables. Adaboost is applied to classification algorithms run multiple times, selecting those variable sets with better outcomes. The dataset is then split into training and testing portions. A random forest or extra

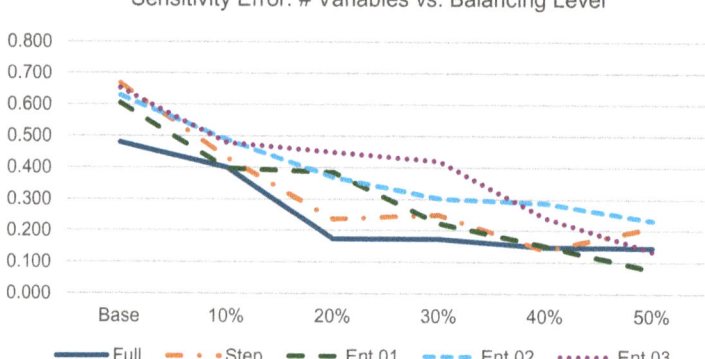

Fig. 9.5 Sensitivity error by level of balancing

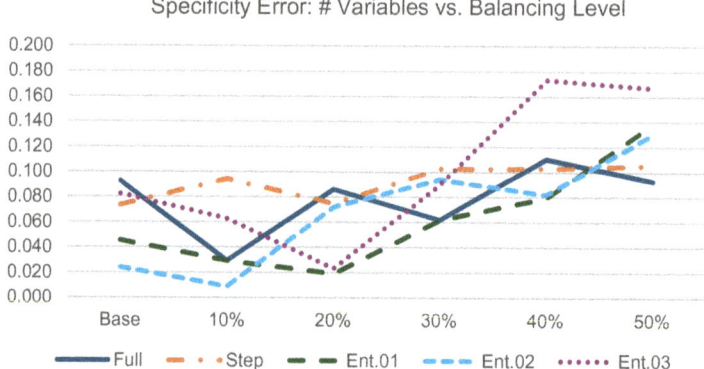

Fig. 9.6 Specificity scores by level of balancing

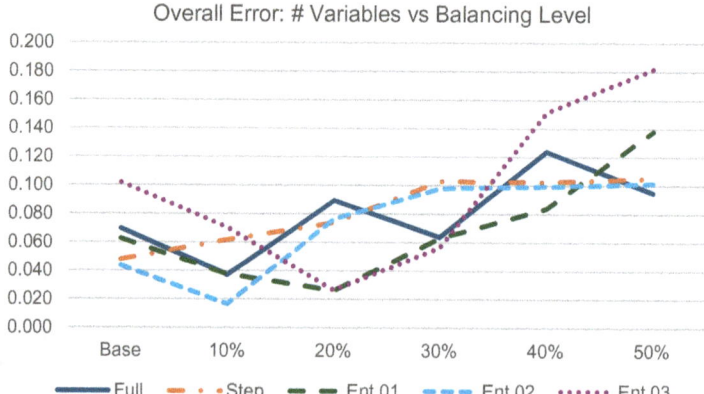

Fig. 9.7 Overall accuracy by level of balancing

9.7 Conclusions

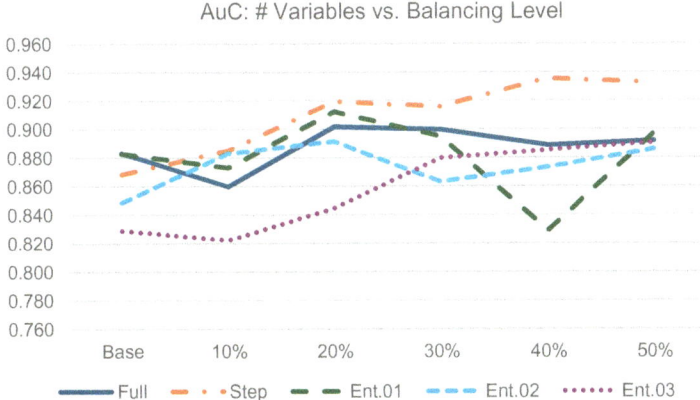

Fig. 9.8 Area under the curve by level of balancing

trees model is applied to the training set, applying bootstrap sampling. The resulting selected model is then applied to the test data.

Data for the Karthik et al. study came from a Brazilian bank consisting of 300,000 samples, supplemented by 100,000 transactions from FICO. The Brazilian bank data was heavily skewed to non-fraudulent cases at a rate of 25.7 to 1 fraudulent. The FICO data had an imbalance ratio of 45.6 to 1 fraudulent.

Dataset imbalance was dealt with by re-sampling. Under sampling loses information. Oversampling risks overfitting. Fit was measured by the area-under precision-recall (AUPR) curve. A logistic regression model had an AUPR of 0.3 for the Brazilian bank dataset, and 0.27 for the FICO data. Boosting improved both to the 0.42 region. Applying Adaboost (using either random forest or extra trees) provided almost completely accurate results for the Brazilian bank data, and over 0.96 AUPR for the FICO data.

9.7 Conclusions

Our results found that in general, the more variables available, the less error, although trimming a few variables improved accuracy performance. The main benefit of balancing was to avoid degenerate models that were obtained with neural network and SVM models (and one case with logistic regression). Our data found little added benefit from balancing to error being more than 10% of total cases. Among methods, we found extreme boosting to be the most beneficial, with random forest models close in relative accuracy. These are models that internally manipulate multiple models. SVM models were next in performance, followed by linear regression and neural networks, the latter two methods yielding very similar results. We note that SVM, linear regression, and neural networks can be fine-tuned to specified data sets, which we did not do, but this fine tuning would take significant computational effort which is not needed by extreme boosting and random forest models.

We have considered datasets with binary outcomes. Datasets with multi-class outcomes create additional complications. For instance, replication of the most imbalanced outcome may create additional imbalance in other outcome categories.

Our basic conclusions can be itemized:

1. Balancing highly imbalanced datasets has advantage, especially in avoiding degenerate models (which predict no bankruptcy). However, complete balancing is not needed—ten percent balancing gains most of the advantage of balancing.
2. Extreme boosting and random forest models were clearly more accurate in our results. Support vector machines had some advantage over linear regression and neural networks, recognizing that we did not fine tune these last three models. To do so, however, would create more computational burden.
3. Variable selection has some benefit, although there is a slight cost in reduced accuracy. The smaller number of variables reduced from stepwise variable selection improved accuracy slightly. The benefits of trimming datasets is that results are much more focused and clearer to apply, at a small cost in accuracy.

Our basic conclusions can be itemized:

1. Balancing highly imbalanced datasets has advantage, especially in avoiding degenerate models (which predict no bankruptcy). However, complete balancing is not needed—ten percent balancing gains most of the advantage of balancing.

The main benefit of balancing was to avoid degenerate models that were obtained with neural network and SVM models (occasionally with decision trees and/or logistic regression). Our data found little added benefit from balancing to error being more than 10% of total cases. Among methods, we found extreme boosting to be the most beneficial, with random forest models close in relative accuracy. These are models that internally manipulate multiple models. SVM models were next in performance, followed by linear regression and neural networks, the latter two methods yielding very similar results. We note that SVM, linear regression, and neural networks can be fine-tuned to specified data sets, which we did not do, but this fine tuning would take significant computational effort which is not needed by extreme boosting and random forest models.

References

Anzanello MJ, Albin SL, Chaovalitwongse WA (2012) Multicriteria variable selection for classification of production batches. Eur J Oper Res 2018:97–105

Dag A, Topuz K, Oztekin A, Bulur S, Megahed FM (2016) A probabilistic data-driven framework for scoring the preoperative recipient-donor heart transplant survival. Decis Support Syst 86:1–12

Drotár P, Gnip P, Zoričák M, Gazda V (2019) Small- and medium-enterprises bankruptcy dataset. Data Brief 25:1–6

References

Karthik VSS, Mishra A, Srinivasulu Reddy U (2022) Credit card fraud detection by modelling behaviour pattern using hybrid ensemble model. J Sci Eng 47:1987–1997

Liang D, Lu C-C, Tsai C-F, Shih G-A (2016) Financial ratios and corporate governance indicators in bankruptcy prediction: A comprehensive study. Eur J Oper Res 252:561–572

Olson DL, Delen D, Meng Y (2012) Comparative analysis of data mining models for bankruptcy prediction. Decis Support Syst 52(2):464–473

Olson DL, Chae B (2022) A study of data mine balancing and variable reduction. J Supply Chain Manag Sci 3(1–2):3–15

Zięba M, Tomczak SK, Tomczak JM (2016) Ensemble boosted trees with synthetic features generation in application to bankruptcy prediction. Expert Syst Appl 58:93–101

Index

A
Accuracy, 2, 13–15, 17, 19, 21, 118, 127, 133–135, 138, 139, 142, 143, 147, 148, 152, 153, 156–158, 160, 161, 167, 169–173, 176, 177, 181, 182, 184, 187, 190–192
Affinity analysis, 41
Algorithms, 1, 4, 5, 10, 12, 18, 42, 45, 48, 49, 57, 61–71, 84, 99, 113, 119, 143, 165, 167, 177, 179, 182–184, 186–189
Anaconda, 37, 38
Analytics, 1, 3, 4, 9, 16, 63
Applications, 4–7, 9, 11, 16, 21, 41, 62, 63, 65, 67, 69, 70, 99, 118, 125–127, 135, 140, 160, 162, 165, 174, 182
Apriori algorithm, 41, 42, 48, 49, 57, 59, 62
Area under the curve, 120, 133, 134, 143, 148, 152, 154, 156, 157, 162, 187, 188, 191
ARIMA, 17, 99, 104, 105, 107, 108
Association rules, 5, 7, 13, 17, 41–43, 48–52, 54, 56, 57, 61, 62, 143
Autocorrelation, 104, 107

B
Big data, 1, 2, 7, 41, 62
Big data analytics, 2

C
Causal models, 100, 104
Classification models, 4, 5, 7, 20, 68, 118, 119, 127, 158, 162, 184

Cluster analysis, 7, 11, 12, 17, 18, 63–65, 68, 82, 97, 119
Complexity, 17, 162, 166, 171, 173, 183, 185
Confidence, 13, 17, 45, 48–58, 61, 62, 145, 162, 173
Credit risk assessment, 6, 68, 69, 160
CRISP, 9, 10, 14, 16, 21
Cycles, 14

D
Data cleaning, 10, 11
Data mining process, 7, 12, 16, 21, 99, 127, 128, 139, 143
Data sources, 11
Decision tree models, 6, 32, 33, 126, 143, 145, 153, 165, 183
Decision trees, 3, 6, 12, 15–17, 30, 31, 67, 69, 125–127, 140, 143, 144, 148, 153, 158, 159, 162, 166, 167, 169–172, 174, 177, 181, 183, 184, 192
Distance metrics, 65, 84

E
Extreme boosting, 20, 126, 154, 169–172, 179, 186, 191, 192

F
Forecasting, 4, 99–101, 104
Forecasting models, 143
Fraud detection, 6, 7, 18, 173, 188

H
Hierarchical clustering, 67

J
Jupyter lab, 37, 38

K
Kaggle data, 108
K-means clustering, 64, 65, 67, 70, 71, 78, 84, 160, 162, 183
Knowledge management, 2, 3

L
Lags, 100, 104
Lift, 6, 45–48, 50, 52–57, 61
Logistic regression, 7, 12, 15, 17, 99, 117–120, 124, 125, 129, 131, 158, 159, 162, 166, 167, 169–172, 174, 176, 177, 181, 183–186, 191, 192

M
Machine learning, 6, 41, 42, 49, 63, 68, 113, 124, 165, 166, 179, 182
Market basket analysis, 4, 41, 48
Multicollinearity, 109

N
Naïve Bayes, 16, 127, 183
Neural network models, 15, 127, 139, 140, 158, 162, 167, 185
Neural networks, 12, 16, 17, 20, 67, 68, 125, 127, 135, 140, 142, 143, 154, 158, 159, 167, 169–172, 174, 177, 181, 183, 184, 186, 191, 192
Nonlinear data, 99, 104

O
Ordinary least squares (OLS) regression, 66, 99, 100, 104, 119, 124, 162

P
Predictive analytics, 4
Predictive models, 99
Python, 7, 23, 31–38, 40, 42, 50, 61, 62, 70, 72, 77, 82, 83, 91, 101, 103, 108, 112, 113, 135, 139, 158

R
R, 7, 23–29, 40, 50, 54, 70, 72, 158
Random forest models, 126, 148, 151, 153, 159, 165, 167, 171, 174, 188, 191, 192
Rattle software, 7, 113, 162, 163
Regression model assumptions, 118, 119
Risk management, 5
R Studio, 23, 57, 75, 77, 91

S
Sensitivity, 176, 181, 183, 184, 186, 187
Self-organizing map (SOM) clustering, 67–69
Specificity, 118, 133–136, 138, 139, 142, 143, 147, 148, 152, 153, 156–158, 167, 169–173, 181, 183, 184, 186, 187
Stepwise regression, 99, 113, 124, 165, 166, 174, 183
Support, 3, 7, 9, 10, 13, 16, 17, 20, 45, 47–58, 61–63, 99, 113, 125, 143, 160, 162
Support vector machines (SVMs), 126, 135, 136, 138, 139, 158–160, 169–172, 174, 177, 181, 183–186, 191, 192

T
Tests of the regression model, 118
Time series, 7, 17, 99, 100, 104, 126

V
Variable selection, 7, 162, 165, 177, 192
Visualization, 14, 41, 65
Visualization tools, 3, 12, 14

GPSR Compliance
The European Union's (EU) General Product Safety Regulation (GPSR) is a set of rules that requires consumer products to be safe and our obligations to ensure this.

If you have any concerns about our products, you can contact us on

ProductSafety@springernature.com

In case Publisher is established outside the EU, the EU authorized representative is:

Springer Nature Customer Service Center GmbH
Europaplatz 3
69115 Heidelberg, Germany

www.ingramcontent.com/pod-product-compliance
Ingram Content Group UK Ltd.
Pitfield, Milton Keynes, MK11 3LW, UK
UKHW021855120625
459539UK00001BA/17